CAMINO LESSONS

Losing Twenty-First Century Fears
on an Ancient Pilgrimage Trail

DEBORAH TERRA WELTMAN

Camino Lessons
Losing Twenty-First Century Fears on an Ancient Pilgrimage Trail
Deborah Terra Weltman
Terra Art Publishing

Published by Terra Art Publishing, Saint Louis, MO

Cover and Interior design: Davis Creative LLC, CreativePublishingPartners.com

Publisher's Cataloging-In-Publication Data
(Prepared by The Donohue Group, Inc.)

Names: Weltman, Deborah Terra, author.

Title: Camino lessons : losing twenty-first century fears on an ancient pilgrimage trail / Deborah Terra Weltman.

Description: Saint Louis, MO : Terra Art Publishing, 2022. | Includes bibliographical references.

Identifiers: ISBN 9798985445701 (paperback) | ISBN 9798985445718 (ebook)

Subjects: LCSH: Weltman, Deborah Terra--Travel--Spain. | Camino de Santiago de Compostela--Description and travel. | Christian pilgrims and pilgrimages--Spain. | Spirituality. | LCGFT: Travel writing. | BODY, MIND & SPIRIT / General. | SELF-HELP / Spiritual. | TRAVEL / Special Interest / Adventure.

Classification: LCC BL73.W458 A3 2022 (print) | LCC BL73.W458 (ebook) | DDC 204.092--dc23

2022

DEDICATION

To Jacque,
whose journey of trust inspired me to attempt my pilgrimage.

To all of my friends and family, to all of my Camino friends,
and to all my *soul friends* along the way:

I honor and thank each of you for your support, encouragement,
and love.

I hope my story will inspire others to dream big and to stand
behind their own dreams.

"I have given orders to guard thee on the way."

— Entryway plaque at a pilgrim's hostel

Acknowledgments

I had help from so many knowledgeable and caring people in the writing, rewriting, and *re*-rewriting of this book! Millón Gracias to all who have been instrumental in the fine-tuning process! Special thanks to my wonderful St. Louis Writers' Guild Critique Group partners who, along with all of their stellar suggestions, offered much needed support and encouragement: P.D. Birchler, T.A. Boyd, and Cynthia A. Graham. I have learned so much from all of you! Special thanks to T.W. Fendley for her repeated encouragements and for getting me to join the Guild… you've made such a positive difference in my writing!

To my original publisher, Winnie Sullivan, from Pen Ultimate Press, thank you for your insights, your vast knowledge, your enormous interest, and the many kindly delivered pushes in the right directions. This story became more interesting and complete as a result of your vision. I enjoyed all the time we spent working together. I hope you are as pleased with the final results as I am, and I hope to always count you among my friends.

To the many kind souls who have read and offered advice… from my cousin Steve, an amazing proofreader, to the many friends, writer friends, past and future pilgrim friends who read and gave their thoughts on some version of the in-process work… I loved getting your helpful feedback along the way! Many thanks!

Thanks to all my friends and family! So many people helped to make my Camino possible. Thanks to my parents who provided support of all types and set the example for me of pursuing and realizing a big dream; to Anna and Erin who were always supportive and proud of their "Hippie Mom"; to my wonderful brothers, Mick and Sandy, who were encouraging and full of good ideas. Many thanks to my dear sis-in-law, Jeanne, my cousin "Doozer," and my friend, Jeanne O., whose generosity and help in creating plane fare from frequent flyer miles made the trip possible. To all my extended family, I thank you for never discouraging my crazy ideas.

Thank you to my dear, dear friends who encouraged me to tackle a scary big dream and helped in so many ways…who gave of themselves to help me do something I *wanted*, not *needed*, to do. And thank you to all who donated to Habitat for Humanity as a means of supporting my pledge walk. I am so grateful for your generosity! I am in awe of all the gifts my family and friends have given me… in both physical and metaphysical forms.

And, now that some years have passed, and I still have my Amigos del Camino in my life, I thank you all too, for the immense joy you have added to my life. Buen Camino to all of you who have touched my life so profoundly! I am so grateful that our paths crossed.

Deborah

CONTENTS

Introduction

*"In life, the same as in storytelling, fantasy
and the improbable are a part of reality."*

Antonio Orlando Rodriguez

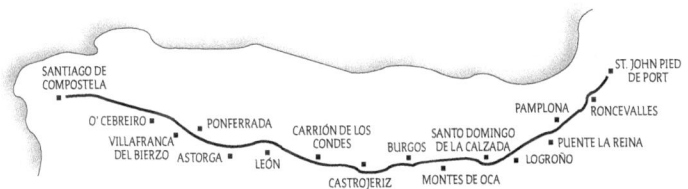

El Camino de Santiago is an ancient pilgrimage trail, walked by pilgrims from starting points all across Europe and concluding at the Cathedral of Santiago, in the city of Santiago de Compostela in northwestern Spain. For a thousand years Catholic pilgrims have walked to Santiago de Compostela. During the Middle Ages, the route became one of the great Christian pilgrimages, and a way to walk off one's sins.

The most well-traveled Camino route is the five-hundred-mile-long Camino Francés, which begins on the French side of the Pyrenees Mountains, goes up and over the Pyrenees into Spain, and then meanders across most of northern Spain. The name, Camino de Santiago de Compostela, translates as the "Way of St. James of the Field of Stars," as the trail winds beneath the Via Lactea–the Milky Way.

Some say the Camino was originally a Celtic pilgrimage route with pagan origins. The Celtic Camino concluded farther west at the city of Finisterre, the "End of the Earth", at the Atlantic Ocean. The Celts passed along their knowledge and traditions orally—there is no archaeological or historical documentation—so we cannot know if these tales of pilgrimage are true or what the purpose of an older, Celtic pilgrimage might have been. Was there, perhaps, a special magic to this farthest western spot in all of Europe? Was it considered a blessing to see the sun set into endless ocean? Were special rituals performed at this sacred site? Whatever the original lure of a Celtic pilgrimage route might have been, the Catholic Church may have woven its own rituals into the walk in an attempt to attract pagan believers into its ranks. According to some sources, churches were regularly built atop sacred pagan sites, holy wells, or springs, and the qualities of the pagan gods and goddesses were absorbed into the Church to become attributes of the local saints. In this way, the Camino de Santiago may have been refashioned by the Catholic Church as a way for a true believer to walk off his sins. Whatever part or parts of the story are true, it was the concept of the Celtic pilgrimage that called to me: a commune with nature, a following in ancient footsteps. It made my heart swell. It felt magical to me. I had not been brought up to believe in saints and their miracles, so as I learned that history of the Camino, I was more than a mite skeptical.

In one origin story of the Catholic Camino, the apostle St. James (Santiago) came to Spain to preach the Gospel of Jesus (40 A.D.). Upon his return to Jerusalem, St. James was martyred, beheaded by Herod Agrippa I (44 A.D.). His body was recovered, the head now miraculously re-attached, and was placed in a stone boat where, with angelic assistance, it floated back to Galicia in Northwestern Spain. There, his body was found shrouded in scallop shells.

In another story of St. James' return to Spain, a bridegroom on horseback was riding along the beach to his wedding just as the boat carrying St. James' body approached. On seeing the boat, the horse became spooked, and both horse and rider were swept into the waters and drowned. Seeing this from the shore, the distraught bride made a plea to St. James for help and was rewarded to see her future husband rise from the sea, his clothing now encrusted in scallop shells.

The body of St. James was buried and, seemingly, forgotten. Hundreds of years later, a shepherd saw a bright light in the sky, and below it, found the remains of St. James. A cathedral was built to house the saint's relics, miracles were said to have occurred, and pilgrims set out along what soon became a well-traveled path to the now holy city of Santiago de Compostela in search of miracles and forgiveness.

In other stories, St. James was seen years after his death, leading battles against the Moors. He was reportedly seen in battles from the year 844 until 1212, when the Moors were finally driven from Spain. In these accounts, St. James is referred to as Santiago Matamoros— St. James the Moor Slayer—and is depicted wearing armor and swinging his sword. In an alternate guise, he is seen as Santiago Peregrino, St. James the Pilgrim, wearing his traveling hat and carrying a walking staff and a scallop shell.

The scallop shell became the symbol of the pilgrim. Worn to show that one was on pilgrimage, the shells may have actually started out as eleventh century travelers' souvenirs, brought back home as a proof that the person had been to the ocean's edge. The shells were also a handy size and shape, a useful tool allowing the pilgrim to scoop up a mouthful of water from a stream or a bite of porridge or stew from a communal pot.

The shell's shape can be seen as a hand outstretched giving alms, a reminder of the handouts traditionally offered to pilgrims along the route. From another symbolic perspective, the scallop shell represents the many pilgrimage routes in Europe, all of which converge at the city of Santiago de Compostela, just as the lines on the scallop shell all converge at a single point.

European pilgrims of the Middle Ages began their pilgrimages from their front doorsteps, walked the entire way to Santiago de Compostela, and then turned around and walked back home—if they were fortunate enough to survive. On their holy walk to the medieval city of Santiago de Compostela, eleventh century Catholic pilgrims would have stayed in refugios (refuges) all along the trail. Many hundreds of years later, the tradition of serving the pilgrims along the route still stands. Modern day pilgrims are accommodated in all variety of albergues (hostels) and offered a "pilgrim's menu" at many restaurants. The bedding is rudimentary. Daily laundry is done a mano (by hand). The toileting facilities are varied and sometimes downright comical. The food is basic and boring, but that said, the Spanish people are warm, welcoming, and deeply spiritual. And I desperately wanted to go.

PART ONE:
Camino Dreaming

A fish cannot drown in water,
A bird does not fall in air.
In the fire of creation,
God does not vanish:
The fire brightens.
Each creature God made
Must live in its own true nature;
How could I resist my nature,
That lives for oneness with God?

Mechthild of Magdeburg

CHAPTER ONE:
Hearing a Divine Calling

*"Not only the thirsty seek the water,
the water as well seeks the thirsty."*

Jalal al-Din Rumi

Sometimes you look from the long perspective and, with hindsight, see life's tiny kicks and shoves, the ones that put you on a particular path or that caused you to study a specific subject, to move to a certain location, or to begin a previously unconsidered career... and then the present makes some sense. But when I look back at how the Camino caught my attention, it's not as if there was a continuous thread of personal history or related incidents that were precursors to a "Sure thing! Let's walk the Camino!" Something in me just clicked. I felt a call to walk the Camino, and my deep connection with the idea never faded, not even over many long and busy intervening years. My plan was to walk the Camino "some day," and "some day" had not yet arrived.

There was no logical reason for me to feel drawn to an ancient Catholic pilgrimage trail. I was raised Jewish and, during my teen years, felt a deep sense of connection with my Jewish faith. In my teens I hated the study of history, found it boring in the way only a teen can be bored. The only knowledge of pilgrimage I possessed came from reading Chaucer's *Canterbury Tales* in my junior year high school English class. I found

I could understand the Old English if I read the stories out loud, and my teacher did an incredible job of helping our class "see" the action. Through Chaucer I was exposed to the concepts of a walking pilgrimage and receiving indulgences, what I would call a "get-out-of-hell-free-card", which one garnered for completing their pilgrimage. But, beyond that limited exposure, I had given no thought to the idea of a walking pilgrimage for more than thirty years.

When I read actress Shirley MacLaine's book, *The Camino, A Journey of the Spirit,* shortly after it was published in 2001, I felt immediately intrigued. Everything MacLaine wrote about her Camino adventure made it sound like a potentially life-changing experience. Even the tough physical grind, the twelve-to-fifteen-mile daily hikes, called to me. The Camino MacLaine described— all but the wild dogs—appealed to me immensely. It sounded like a made-for-me adventure: a spiritual quest, a silent retreat, a connection to centuries of seekers, a walk through history…and all while passing through an ancient and breathtakingly beautiful part of the world.

I felt a draw to quiet time, to time alone walking in ancient woods, and hopefully, to having a spiritual encounter, as had MacLaine. Though I felt the Camino's pull, I did not move forward… not for ten years.

Why not follow an easier path to hear Spirit? Why travel across an ocean? Why walk twelve to fifteen miles per day? Why not instead go to a local convent to sit and meditate? Or even do walking meditation in my backyard labyrinth? Why not walk around my neighborhood and allow God to speak to me here? There was something more calling to me, something even beyond wanting to hear divine guidance. I wanted to be in Spain. I wanted to be in the ancient woods, with the swirling Camino path in front of me, beckoning me to follow wherever I was being led. What I felt sure of at this point was that my personal growth lay on the far side of the Spanish Way.

I spent the next ten years with the Camino nestled in my unconscious, only to have it pop up in the form of gentle nudges from God, Spirit, the Universe, or whoever is in charge of gently nudging. I would spot books on the shelf at the library or at a garage sale that focused on the Camino, on ancient pilgrimage trails, on the Knights Templar whose duty it was to protect the pilgrims. I mentioned my desire to my next-door neighbor, a high school Spanish teacher, and was delighted to learn that he had taken students to the city of Santiago de Compostela. I met people who knew people who had walked the Camino. My eyes and ears were subconsciously on high alert so that a Camino/pilgrimage reference would not pass me by. But, still, I had not gotten serious, not until 2011, the year of my sixtieth birthday.

CHAPTER TWO

Divine Direction and Family Drama

*"The call to adventure signifies
that destiny has summoned the hero."*

Joseph Campbell

The hero's journey is begun when the hero is summoned. It's hard to think of myself as the hero, but I did receive a call. The story of what happened and how it happened still surprises me. I choose to see it as a masterpiece of planning by a Higher Power, complete with a very motivating threat.

In 2008 I began to read and study *The Artist's Way: A Spiritual Path to Higher Creativity,* the creativity course by Julia Cameron. I blossomed by doing the work, journaling three pages of "download" every morning and taking myself on a personal and private weekly "artist's date" to fill my creative well. I read the chapters and did the assigned tasks at the end of each one. I learned whom to trust with my precious artistic creative works and whom I should steer clear of. I was introduced to the concepts of synchronicity, healthy anger, compassion for self, and the benefit of losing a perfectionist mindset. Most importantly, I learned that God wanted me... wanted us *all*...to be creative. I was introduced to God the Great Creator. "How wonderful!"

I thought. I co-led my first *Artist's Way* group and eventually went on to teach the course. As I wrote my daily journal pages, I became comfortable with receiving input from the Divine. In both my writing and in my teaching, words would flow through me...stories would unwind...the perfect exercise would present itself to help my students over a hump. The muse has long been available to work with artists and others with ears set to hear. I was beginning to know what this type of creative download felt and sounded like: effortless, direct, and clear. One day, while writing in my *Artist's Way* journal, the ten years of unconscious, but consistent, Camino prodding went from intangible to an all-out: PAY ATTENTION – BEEP-BEEP-BEEP – CRITICAL MASS HAS BEEN REACHED – PAY ATTENTION—BEEP -BEEP-BEEP–EMERGENCY!!!

I'd made no real world plans for a Camino trip, had never saved any money, never worked on getting into great physical shape. One chilly St. Louis January morning I sat on my old floral living room sofa to meditate and to journal. I remember thinking about the Camino and immediately knowing that this was the time...that I needed to walk the Camino this year, 2011, the year I would turn sixty, "or your life will be forfeit." I heard that last thought come floating through my head, but I was not its thinker. The words came from beyond me. They were spoken to me. I did a double take. Where did that come from? For a split-second I felt afraid. A divine threat? Will I die if I don't walk the Camino this year?

I had experienced this type of unsolicited input before. The divine offerings I'd received in the past were always of a loving nature: a bit of helpful advice, a suggestion about showing compassion or kindness. I realized that what I heard did not feel like a death sentence. I wasn't being told that if I didn't walk the Camino this year I would die. I felt that if I didn't go, my purpose in life would not be realized. My life would stagnate, or worse, I might lose strength, ability, and personal power. And, as a corollary, I felt clear that if I were walking the Camino on my sixtieth birthday I could do *anything!* The rest of my life would be wide open and limitless. I was paying attention! The fear of not going, of not having a powerful rest of my life, of *forfeiting all that I had come to this life to be* was a super-sized motivator!

I decided I would write my travel dates in my calendar. I would make a commitment: *EL CAMINO: March 28 – May 9.* Almost six weeks of walking and travel time, probably not long enough to walk five hundred miles, but I would research and adjust as needed. Perhaps over all these years I had been waiting for a sign: a chunk of money coming in? An opportunity that presented itself to me on a silver platter? Some kind of divine push? And perhaps the words in my head were that push. Writing down the dates in my calendar wasn't necessarily my strongest message to God to show my commitment to going, but I felt a need to do something, even if it was only symbolic. I then brainstormed some go-walk-the-Camino ideas in my morning journal pages: thoughts on budgeting and possible ways to bring in extra income. I decided to ask the boss at my part-time sales rep job if I could work double-time for a month before and after my Camino to make up for the time I'd be traveling. He would either say "yes" or "no" and, of course, I hoped for a "yes." And then there was the thought to ask for financial help from family and friends… now that felt daunting.

I continued writing in my journal:

Had an unhappy chat with Erin [my twenty-one-year-old daughter] *last night. No yelling, not a fight. She did not want to hear what I had to say, "Be honorable with your word. If you say you will do it, do it." Talking about "saying it/ doing it" for myself, this brings up fear about walking the Camino. I want to do what I say I will do. If I commit to going, I want it to happen. If I tell everyone I know that this is what I'm doing, and I ask for their help to do it, I want to succeed. I want to become an example of what "creating one's life" looks like. And, I don't want to fail, to feel embarrassed.*

I remember making a promise to myself, when I failed the written driving test at age sixteen, to never tell anyone beforehand again. My thought had been that, if I failed, at least I wouldn't feel embarrassed by people knowing I had failed. Now, if I am serious about walking the Camino, I need to lose that fear of being embarrassed. I will likely need tons of help to pull this off, and fear of embarrassment will hold me back! Money feels like a huge hurdle to me. Think trust, Deb. Just see how it plays out. Meanwhile, I must do the work of preparing my physical body, doing research, exploring possibilities, being open to what comes. Everyday I must do something that moves me forward. Could I auction off some household goods? Who would buy? Divine Source, could you handle that part?

After my journaling I went to my pocket calendar to write the Camino dates in it. I happened to glance inside the cover of the 2010 calendar, which was rubber-banded to the one for 2011, and came across a notation from a friend's birthday party eleven months earlier to "call Bill who walked the Camino in 2009." Ha! I had totally forgotten that I had been given Bill's name and number! Pretty funny that it was there in front of me immediately after writing the Camino dates in my calendar, after making a commitment! I called Bill. He was receptive, and we made plans to meet for coffee and conversation the following Monday. Bill agreed to tell me about his experiences and to share his photos. I was so excited! I composed a long list of questions and came armed with pen and notebook, prepared to write down every precious bit of wisdom offered: What was it like? Climate? What time of year did you travel? Solo or in a group? Did you walk the entire Camino? How long did the walk take you? Which route did you walk? What to bring? What to skip? Costs: plane, other travel, and day-to-day expenses? Where to find the best, most updated info?

Bill gave me invaluable information. First, my planned dates were too early in the year. He said that in late March the path crossing over the Pyrenees Mountains from France into Spain, the route known as the Camino Francés, might not be safe due to seasonal storms. He told me to wait until mid-April to begin. Bill suggested that my walk would probably last for forty-five to fifty days depending on my pace, my endurance, and how happy my feet were averaging ten to fifteen miles per day. Bill said to get good hiking boots at once, to break them in by walking two to three miles per day, and to work up to walking while wearing my backpack. He suggested that I plan to stop at the refugio (shelter) at Orisson on my first day out, about halfway up the Pyrenees, rather than overdo at the start. He gave me a list of guidebooks, organizations, and a list of which albergues (hostels) to pass up because the facilities were subpar in his opinion. And, most helpful: he told me how to use moleskin to avoid blisters!

I lusted after the experience of a walking pilgrimage the way others look with desire at cruises or trips to the beach or the mountains. I just knew the walk would make me happy, fulfilled, and in some fashion, comfortable in my skin. After holding the Camino in bucket-list status for so many years, I heard a story that felt like a call to action. An Artist's Way friend had gone on a silent retreat to a central Missouri monastery where he hoped to process his grief and begin to heal after the recent death of his beloved spouse. Hearing him describe his retreat experience, I felt an immediate draw to the idea. I just knew I, too, would love being immersed in quiet, being completely available to my self, with no outside pulls on my attention…except if the Divine wished to communicate with me.

The thought of time for me only—to do something just because I wanted to, especially something quiet and peaceful—sounded immensely appealing. My life at the time was kids and customers, family and friends, people whose needs I dealt with according to their requirements and their schedules. My own needs had played second fiddle to the music of others' souls for so long. From childhood on, both my mother's and my sister's needs had regularly trumped my own. This was not the biased remembrance of an Oedipal complex or a sibling rivalry; my mother suffered from depression and my sister was born with physical and intellectual disabilities.

Growing up, I questioned whether my mother was my parent, or if I were hers. From my childhood perspective, Mom appeared to wield her emotions like a weapon in an attempt to control others, to get her way. In her defense, she was a very young mother, caring for young children and with a husband whose job took him out of town every other week. She must have felt the weight of the world on her shoulders. Mom worked hard at cleaning and cooking and caring for us. She tried to be the perfect postwar wife and mother. We were always well cared for physically, but sometimes she would just lose her attachment to adulthood. If she decided we kids had watched too much television, she would scream at us, and when that didn't have the desired effect, she would unplug the TV and, literally, cut the TV's electrical cord in half with scissors. There were times when she would run to her bedroom, slam the door, and we would hear her loud sobs coming from the room. My brothers and I wondered who had caused it, who was to blame. From my perspective, Dad and my grandparents appeared to give in to Mom rather than to encourage the responsible adult in her. Many a time, when her desires and my own butted heads, I was told to just go along with her because she "has problems," or I was warned that I could "win the battle, but lose the war." "What battle? What war? What is wrong with this picture?!" I wondered.

I trusted that my physical needs would always be met and that I was in some fashion loved, but I never trusted that anyone would meet my emotional needs. I never thought anyone would ever tell me that I was important or say what wonderful strengths and attributes they saw in me. I never felt at, or even near, the top of the importance pecking order. That space was reserved for Mom, and later, for my sister.

After my sister's birth, Mom went for stays in the hospital to "rest." It appeared that this fourth child, born with physical and intellectual challenges, was more than my not quite thirty-year-old mother could manage. A year later, when the pediatrician confirmed my parents' fears— that my little sister was not progressing well, that she was "mentally retarded" to use the language of the time— my already stressed mother was even less available to my brothers and me. Our physical needs were still met, we were always fed, clothed, and sheltered, but it appeared to us that our baby sister now consumed all the emotional energy Mom could muster. There were no "girl talks" between Mom and me, no discussion of my schoolwork, my successes, or my challenges. Plus, I came to believe that there was a family expectation that I would be my sister's caretaker. I did not wish this. I felt embarrassed just to be out in public with her. I felt distraught that the sister I got was not one

I could bond with or share life's lessons, joys, and triumphs with. I was p-ssed off with God for bringing me a defective sister.

I later learned that it is quite common in families for a child with exceptional needs to absorb the major part of the parents' attention. Unfortunately for my brothers and me, at that time there were no support groups for siblings. We were left to our own devices when it came to understanding and accepting our feelings of resentment and loss. As adults, we have compared lots of notes and have been blessed to become our own "support group." We all wished we'd received loads of "attaboys" and "attagirls," and we all came to understand how that lack of encouragement might have contributed to our late bloomer life paths. As much as I loved my dad, my grandparents, and my aunts and uncles, and I knew they loved me, I also wanted empathy. I wanted someone to really listen to me and to reflect back to me that, "Yes, living with your mom is difficult. Yes, sometimes we ask you to go along with your mother's wishes for the sake of peace in the family. And yes…sometimes you are right and she is wrong." They did say to me that I had a right to be upset, that Mom was difficult, but I wanted things to change. I wanted a defender who would say to Mom, "Your daughter is right, and you are wrong. Grow up already!"

I played second fiddle to my husbands' needs in all three of my marriages as well. In the 1970s my first husband and I moved from the college town, where we had met and married, to my hometown of St. Louis, Missouri, seeking job opportunities. We later moved to Boston for my husband's education, and still later, to Bahrain, in the Middle East, for his Ph.D research, now with a toddler in tow. Divorce brought me back to St. Louis and into an almost self-directed life choice: I went back to college to get a fine arts degree. Even this stellar idea came from outside of me, from my soon-to-be-ex-husband's kind suggestion that "you have always loved art and so…"

His idea: that after our breakup I might want to explore the arts formally. As unaccustomed as I was to going within, to paying attention to my own deep desires, I'm not sure I would have come up with the art degree notion on my own. Because I had been encouraged to be attentive to the happiness of others, to support the needs of my mother and my mentally challenged sister before my own needs, I just wasn't used to thinking about what I might want. I felt angry and acted rebelliously, but still I walked through life with that bit in my mouth, not free to think of my own desires first, told I was being selfish when I tried.

My post-divorce plan became: get an art degree, get teaching certification, and land a job teaching in an American school overseas. I had loved living abroad! So, yes, I had become aware of one personally sourced desire…only the one. After completing my degree, I moved, not to an American school overseas, but to the Gulf Coast of Florida with soon-to-be-hubby number two. Florida had a much larger need for art teachers than St. Louis at that time, and my fiancé's ex-wife had recently moved to Florida with their children. My child and I moved to a new state because of my intended's ex-wife's desires…and the possibility of a job opportunity. Fortunately, I loved Florida—the warmth, the beaches and tiny islands, the different lifestyles: Greek sponge-diving villages, Clearwater's older downtown neighborhood where we would walk to the dock and watch the sun set, or take the catamaran out for a ride in the Gulf Coast waters. Even an impending hurricane was new and strangely exciting.

Divorce number two, a new husband (number three), and another baby on the way preceded the move to a Georgia military base. Life went on, the third marriage went awry, and, once again,

I was back in my hometown of St. Louis, now age forty-four, with two children, single-parenting again, and still looking for my life, what was right for me, what called to me.

I had recently begun a new business and moved with my kids into a dear friend's very small, three-bedroom home, where we squished in along with my friend and her son. She was gracious to offer to share her home with us as my marriage fell apart... unfortunately, also a moment of deep rift between my parents and me. My mother had again "lost it" with me as I divorced this third spouse. He, too, suffered from depression, and I think Mom may have felt threatened by my divorce, as if the fact that I divorced a depressed spouse clued her in to the possibility that my dad could also divorce her. We never discussed this. She never explained her fears and concerns to me. This was purely conjecture on my part.

I was at a low point, surviving on personal will, on resolve to be a responsible parent to my children. And, I was surviving financially on child support, as new businesses often take months or years to become profitable. After the first three months in my new custom framing business, when I was able to take thirty dollars out as salary, I felt a tiny tingle of excitement. Perhaps I would be able to make a go of this business!

Meanwhile, my friend became increasingly morose and decidedly unfriendly. The kids and I kept her from having the downtime, the quiet, the peace that her home had previously afforded her. As my monies ranged from tight to nonexistent, we ate her Christmas cookies, and sometimes her stew and her fresh-baked bread. I knew she loved my kids and me and that she was incredibly generous to have invited us into her home in the first place, but she had bitten off more than she could chew. Six months into our communal living arrangement she asked us to leave.

I fell apart. I cried and was hysterical, picturing my kids and me in a homeless shelter, out on the street, or, at best, living in the back room of my store, on makeshift beds, showering in the sink, and eating cheap meals out since we'd have no way to refrigerate foods and nowhere to cook. I didn't have the income saved up for a move: first and last month's rent, plus a security deposit. Of all times for my parents to be angry with me! I could not go to them for help.

They hadn't called me. When I called them, they said they didn't want to talk. They hadn't even communicated with their grandchildren for months! I understood this to be a side effect of my mother's depression and whatever other emotional disorders troubled her. The fact that her illness overshadowed her familial bonds of love and required my father to side with her to maintain peace in their home, left me without resources at a time of deep need. Fortunately for me, my friend relented and agreed to shelter us for a couple of months longer, rent-free, so I could build up the funds we would need to move into our own place.

The way Mom finally "apologized" to me after this ten-month-long estrangement was to call me, out of the blue, to kindly report that she had been diagnosed with breast cancer, that she needed to let me know because now I was at increased risk. "They caught it early," she told me, and she would only need surgery, no chemo or radiation. I was astonished: this woman, my mother, had to grow cancer cells in her body to show me love? To attempt to recreate a bond? That's how it hit me…she appeared to me to suffer from an extreme deficit of emotional self-understanding.

In my early fifties the last major altercation with Mom occurred. My now teenaged daughter got into a political conversation with her grandparents over the Israeli-Palestinian conflict. My daughter and her grandmother had a very special relationship. She could speak her mind, and Mom would accept it. No one else in the family could say what Erin said and avoid Mom's wrath. Mom loved her that much. It was when I tried to add support to my daughter's side of the conversation that the discussion escalated into madness. Mom screamed at us as we hurriedly said our goodbyes and walked to the car. She followed us outside, continuing her rant even as we sped off. After that incident and after multiple conversations with my brothers, all of us agreeing to remain forever mute on the topic of Middle East politics, my brothers tried to coerce me into writing a letter of apology to Mom, to once again "make peace with her because she has problems." I blew up.

Fortunately, I was alone in the car when my emotional explosion occurred, cursing loudly while driving on a sparsely populated highway. By the time I reached home, my anger was spent. At that point, after four months of estrangement and emotion-filled family drama, I'd had enough. I was an adult, and I would handle things in my own way. I invited the entire family over to my home for dinner where we pleasantly swept the preceding months of outrage and furor under the rug. My mom would never admit to having done anything wrong, and I was just done with the whole stupid conflict.

I vowed never to be one who would use the wrath of her emotions to control others. I vowed to myself that I would never seek attention through mental or physical illness. And, yet, there were times I had used my emotions to try to control others in relationship. It hadn't worked; it had contributed to the three divorces, but this was the family relationship model I had absorbed.

What I had *not* learned from my family was to pay attention to my own needs, to my own desires. Maybe because the Camino had called to me so loudly and so persistently, I had finally noticed this deep, personal desire.

Stunted by my feelings of unfairness at having to navigate through life saddled with a "crazy mom" and my early fear of life-long responsibility for my sister, my relationship with the Divine felt lots like my relationship with my earthly parents: estranged. And, in both cases, with Mom and Dad, and with God, I wanted a different relationship…not estrangement, but a cautious *pas de deux*, where we would gradually get to know each other again, and at a different level…this time with me as an adult. I was ready to take full responsibility for my part in our differences, carefully choosing when and where I would engage, committing to what felt right for me, and controlling from my end as best I could, knowing that I had no control over Mom, Dad, or God, but only over myself. Yet, while a desired change in relationship with my parents was clear in my mind, the getting-back-into-relationship-with-God part was not a clear thought. It was resting in my unconscious. Looking back, I see my soul-self wanting to believe again, to trust again, wanting to be given proof that God existed, that God would always be there to support and love me, even when Mom and Dad did not.

CHAPTER THREE:
The Year of Trusting

"Carefully observe the way your heart draws you and then choose that way with all your strength."

Old Hasidic Saying

The remainder of January was filled with Camino thoughts: Where to begin my walk? Where to find resources for further information? How to get the Camino funding going? I needed to get an idea of the costs and then, armed with that knowledge, I would brainstorm ways to bring in money.

With a quick head check of expenses, I estimated it would take between $5,000 and $6,000 to cover both my trip and the home expenses in my absence. I hoped to have a $1,000 to $2,000 tax refund coming in, so that meant I would still need to come up with an extra $4,000 or so.

I shared my Camino desires with friends from my *Artist's Way* group at our mid-January meeting. These were my friends from the original group. We had been meeting regularly for three years at this point, doing "check-ins" and dispensing advice, offering support, and sharing what we were learning on a twice-monthly basis. The group was very willing to help me brainstorm Camino ideas. Some suggestions were: to raise money per-mile-walked for a good cause, to get a shoe store to sponsor me with great walking boots. They liked the idea of getting a local paper to pay me for a series of Camino stories. Since this was our first meeting of the year we also talked about our "Year of_____."

In 2008 my friend Kim first introduced her concept of the "Year of_____" to our *Artist's Way* group. Kim explained to us how she selected a new topic every year to study and learn about in every way she could think of: taking classes, reading, traveling, purchases, job direction, journaling, whatever she could imagine. We all loved the idea and committed to a new "Year of_____" at the start of every year. The year 2010 had been my Year of Gifts and Genius in which I explored my own areas of giftedness and created a curriculum to help others explore theirs. While journaling during December 2010, I came up with my "Year of _____" idea for 2011. It turned out to be perfect and a real doozy of a challenge! I had determined that 2011 would be my Year of Trusting. I liked the active verb *trusting*. I hoped to be able to gear up my current paltry level of trust in God/the Universe. I hoped the Divine would shower me with whatever was perfect for me. I hoped that all the right lessons, insights, nudges, helpful people, opportunities, and support would manifest in my life, and be such an obvious show of divine planning, that I would be forced to see it and forced to believe in divine intervention, forced to see trusting as a legitimate way of navigating through life. This is what scientifically-geared, still-questioning seekers do: we set up experiments to prove that trust in the Divine is a viable option. I also wished to once again become trusting in relationship. And, I would focus on trusting myself, my vibes. A juicy challenge!

I hadn't felt trust in anyone but myself for a long time, and I didn't trust myself in the area of relationships. Having been divorced three times, I felt embarrassed by my lack of insight into how to create a healthy relationship. I also had not built up any self-trust in the area of finances due to years of living with low income.

Trusting also felt hard because I'd been let down so often. I trusted my family, but only so far. I never trusted them to totally "have my back." There were myriad people who had disappointed me throughout my childhood, people I started out trusting and then lost trust in.

In my teen years my feelings of spiritual expansion and relationship with God had been unceremoniously stabbed and left for dead. There are no perfect people. I now know this because God once whispered it in my ear as I was bemoaning my loss of trust in someone I had formerly respected. God told me I was to love this person anyway: a needed lesson. But, back when I was in my "observant teen Jew" period, I was a long way off from hearing this message. Teen me was enjoying learning and practicing Jewish customs, rituals, and prayers. I loved to follow along in my prayer book, reading the English and the Hebrew, and attempting to translate and learn individual Hebrew words. I loved the Rabbi's Torah discussion held for scholars after Saturday services, a Jewish philosophy debate that I was occasionally privileged to hear. During this period two different rabbis failed me…failed at being the spiritual support I needed.

The first rabbi rudely ousted my mentally challenged sister and me from the Sabbath services because my sister, not understanding what was expected, persisted in talking while the rabbi attempted to deliver his sermon. "Will someone please take that child out of here?!" I will never forget the anger in his "Rabbi/Diva" voice. I was both hurt and embarrassed. Here I was trying to do something nice…to spend time with my retarded sister and give my folks a break…and what did I get for my trouble?

The second rabbi, in front of a large audience of teenaged United Synagogue Youth members, failed to answer a Big Question: "Why does God cause people to suffer?" a question I asked, giving the example of my disabled sister. This rabbi ignored me. Although it was obvious that he did not have an answer to this very difficult question, he could have said that, regretfully, he didn't know…that the way of the Divine wasn't always clear to humans. He could have offered to talk with me after the group meeting, hearing my genuine unhappiness. Instead, he turned away, he literally turned his back to me, as though I and my question never existed. He lost quite a few youth group members that day.

I felt savaged by both rabbis' unkindness, by their imperfections, and removed myself from all things Jewish and all things religious for the next twenty-five years. It would have been wonderful for me if the synagogue youth group had been able to answer my spiritual needs, my early challenges, my discomfort with a God who would make my sister so not what I wanted. And, as much as I craved a spiritual life, a peace coming from divine support, a mystical experience…what my spiritually inclined teenaged self got were figurative smacks in the face from some of the adults I looked to for spiritual guidance.

Though soured on Judaism by the unfortunate experiences with the two rabbis, and rejecting all forms of organized religion as being responsible for war, for exclusion, and for hate, wanting no part of any flawed belief systems, I remained open to the spiritual and the mystical.

The magic of Mother Nature, of first green daffodil shoots poking through mud, always delighted me. From early childhood I had loved the plant world. My adult shots of spiritual connectedness were few and far between… mostly showing up as interior feelings of expansion, related to magical places, starry nights, and plant-filled vistas. I felt spiritual tugs, pulls to parts of the world with deep histories.

Exploring burial mounds in the Bahraini desert with my first husband, I had felt a deep connection in that long hallowed place. Seeing a slide show brought back by a friend, one of the first Westerners to tour China in the 1970s, I imagined walking the Great Wall of China and visiting ancient temples...the Forbidden City... places where one could feel the mystical, feel the wisdom of the age, undiminished by modern human touch. I wanted to explore places that felt peaceful, with a connection to something older and greater. I wanted to feel lit from the inside. I wanted more, but I didn't have the words to describe what I sought. Nor did I have the quiet time to seek.

I left my spiritual self behind for decades, relishing the occasional spiritually expanded moment that presented itself for me to experience, but mostly, I felt spiritually alone and abandoned.

My Year of Trusting began with the exciting news that my daughter Anna desired to go to grad school. "That's wonderful," I told her. "It will happen. We don't always need to know how, but just go forward a step at a time and trust that there is a way." I was talking to myself here more than to Anna, trying to solidify my own ability to trust. I loved the thought that I might be taking others along with me on my Year of Trusting journey. I hoped that my kids, other family members, and my friends would all get to see me trusting and taking the steps toward my Camino big dream. I wanted to realize my dream and in doing so, inspire them to go after their own dreams!

I was excited and, yet, afraid that I wouldn't be able to pull it off. As much as I was trying to stay with my feelings of excitement, my actual focus was on lack of money. My daily money fears even entered into my dreams. Since I knew this worked against me, I created a very loose three-step plan in my journal:

1. *Pray and very consciously attempt to let go of worry. As an ongoing, day-by-day process, I will attempt to notice and drop worrisome thoughts as quickly as possible.*

2. *Have my planning-for-the-year reading with Nikki, my intuitive adviser, and ask her to use her amazing intuitive gifts to give me needed guidance.*

3. *Do my personal accounting and find exact trip costs. For me, usually, more information is helpful. Having no idea how much money I will actually need is stressing me out. I warrant that having some figures, beginning to visualize the "thermometer," and seeing the money level rising to the top, will be an antidote to my current fearful focus.*

During my yearly reading, I received Nikki's usual spot-on and helpful information. It always feels like she tunes in to a specific heavenly frequency and gets useful feedback for me from my angels and my divine teachers. Nikki said that last year I had gotten clear on what I wanted, on my deep desires. This year, Nikki said, would be about "standing behind your deep desires," allowing them to be heard out in the world. This turned out to be a critical piece of information in my Camino quest. Many times before and during the pilgrimage I'd have to gird my loins, go past my fears, and ask for help. Or, I'd have to get on a plane, a train, or a trail, not knowing what would happen during the day's trek or when I would reach my destination. I would come to find immense personal courage in this concept of standing behind my deep desires, of being so aligned with my goal that nothing would deter me from it.

I often awake to a mental "sound track." The next morning, after my intuitive reading from Nikki, these lyrics were playing in my head. Had I heard this song in the grocery store the day before or on the radio?

I didn't know if I had the lyrics right, didn't remember whose song it was, but I understood the meaning for me. If the Camino represented Spirit/Divine, if I would be walking with Spirit, it made so much sense:

"With you (Spirit) by my side, you know the way I feel.
With you by my side, your (Camino) secrets to reveal,
For you are the magnet and I am steel..."

I felt forcefully attracted, magnetically pulled to this path where Spirit knew my feelings and understood my deepest desires, where secrets would be revealed. Part of standing behind my deep desires, in this instance, was knowing that if I did go, my life would move forward on the path my soul had selected. And, if I didn't go, I would sit and feel blocked. I desperately wanted to go walk the Camino!

CHAPTER FOUR:
A Divine Download

*"It is quite possible to leave your home for a walk
in the early morning air and return a different person—
beguiled, enchanted."*

Mary Chase

If I wanted to be able to comfortably hike ten to fifteen miles per day on the Camino, I would need to do more than just tone and tighten! And walking two to three miles per day was the preparation Pilgrim Bill had suggested, so…

Many blessings are gained by doing regular exercise: healthy lungs, strong muscles, and other happy body parts; time to think and reflect; peace of mind; and of course, endorphins, the feel-good hormones that exercise releases. I don't know that I was surging with endorphins, as slowly as I walked, but with regular walks I began to notice small health improvements. During the first few weeks of my Camino prep, I would feel a burning sensation in my lungs. Whether from the cold January air or from my years of inactivity, the pain caused me concern. The burning feeling would go away after walking a half mile or so, and in time, I didn't feel it at all. Every day was a struggle to "just do it!"—to put on my boots and my coat and go outside to walk. Once I pushed myself out of the door I was fine. I came to enjoy my walks immensely.

I usually walked one of two neighborhood routes: the first, mostly flat, or, the second that featured a steep downhill trek. As I knew I would be climbing the Pyrenees Mountains at the beginning of my pilgrimage, I opted for the pitched walk except on days when there was ice or snow cover on the ground. I would descend, go up the other side, turn around, and walk back down and back up, a trek of two or more miles depending on which route I took heading home. I first walked in my old boots…more a fashion style than a real pair of hiking boots. When I finally got around to purchasing good hiking footwear, I had barely enough time to get the new pair broken in. A big oops! I was running very late in my preparations. I didn't get around to walking while wearing my backpack until the last few weeks before my departure. Consequently, I found walking while wearing only a modestly heavy backpack to be a challenge during the whole trip. A friend lent me her backpack and the kind REI staff checked it out for me to make sure it was a good fit. It was fine with a few adjustments, but I was still learning backpack-wearing lessons well past the middle of my pilgrimage. There is no substitute for experience! My preparations were barely acceptable, and I ended up paying the price.

There were many pre-Camino days when I walked with friends, but most days I walked alone. I enjoyed my solitary walking time. I kept to my own pace, noticed the scenery, the bits of brown-green grasses peeking through the melting snow. I became adept at watching out for black ice and doggie droppings. When the weather was just too miserable to walk outdoors I would mall-walk. A huge blessing for me was that when my body was walking, my mind was free to explore, to imagine.

One sunny, but chilly morning, an idea for a guided meditation came to me as I walked. Perhaps it came as a result of my extreme Camino-focus, or perhaps it was a divine download.

Perhaps I was being prepared to "hear" it as part of my Camino prep. As I walked, my imagination took my well-bundled-up self to a lovely (virtual) neighborhood park where in my mind I saw myself gliding across the icy paths feeling very in control of the glide, until the path dipped down, and I found myself falling into an Alice In Wonderland-type rabbit hole—falling, falling, falling—and eventually landing gently and unharmed. In my imagination, I looked to the side and saw a lush, green landscape, beautiful open countryside, and a path leading to a mountain.

The mountain seemed to pull me towards it—just like the song lyrics: "you are the magnet and I am steel." The meditation continued with me walking to the mountain, finding my special path to climb, and in the process, meeting those who would offer me advice, who would make clear my own inner wisdom. I received symbolic gifts. I shed old fears and hurts. And, best of all, I received my heartfelt dream. After the meditation ended I felt calmer and less burdened by current worries. "Thank you, God! Thank you for the inspiration!" After I had completed my walk, back at home in the real world now, I began to write it all down. Many handwritten pages later, it felt complete. I had remembered all of it. [The Pilgrimage to Essence of Self Guided Meditation, is in the Appendix, on page 274.]

My pilgrimage had begun, though it would be months before I set foot on the actual Camino. I was in pilgrim mindset; feeling what a pilgrim feels, open to adventure, to new people, and to new ways of seeing myself. I think the divine download of the guided meditation—that's what it felt like to me—came about as a result of my willingness to receive: words, monies, new friendships, life lessons. I was ready to learn about life's mysteries and about God's (sneaky) plans for me.

CHAPTER FIVE:
Divine Fine Tuning

*"All will be well, and all will be well,
and all manner of things shall be well."*

Thirteenth century Christian mystic, Dame Julian of Norwich

When one has finally gotten in touch with a deep desire, a big dream, what should follow is a series of actions leading the person directly to their heart's desire. I don't believe this is how life proceeds for most of us though. For me, the time between making the decision to go on pilgrimage and the time I finally got on the plane was fraught with fears, full of discomforts, and yet, in some ways, astonishingly joyful. It was as if the Divine was continually giving me tiny kicks in the hindquarters... some to move me in a totally new direction, and some to only slightly alter my course. It seems I needed a great deal of divine fine tuning.

I began to wonder if this was actually a Skinnerian-type experiment in divine positive reinforcement. At times it seemed to be just that. Every time I would revert to my habitual fear-based response to lack of money, and instead manage to "flip" to finding a way to trust that my needs would always be met...that I would always be cared for...every time...the Great Psychologist in the sky would reward me with some sort of "treat." My problem: I was far less adept at learning the Experimenter's lesson than most lab rats!

During this early stage, a part of me was completely clear that I was supposed to go on pilgrimage, and that God appeared to be showing up and doing His Work in the much heralded "mysterious ways." Unfortunately for my peace of mind, there was always the more skeptical and fearful part of me trying to peek behind the Great Oz's curtain, looking for proof of a divine commitment to me. I struggled with the concept of "trusting" for a full three months before I left for the Camino and, although I would have some fabulous successes in my experiences of trusting, I remained tightly bound to my fears and never learned to "think trust" as my initial go-to response throughout the entire journey.

⌒

The notion came to me that I must be in complete integrity with my Camino desire, that I must be one hundred percent committed to it, or I would never be able to get anyone else to support me in this venture. And, I knew I would need help from my family and friends to make this journey happen. I composed a long letter describing my deep desire to walk the Camino and all the types of assistance I would need in order to realize this dream. I wrote, added to, and re-wrote the letter over and over again. I seemed to have a mental block when it came to sending it. Although I had received glorious support when sharing my Camino desires with my *Artist's Way* friends, I felt fear at the thought of sharing my plan with my family.

There was a history of tension in my family concerning different-from-family religious beliefs. It began in my early childhood, the years before Teenaged Me became excited by Judaism. In grade school I was pushed towards Judaism, forced to attend Sunday School, and it was expected that I would be bat mitzvah-ed. I pushed back strongly. I did not have an interest in Judaism or Jewish studies at that time. When I later became involved in my synagogue's teen youth group, the tables turned: then I wanted to go to Sabbath services, to sing the rich melodies of the Hebrew prayers, and to see my friends. I met other teens from local synagogues and from all over the central United States. We met at yearly conclaves, at summer camps. I corresponded with new friends from Denver, Minneapolis, Kansas City, and Des Moines. The United Synagogue Youth were creative and smart; they loved music, plays, and parties, and they also felt called to religious practice and deep conversation. Now I was the one pushing my parents to be more observant: to attend regular Sabbath services, to keep a kosher home. We were never in synch, my parents and I, always wanting something more that the other could not—or would not—give.

In my adult years I'd seen painful family division and rancor when my brother converted to Christianity. My three non-Jewish husbands had been held at arm's length until my parents grew to know and respect them. Of course, political comments about the state of Israel, if different from my parents' beliefs, had become off limits due to the friction and estrangement they caused. I had long since learned to keep my spiritual beliefs private for fear of stirring up family conflict. My parents must have been avoiding conflict, too, because they never asked me to share about my beliefs. And now I was going to need to expose at least some of my hidden self. A Catholic pilgrimage trail for a little Jewish girl? *Oy vey!*

Tuesday, Feb. 1, 2011, Journal

I finally spoke to Mom about my Camino desires last night. She seemed interested! Isn't it funny that the question my brother Sandy said she'd ask first was correct: "Are you going alone?" So, her concerns center on fear/safety issues. My guess is that both safety and money issues will come up with Dad. But, I gave Mom info to Google, and

I'm sure she'll have lots of questions to ask me later. I purposefully didn't share much about the Catholic aspect of the Camino. Mom can see the benefits for my physical health, and she is very supportive along those lines. Can I be up front with Mom and Dad about more of the real me? Past lives, heart-centered beliefs vs. religious dogma. This will be interesting. Anyway, I am totally pleased to be getting such a positive initial response to my plan. Before bed last night I had the thought to ask former pilgrim Bill about the safety of the drinking water on the Camino. Also, about medical needs, ATMs, and Internet cafes.

Thank goodness that at this point my mother seemed to have mellowed somewhat. She hadn't flown off the handle at me for years. She was, we later realized, being affected by a neurological illness that was causing her to frequently lose her balance and, on occasion, made it difficult for her to speak her mind, to get her words out. She was likely aware that something was "off" regarding her health. In hindsight, this period was actually a blessing for Mom and for me as we had a chance to do some fence mending. I had opportunities to willingly be of help to her, and she had chances to "attagirl" me.

I had gathered together my income tax paperwork and sent it on to my accountant to work her legal magic. I was praying for a hefty tax refund. And, after weeks of writes and rewrites, a polished and heartfelt Camino letter to family and friends was typed and ready to go out. In being so open I was making a huge commitment to myself to actually go through with this adventure.

I knew that in making this very public request for help, I would be watched. If I sent out the letter, and then changed my mind, I would be labeled a "quitter" in the eyes of many. Even more important, I would be a quitter in my own eyes… and my life *would* be forfeit.

I finally e-mailed the letter below, in batches of sixty, to two hundred thirty friends, family members, and acquaintances, even to a few folks I barely knew, but with whom it felt right to share. I was so nervous I had to say a prayer each time before I hit the "send" button. I was laying my thoughts and desires out there for all those in my life to read. I had never felt so exposed, so completely open in my entire life. This was the real source of the extended delay in sending out the letter: my fear. But in the end, it was all perfect, even though I did not, at this point, know why.

Sunday, 2-13-11, E-mailed letter, sent out to 230 People!

Dear Family and Friends,

Over the last ten years I have had a persistent and consistent desire to walk an ancient pilgrimage route called El Camino de Santiago de Compostela or The Way of St. James of the Field of the Stars. The Camino trail begins in France, crosses immediately over the Pyrenees Mountains into northeastern Spain, and continues across northern Spain to the city of Santiago de Compostela, a journey of approximately five hundred miles. If time permits—the time frame I am planning for is from mid-April through the month of May—I will then continue west past Santiago to Finisterre, the End of the Earth, on the Atlantic coast of Spain before heading home.

I feel a strong calling to do the walk this year. I will turn sixty in May and my deepest desire is to be walking El Camino on my sixtieth birthday. I believe this will set the tone and set my intention for the balance of my life: to be a strong, healthy, able, adventurous, and heart-centered woman, to be always a seeker of truth, peace, love, and understanding. I can't say exactly why I am so drawn to making this journey. Perhaps it is a past-life connection. That feels true, but

I believe there's more. There is something here for me to learn about myself and about my place in the world.

I go as a spiritual pilgrim, not a religious one. I make no vows and I receive no indulgences, no remission of sins, as an eleventh or twelfth-century pilgrim might have done. I go with a deep desire to learn from this experience and as deep a desire to share what I've learned on my return. I feel a call to teach, and whatever I am to teach, I will learn on the Camino.

I need help to make this happen. Please support me in whatever way you comfortably can. If you have items I can borrow or use, if you have ideas, frequent flyer miles, or money, whatever. Believe me when I say I have never made a request like this for myself before, and I would not if this were just a passing fancy or a lark. This is me creating my life…me stepping into the life I came here to lead.

Thank you from the bottom of my heart for your help in whatever form. Prayers are definitely welcome. Speaking of prayers, for anyone who would like me to deliver prayers, either in written form to the cathedral in Santiago de Compostela or to simply express your prayers for world peace, for repair and renewal of our home planet, for more love, compassion, and understanding, as I walk the path I will gladly deliver them. I hope to spend time in prayer and contemplation each day.

Please call or e-mail any ideas you have for ways I can fund this journey: through income-earning opportunities, through gifts, grants? I am open to receiving in all ways. Please open the attachment to view a list of what I currently know I will need to make the journey and to see how you can pledge to Habitat for Humanity based on the total number of miles I walk.

With much love and gratitude,
Deborah Terra Weltman

NEEDS LIST *[the attachment]*

From REI or other hiking/camping supply store, or, if you own and can lend:

- *Water-wicking/quick-drying clothing: 2 pair zip-off pants-to-shorts, 1 long-sleeve insulating t-shirt, 2 short-sleeve t-shirts, 4 pairs each thick socks and sock liners, undergarments*
- *Fleece vest, gloves, and hat*
- *"Hump-back" poncho to fit over backpack*
- *Fold-up, lightweight sun hat*
- *Micro-fiber travel towel*
- *Waist belt pack to store valuables*
- *Thin and very lightweight sleeping bag with a cinch sack*
- *Camel-back (bladder) water carrier to fit into backpack*
- *Mylar thermal blanket*
- *LED flashlight with a whistle on a lanyard*
- *Hiking boots with orthotics—need ASAP so I can get them broken in*
- *Small digital camera with a waist pouch*
- *Foam ear-plugs for sleeping in hostels with snorers*
- *Various emergency medications: antibiotics/Z-pack, Imodium, Arnica Montana*

BIG HELP NEEDED!
- *Visits with a personal trainer to get in top shape*
- *Lots of folks to walk with me!*
- *Frequent flyer miles. Enough to cover segments of the trip—OR—other ways to travel cheap/free—OR—an actual ticket! Money to cover bus and train travel in Europe, travel insurance, and help to set up tickets and insurance policies*

- *Money to cover costs in Spain: approximately $25.00/ day X 45 days= $1125.00*
- *Money to cover home bills: approximately $3500.00 for 2 months*
- *A "business manager" to help with various money-related issues, to make sure the bills that I can't pay in advance get paid on time, etc.*

Yes, I can use money. If you can gift me funds towards this trip, I will so appreciate it. I will use the funds with great care and with huge joy! I can also use REI gift cards, travel arrangement help, body training help, items from the "needs list," and ideas: how I can use my home to make money while I am gone, e.g., rental for events, etc. Please spread the word. And, of course, if you need framing or interior decorating, please schedule an appointment now so I can earn as much as possible before the trip.

One last thing: I will be adding a fund-raising component to my pilgrimage. Please consider pledging 5 to 10 cents per mile (or more) towards funding a home for a deserving family through Habitat for Humanity. I hope to walk about five hundred miles, so that would be a pledge of $25 to $50 (or more)! The local Habitat office will take the names, contact info, and pledge amounts of all who agree to participate. Then, after I return, they will send out a pledge form to return with your donation. After receiving your pledge, they will send you a charitable donation receipt.

I have always felt huge admiration for the work done by former president Jimmy Carter after he left office, including, at age sixty, becoming involved with Habitat for Humanity as a volunteer—their most famous volunteer—great publicity for Habitat! As I will be turning sixty on the Camino, doing a "pledge-pilgrimage" for Habitat feels perfect to me!

If none of the above requests is do-able at this time, I ask you to send me your blessings and prayers. And please tell everyone you know about my pilgrimage. Maybe you know the perfect person who will be of great help to me! I am trusting that all is perfect here and that everything is being put into place for the highest good of all concerned. Thank you for your thoughts, your help, and your prayers.

Deborah

Equal Portions of Love, Fear, and Excitement

*"It is never a mistake to search
for what one requires. Never."*

Clarissa Pinkola Estes

Valentine's Day was amazing! I was overwhelmed by the generous response to my Camino letter! Because my "request for help" letter had inadvertently gone out on February 13, I began receiving gifts on February 14, Valentine's Day! Yes, I took in the symbolism. I was receiving gifts of love.

The first e-mail of the day was from my early bird friend Cheryl, also my chiropractor, saying she would treat me once a week for free until I left for Spain, so I would arrive on the Camino in the best physical shape possible. Gifts and offers of support arrived hot and heavy on Valentine's Day and continued to arrive almost daily for the next two months. It seemed I had touched many people with my request and many wanted to help me, wanted to be part of my adventure.

I received money; frequent flyer miles; small necessities: a travel towel, a money belt, a Spanish-English pocket dictionary; and some small encouragements: a pendant with the Rune symbol for courage, a tiny travel-sized meditation book. Over the next two months, in addition to regularly receiving gifts of funding, I was loaned travel gear: hiking clothes, a backpack, a small camera, and an international phone. I was gifted visits with a personal trainer. There were gifts of travel packs of medications, nut butters, and gift cards. People came forward with offers of work. Some even pre-paid for work to be done after my return. I received three months free in a networking group where I met more people who wanted to help me. I received an offer to Feng Shui my home-based business for increased growth. A new friend set up a website to collect monies for my Habitat pledge drive. I received multiple intuitive readings, offers of places to stay in Chicago or New York, depending on where I departed. Friends helped me to buy the right hiking boots, and many friends took turns walking with me. In the end I had received help of some sort from more than sixty generous and loving people!

Even as my Camino planning moved along smartly, my fears continued to surface. Virtually every post to my daily journal began with a downpour of negative feelings: anxiety, "going to the dark side," or feeling insecure in some fashion. My state of mind fluctuated wildly between extreme excitement and extreme fear. It was definitely not all "lollipops and roses." Each day I searched for ways to calm my worried mind, and to move forward.

Wednesday, 2-16-11, Journal

I'm reading the Camino guidebook in earnest now. Need to know more about the costs, the distances between albergues. I am noting the comments about the availability of potable water, sections to avoid walking, if possible, because they are too close to the highway, etc. I am highlighting important info.

I had purchased a wonderful book: a combination map and guidebook of the Camino route I would be walking. "Camino de Santiago" by John Brierley gave distances between albergues, the daily walk's elevation, and suggestions of what to be aware of on each day's route. It was written in English, Spanish, and French to aid in communication between language-challenged pilgrims... allowing us to share info even when we couldn't do so directly. Best of all, this was the "skinny" guidebook. It ended up fitting neatly into my slung-over-the-shoulder travel purse—my perfect-for-pilgrimage Baggallini—and was easy to pull out and check details along the trail...so much easier to access than stowing it in the backpack! The travel guidebook weighed almost nothing. It was perfect! I loved it from the first comment on the opening page: "The Camino's ability to transform and elevate human consciousness remains undiminished over the centuries."

I was drawn to read the entire guidebook immediately. The bits of knowledge were helping me to visualize a somewhat clearer version of what I was heading into. Once on the Camino I would reread sections of the guidebook every day to plan my day's route, to gauge how far I had come, and to make notes. Often, the guidebook and my Spanish-English pocket dictionary were the only reading matter I had on the trail. I sorely missed my stack of books at home!

Thursday, 2-24-11, Journal

I went boot shopping today with Erv and Marilyn. They are so generous. Not only did they contribute monies towards my boots, but they also took me shopping to their favorite sporting goods stores so I could benefit from their knowledge. We saw a pair of boots at REI that I am considering. Robert, the shoe salesman, was very knowledgeable. He showed me how to put the boots on, to gently bang my heels into the floor to settle my feet in place before lacing them up.

This particular pair has great ankle support and fits the best of any I tried on. I will still need to get customized inserts to support my flat feet. The combined costs will make these boots some mighty expensive footwear!

Friday, 2-25-11, Journal

I had a good second meeting with Pilgrim Bill yesterday. Lots of helpful info: costs, phone communication, and lots of other stuff, but the walk itself is feeling scary now. Can I do it? I kind of wonder about my sanity. Why do I want to do this, and why do it alone? And I worry about my health and fitness. I am afraid of not finding my way, of missing connections. And my Spanish skills need help! Then, there's all the prep work to do: having the clothes, the gear. What else? Fears of coming back changed? No, I feel that the change will be beneficial for me. Missing out on _____ while I'm away? No, it will all be perfect. Those seem to be the main fears.

[But one fear was hiding. Once I became aware of this fear lurking inside me, I did a bit of "direct writing," to calm my fears. Direct writing, also called automatic writing, is a journaling method used for contacting an inner or a divine source of wisdom. Using my morning journal time, I asked for answers about this fear.]

Saturday, 2-26-11, Journal

Question: What if I don't like doing the walking pilgrimage?

Answer: You will. There will be moments that are unpleasant, but, by and large, you will gain enormously from doing this work. Your mind will be occupied with song, with birdsong. Your breath will take care of itself. You will manifest all that you need. Your mouth will be happy. You will make friends. Your way is blessed. You will have energy, strength, and appetite for life. It will not be boring. You will find much upon which to focus. Your path is clear. Your path is long, but it is right for you. Go towards it with joy. Fears are false. Please have fun now.

Question: Are you saying to lose my serious attitude?

Answer: Yes, this is for fun. You will always remember this trip as joyous! Bring a sense of humor! Bring your sense of adventure… whatever size it is now, it will be expanding. You are one… a part of the Greater One. Be comfy with yourself. And one more word: smile. It will get you where you need to go! That is all.

[In retrospect, this answer most definitely came from beyond me. It was accurate and useful. The injunction to "smile," simple as it was, made a huge difference in my Camino experience.]

Thank you! I continue to feel better and better. All is perfect: the amount of prep time I will have, the gifts and the help I will be given. The trip, the journey, the pilgrimage will be joyous!

Sunday, 2-27-11, Journal

Yesterday I did a really good job of moving out of fears and into excitement. The successes occurred when I did direct writing and listened to enlightening music, the CD my friend Nayana sent me. Nancy, my travel agent friend, says it will be much easier once I am there and "in it." That is a great thing to know 'cause right now the more I learn, the more anxious I get. This will pass. It will be easier once I'm there!

For today, I will keep returning my focus to: fulfilling my path, moving past "stuck" and into whatever ways I am to serve next. I was discomforted by Pilgrim Bill's revelation that he quit work to be able to walk the Camino and hasn't worked since. He and his wife had plans for a business, but it didn't work out. Now, they are living "off the grid." I wonder if he's given up on a passion, a big dream. And, what would it look like if he had a big dream again? It was scary to see someone who had walked the Camino now stopped in his tracks. Could that be the outcome for me? I have always believed I'd be okay, that I would have all my needs met…up, into, and through my old age. How this will happen, I don't know… Through my writing or teaching? Framing and décor? Sales rep or other jobs? I think I'll just decide not to be fearful about what life after the Camino will look like. I don't know to what Bill dedicated his Camino, but mine will be dedicated to: My life from age sixty on. I will be my authentic self. I will continue to learn and to grow. I will do that which I feel called to do. I will love deeply.

Ellen, my friend from grade school days, called. I had asked her about visiting her daughter in Madrid at the end of my trip. She will check with her daughter and get back with me. Is it fair to ask Jeanne to research other fares, dates, or should I just go with the reservations I've got?

[My sweet sister-in-law, a special cousin, and a dear friend had all helped me by donating frequent flyer miles, enough to cover my entire round-trip airfare, and they also helped me with making the airplane reservations.]

This is the Year of Trusting. How does that apply here? Am I to trust that it's OK to let go and let it unfold as it may? OK, then. I just e-mailed Jeanne and thanked her for all the research she has done. I said to proceed with the dates she has reserved for me. If I want to move forward and to lose my fears, I will have to first acknowledge them. No hidden fears allowed. I want to walk through to the other side, to feeling fearless, to feeling God's love and support. I am always moving forward, sometimes supported by a gentle breeze at my back and sometimes through sticky mud, but I am moving forward.

[Here I was "seeing" into the future…visions of muddy Camino walks to come.]

It was no accident—and this I trust completely—that I decided to go on pilgrimage during my Year of Trusting. Rather, it seems a bit of lighthearted divine humor that led to my many synchronous experiences. I can almost hear God chuckling, "So, she wants to learn to trust? Okay, girlfriend, here are some trust lessons that will knock your socks and your hiking boots off!" The pre-Camino months led me to divine guidance in song lyrics, symbolic dates, sneak peaks, encouragements, and ideas. Everything held clues that more was going on than just the physical world life I could see.

I used all the spiritual and motivational tricks I knew to move myself away from fear and into excitement. I had heard on a radio program that, chemically, fear and excitement are identical in the human body...that we can choose which label to attach to the feeling and, in that way, maintain some emotional control. I regularly practiced "flipping" from the fear label into excitement. In addition to my daily journal pages and my walks, I often practiced direct writing to contact my unconscious or my Higher Self in order to gain insight. I did an exercise known as a focus wheel to ramp up my excitement. And what worked like real magic for me was my dream board, a visual imaging tool used to focus on and draw to one's self what one deeply desires. Previously, I had loaded up my dream boards with tons of images, quotations, and photos, only to find myself scattered and lacking in focus. Because I was feeling very clear about my current desire, I decided to create a simplified, single-image dream board: a photo found on the Internet of a Camino pilgrim wearing a backpack and heading down a swirling Camino path.

As the person in the photo was shown from behind and wearing generic hiking gear, I could easily imagine myself as the hiker. I printed up the image and placed it directly across from my bed. Every time I saw the photo, first thing each and every morning, I would feel an intense excitement. The Camino magic was pulling me in. I also found an image that seemed Camino-like to use as an online banking security photo. I labeled it "El Camino" and was later rewarded by seeing this exact scene when walking the Meseta, the flat plains of the Camino.

Monday, 2-28-11, Journal

Yesterday was an awesome day! I talked with Ellen, and she says her daughter will show me around in Madrid. Erin got her part of the financial aid form almost done. And my taxes are complete. Oye! Such low income! But, I have a nice refund coming! And I had the thought about the Camino: "I can do this!"

Last night Erin went to bed early, frustrated by computer issues. She planned to handle things at school in the morning. I was having a lovely long-distance chat with daughter Anna, when the tornado sirens sounded. I woke up Erin and we went to the basement. We chatted. She texted with friends. We went upstairs after the alert was over, checked weather online, and I checked my e-mail. Jeanne had confirmed my flights! I am set! When I finally got into bed I discovered that sly Kim, who had been over earlier in the day for our Artist's Way group meeting, had slipped a check under my pillow with a note that read, "Pleasant dreams of the Camino!" I went to bed laughing!

I awoke from my dreams this morning with a tiny image of Dad's death. I asked God to please wait, to let me do my pilgrimage, to let us have our family reunion this summer, and to let Mom and Dad get moved to their new senior living apartment. When I looked out the back window I saw that a tree in my yard had been blown over by last night's storm. It didn't crash. We heard no sound. It's still holding on by its roots, gently resting on the neighbor's fence. Unbelievable. I cried and called my insurance agent. I woke Erin and we cried and hugged. Maybe the tree came down as a sub for Dad, a sacrifice? Or, maybe it was the tree's death

I saw? Or, maybe the downed tree, damaging the entrance to my backyard labyrinth, is a sign that it is time for me to do something new: the Camino. A sign that an old chapter is closing and before a new one is opened there will be things that need to be uprooted: trees, old belief systems. There will be the need to replant: trees, faith, a new me? I can take the symbolism: a part of me must be uprooted to make room for the new, for the next step whatever that may be. But for right now, I'm still attached to the same ground. I'm still very sad about my tree, but I thank you God, for protecting me and Erin and our lovely home. I am so grateful that we are safe.

CHAPTER SEVEN:

Focus!

*"Obstacles are those frightful things
you see when you take your eyes off the goal."*

Henry Ford

Tuesday, 3-1-11 Journal

Yesterday I had a wonderful meeting with Jill, the personal trainer. She gave me lots of muscle-building exercises to do and put me through my paces: walking on an incline, walking steps, stretching. Very helpful! I have a couple more questions for her about using walking poles and an exercise to avoid plantar fasciitis. I want to deal with an occasional troubling foot pain ASAP. I will call her today to ask. So glad I went. She says I'll do fine, long legs and all.

Friday, 3-4-11, Journal in Portland, Oregon

Arrived yesterday in Portland, Oregon. Happy and excited to be here! My old Artist's Way buddy, Alex, and his new bride, Mary, are supporting my Camino big dream by paying me to come to Portland to do some décor work in their new home. My anxiety level about the Camino has fluctuated wildly since I got on the plane. I started out feeling very nervous, fears of in-flight ear pain. Perhaps imagining my trip to the Camino in the near future? Eventually I relaxed into the flight and read a Camino book. Since arriving, my right foot has been really unhappy. I'm having some surprising shooting pains. I can now get to the Camino, the tickets are in place, but please God, let me be able to do the walk! I am so ready for new boots. These shoes are not feeling comfy: one blistery area—good practice for dealing with future blisters on the trail—and the foot pain! Please God, help me get my body ready for this journey. Help my body be able to support my soul so I can have the experience I came to this life to have.

On the plus side, Alex and Mary are incredibly kind to me, and to each other. It makes me want to be in that type of relationship. I love their ease and joy in being together. I envy their financial comfort, but that is a by-product of all their years of hard work and of having joined forces. Lucky for me, neither one likes the other's artwork. That's why they've asked me to come… to find a way to place their art that makes them both happy. They are comical, and it is a joy to observe their interactions.

Sunday, 3-6-11, Journal in Portland, Oregon

Tomorrow at this time I will be on a plane back to St. Louis. This morning, at 6:10 a.m., I was awakened by a rogue alarm clock which likely became hidden when we moved furniture and accessories around yesterday. I may have a cold coming on, but I am knocking it back with the saline nasal wash. My phone is charged. My hair is washed. I hear birds chirping outside.

We have successfully hung art where it looks best in each room. We have used both partners' precious items, even using some of Alex and Mary's art together in the front office to good effect. I feel my job here has gone well. Alex and Mary both seem pleased. I am so grateful they invited me. In addition to paying me for my work and travel expenses, Alex and Mary have taken me out to eat. I had a gluten-free pizza, my first real pizza for many months. Yum! Then, sweet Mary decided she would take her yearly REI membership refund and put it on a gift card to give me…said she didn't need anything just now.

She and Alex are both so generous! And, as a bonus, going up and down the staircase many, many times, bringing art up and down to try in different locations has loosened up my painful foot. Thanks, God!

Wednesday, 3-9-11, Journal

I'm so glad my focus is squarely on the Camino now. I am willing to let go of many of my usual activities and even my relationship desires, for now. There are still so many Camino details left to handle! One month plus two days until I head out. I'm scared and excited! The thought "can't wait until it's over, 'til I'm complete" has got to be replaced. I want to be totally present with every aspect, with every moment of this pilgrimage. I want to appreciate every barrier I've overcome, every check off my "to do" list.

It's warm out today (high 40s to 50s), but overcast and windy! I will walk later at some point if I'm not coughing.

Thursday, 3-10-11, Journal

I want to clean and clear out sickness. Maybe I'll focus on that today and help myself to heal. I'll vacuum, neaten up, light incense, ring bells, and create an altar for my Feng Shui "helpful people and travel" area. It's nasty grey out again. I crave sunshine! It feels wintry, cold, ick! I know I have tons to do, but part of me wants to stay in bed, in my jammies all day to rest and heal. I'm just so sick of being sick! I'm past a desire for Chinese veggie soup and hot tea with honey. I want chocolate and curry and flavor! I do feel better than yesterday. I may make a medicine run to the drug store, but mostly I will rest and renew. So much still to do…aargh!

Friday, 3-11-11, Journal

I did my accounting yesterday. I feel lots closer to my Camino goal. Assuming my figures are correct and that my commission check, framing sales, and promised gifts all come in, I am very close. Thank you, God, for resources. I am only about $600 away from all I will need for now through 6-2-11!

So many items still on my "to do" list. My goal for when I'm on the Camino is to: be on the Camino. Be here now! If I get everything handled that I can now, I will be able to let go when I'm away. Someday, and I so look forward to that day, I'll have regular income and enough of it to be able to set up all my bills as auto-pays online and just GO when I want to go. Heaven!

CHAPTER EIGHT:
UN-worrying

*"The problem is that we're focused on problems!
All our energy goes into thinking about, worrying about,
and trying to fix our concerns. What we should be doing is
shifting our perception to a higher level so that we can tap
into our courage and imagine a world that isn't beleaguered
with issues—and actually dream it into being."*

Alberto Villoldo

What is there about worry that we find so attractive? Do we think that worrying about another person is a way of showing love? Is worrying about self a way to become more productive? Is worrying about the future a human attempt at controlling fate? Speaking for myself, my family, and my friends—the people I know best—I would have to say "yes" to all three. We must believe that worry does show caring, that it serves a purpose, and that it changes outcomes. Where did we ever get these notions?

In my family we inherited the worry gene. My grandparents worried about my parents—who worried about me—as I now worry about my own kids. Wait. Make that past tense. As I was preparing for my Camino experience, my plan was to focus on not worrying. After almost sixty years of practice in the art of extreme worrying, I knew I would not be able to flip the switch to "off" or even to dial down the worrying…not without lots of conscious thought and much mindful practice. I went back and forth a lot. Some days I worried until I walked and then I felt better. Sometimes I made lists and worked my plan. That helped. Some days it was all I could do to remind myself that worrying would not help, that worrying would drain my energy and drag me down. The Camino prep, planning, and final push became the perfect opportunity to practice un-worrying.

I eventually came up with a mantra: Planning solves. Worrying dis-solves. I gave myself permission to plan, to write lists, to journal my concerns, to talk with friends, to research, to brainstorm, to pray, and to listen for divine wisdom. What I attempted to remove from my days and nights was any emotionally draining form of worry: "Oh my! Oh dear! What will become of me/you/he/she/it/us/them?"

Baked into the Camino un-worrying course work was the additional ingredient of handling others' worries about me. The most frequent comment I heard when telling people about my Camino plans: "You're going alone?" Who knew that the idea of going someplace alone held such fear for so many? That was the one thing I wasn't worried about!

Monday, 3-14-11, Journal

I woke feeling anxious again today. I know that a daily walk will handle the anxiety and yet, I did not walk yesterday. Instead, I was home when Mom and Dad called to say I should stop doing other things and walk! I don't handle their worry/advice well, even though I know it is given with love. At least three other people talked to me recently about the importance of a regular daily walk. I already feel conflicted. This is not helping. What can I say to Mom and Dad though? Their worry about me drags me down. And I don't like being given advice except when I ask for it. But, I'm not going to change them or their thinking, so what can I say in response?

Dear Mom and Dad,

I know you love me and you want me to succeed at this. If you think there's something I don't know and need to know please tell me. Otherwise, please trust me. Trust that I am doing the best I can and handling things in the way that makes most sense to me. Right now I don't need advice as much as I need support. Your financial support is so appreciated, and also the support of knowing that you trust me to do my absolute best, to know you'll be there for Erin if she has needs while I'm away in Spain. It's okay to ask me questions, but know that I may not be able to answer them well at the moment. My brain is dealing with thousands of details, and I am feeling lots of anxiety. Yes, I have lists of what I need to do. The details are written out. I just feel fragile. Like my Self is full up and can't take in too much of the outside world.

Love,
Deb

I never sent this letter to Mom and Dad, but writing it helped me to understand what I was feeling.

I really need to keep a laser focus on this trip. But first, I still have jobs to complete, a one-day women's program I'm leading for adult ed at the U. of Missouri, family get-togethers, walking with friends, and money details to wrap up. Money…that's where I would love the log-jam to break. The moment the last financial details are in place I will relax but, meanwhile, I owe!

So God, here's my prayer: Let the struggle ease. Let the log-jam break. Let the monies flow. Let my days become manageable. Let me create what I came here to create. And, give me the courage, will, strength, endurance, and support to do my pilgrimage.

Time to move on, to meditate, and make my phone calls. Then, I will either take a snowy walk or a mall walk to exercise my body and to free my mind from anxious chatter.

We laugh about how weather forecasters love St. Louis, as they are never bored here. The classic St. Louis weather wisecrack is that if you wish to test plants to see if they can survive temperatures on the moon, you try them out in St. Louis first. This spring's weather had been typically irregular: 60-degree days in February, big snow in March. In St. Louis it is normal to have four to six inches of snow one day and for it to have melted a day or so later. Because of this weather irregularity, where I could walk was often an issue.

Tuesday, 3-15-11, Journal

I ended up taking a wonderful walk in the slushy snow yesterday. I was warm and dry with my new boots protecting my feet. Now I need to walk each and every day until I leave…in less than one month! Enough time, I hope, to get my new boots broken in.

I'm glad that both of my adult children are so fully engaged with school. I just don't have the time or energy for lots of involvement with them right now. I guess I'll retrieve my dirty clothes from yesterday, get dressed and go for a walk. I can wash when I get back and will feel good for the whole day!

Wednesday, 3-16-11, Journal

It's supposed to be a beautiful day, in the 60s! I'm not feeling like writing at all. I am not feeling creative flow at the moment. Feels like too much else to do. I opened the book, "Creating Money" by Sanaya Roman, at random to get direction on what to do re: money worries. I opened to: "…see myself in the picture and find the 'essence' of what

I want." What is the essence of what I want to do, to be on the Camino? I think it's about creating me, seeing who I am with all of the familiar stripped away, finding the core of myself. It's also about having a spiritual awakening/knowing/understanding, a completion of one segment of life and moving on to the next.

Now I feel like crying. Why? Saying "goodbye" to this life segment? Fear of the unknown? What if there's nothing for me on the Camino? That can't be, there's always an opportunity for learning. I will learn. For now it's just unknown what I will learn. Today I will strive to stay in the present where I can get things done.

I will be so relieved to leave the moneymaking and bill-paying world for seven weeks to see if I am different when I don't have those constraints on me. How will I be different? Less stressed? Walking off the stress I do have? How will I be as far as missing family and friends? I know it seemed like forever last summer when Erin was gone for five weeks. Somehow I don't see myself becoming homesick. I have always felt excited when I was away on an adventure. I think it is usually harder for the folks left at home missing their loved one.

Thursday, 3-17-11, Journal

Yesterday was a big day. Walked four and four-tenths miles on the hilly trails of St. Louis County's Queeny Park with my friend Sandy. It was nice to have Sandy do most of the talking while we walked. I did fine with the walking except when trying to walk and talk simultaneously. Perhaps my lung capacity will increase with time. I'm sure it will. We walked lots of hilly terrain. My boots felt great although my hip and knee were uncomfortable towards the three-mile mark. It was perfect to go to the specialty shoe store immediately after. There were no other customers present when I arrived and all the staff helped me. They all said I was walking crooked due to a shorter right leg and fixed me up with a heel lift in my right boot. Wore the boots the balance of the day. They felt good! Today I will test out the new heal lifts on my morning walk.

It is sunny and warm this morning. I will enjoy walking in this spring weather. We are only a couple of weeks from April. In fact, spring officially begins in less than one week. Today is St. Patrick's Day. I don't think I have any green clothing except for a green sweater, and it's supposed to be in the upper 70s today— too warm for a sweater. 8:10 a.m. Time to get out on the neighborhood "Camino" and walk!

Monday, 3-21-11, Journal

I have walked every day for the last week. I still have to push myself to begin, but I am happy once I get going. Yesterday Mom and Dad gave me a check, Camino money, and so did Uncle Norty. Very generous of them all! Got to see the extended family at the Butterfly House, where we all went to honor Aunt Ann with a bench in her name. It's such a lovely place: an indoor butterfly preserve with Blue Morphos and loads of other butterflies landing on dishes of fruits and on us…magical! Then, we went out to dinner, a barbeque restaurant. Not a vegetarian haven, but Erin and I, both committed vegetarians, ordered side dishes and it was fine. I was glad the whole family was able to get together. I also walked and worked in the yard a bit yesterday. All good.

I am finding it less and less interesting to write these morning journal pages. I feel as if I'm preparing for a "flip" in lifestyle to the Camino. There, I hope to walk first, and write later in the day, to journal where I've been, what I've seen, the thoughts, feelings, the "knowings" of the day. I look forward to that very much! Three weeks until I leave!

Thursday, 3-24-11, Journal

Went for a delightful walk this morning—33 degrees, tiny snow crystals, but I felt good! I stopped and stretched when I felt off, and I had a book idea: "Walking El Camino and Other Stories of Asking for Help and Receiving It!" This would be the story of my experience of asking for help to make my big dream happen, plus others' stories of times they asked for and received help. The book would encourage big dreaming. It would discuss the benefits of asking for help to achieve a big dream. The reader would see that asking for help could lead to getting to do what is personally meaningful, to becoming aware of how much one is loved, and to increased self-esteem and happiness. There would be a section on how others benefit from supporting us, too. Here's the opening: "In addition to counting on the kindness of strangers, how many of us trust in the kindness of our families and friends, trust that those special-to-us people will be there to assist us when the time comes...when we want—not necessarily need— but want help to accomplish a big dream? I knew I was loved by my family and friends, but I didn't know my real value, I didn't really 'feel the love' until I asked for help to realize my big dream."

I guess I'll decide how this idea feels after my return. It feels exciting now!

Friday, 3-25-11, Journal

Last night a dear intuitive-healer friend, Julie, gifted me with a treatment to adjust my legs and hips, and, to remove the energies of others' worries from me. She says I am to ask them to shift from surrounding me with heavy, negative energies of worry, to praying for me. I love that!

Julie described worrying about others as adding "snakes of worry" surrounding their heads. Like Medusa. What a visual! When I thought of worry in those terms, there was no way I wanted to have anyone put even a tiny dollop of worry energy on me, nor did I want to place any of that awful, heavy, weighted-down energy on anyone else, especially not on someone I love!

Wednesday, 3-30-11, Journal

I haven't written regularly for the last couple of weeks. Instead, I have gotten out and walked. Writing morning journal pages and working on my writing project have been put down. Some of this is the shift to the Camino where I will walk in the morning and write in the afternoon. I am eager to be there, but also, I am experiencing fear of the unknown. For a while I was in a very good place. I could just tell that I would be provided for, looked out for, guided. I could tell that the Camino would hold magic for me. At the moment, I am focused on the physical: telescoping walking poles, travel towels, a backpack that fits well, getting from Paris to St. Jean Pied de Port where the Camino Francés begins...the route I have chosen. I wonder (and worry) about where to begin my walk: at St. Jean in France or up and over the Pyrenees in Roncesvalles, Spain. At this point, I can let that last worry go and assume that I will know what I need to know when I get there. It will depend on the weather. If there are late spring storms I will not be allowed to make the Pyrenees climb.

In the movie, *The Way*, starring Emilio Estevez and Martin Sheen, the son dies on the Camino as the result of just such an early spring storm. The movie came out in the U.S. right after my return home from the Camino.

I wonder whether my perfect walking companion will present or if this is for me to do alone?

Thursday, 3-31-11, Journal

About one and a half weeks to go. I feel anxiety, but things are going well. Walked again yesterday with Sandy, about four miles around Queeny Park with the backpack! I did great! I was tired going up a steep hill, but recovered quickly, and had energy to watch my niece Grace later in the day.

CHAPTER NINE

Generosity, (Arch) Support, and Lightheartedness

"I ask for the health my body requires
to serve the purposes of the soul."

Aelias Aristides

The entire experience of asking for help—from both human and divine sources—was a revelation to me as so much went right! In addition to the sense of divine right timing, I had a feeling of intense passion, and of being moved forward. The "rightness" feelings were so strong that I was even able to overcome my fear of asking for help! The most special part for me was the experience of the "right" people showing up at the "right" time. I love the thought that we act as angels for one another! I have thoroughly enjoyed the blessings my many "angels" have gifted me.

Below is what I wrote for my May business e-newsletter before leaving for the Camino:

Three Stories of Pre-Camino Generosity

As you read this I am walking the Camino de Santiago de Compostela, across northern Spain. This is being written in April, before I leave, so I can't yet tell you about the trip, but I want to share three pre-Camino stories that are meaningful to me and that have clued me in to the possibility of divine intervention…not earthshaking divine intervention, but a type that feels personally meaningful.

Story #1: I listen to the answering machine messages at the end of March. There is one from a woman I've never met, but I do recognize her name. I had gotten Peg's name and e-mail address from the art gallery in Eureka, Missouri, where I was teaching *The Artist's Way*. Peg was considering signing up for the class. I put her on my e-newsletter list so she would know about future classes. The answering machine message from Peg says that she's been reading about my Camino pilgrimage, that she has gone to REI and has purchased some of the items I still need. An almost total stranger has bought me gifts to support my big dream! I laughed and called Peg back. We have since had occasions to meet and talk, to begin a friendship. My lesson: There is larger support for me, even beyond family and friends. There are "angels" working on my behalf.

Story #2: Coming back home from an event at the U. of Missouri-St. Louis during a crazy-heavy freak snow storm at the end of March, I couldn't see the boundaries of my friend's driveway and backed directly into the edge of her stone wall. I drove home, checked, and no damage to the bumper. I called Samantha, the owner of the stone wall, to say, "Check to see if there's any damage to your wall. If there is I will take care of it." Fortunately, the wall was fine. But the next morning my tire was pancake-flat. The Auto Club guy came out to put on the spare. Another Auto Club guy came out the following day when I couldn't get the car started to take it in for tire repair. I was hoping the car repairs would cost little, as I wanted to keep my monetary focus on my trip. I was mindful that worrying would not help, that perhaps all of this had happened for a reason; that all was perfect even if

I didn't know why. Later, I got a call from the repair shop. They could find nothing wrong with the starter, the battery, nothing. I may have just flooded the engine they told me. And, they replaced my tire for free because it was still under warranty! My lesson: I am being supported and watched over. There will be help available if I need it.

Story #3: I met Lisbeth at a Your Collaborative Board meeting: a three-month membership generously gifted to me by Karen, the leader and coach, as her contribution to my big dream. Lis heard about my trip and my desire to create a fund-raising compo-nent: pledges per miles walked for Habitat for Humanity. Lis, also someone I had not met before, decided to offer her support by creating a website about my Camino pilgrimage to register pledges. The website was done within a week and beautiful, and I was thrilled to work with Lis. It was an easy and enjoyable expe-rience. My lesson: There is help/support when doing good in the world.

Through all these end of March lessons, I was also supported in physical ways: gifts of equipment and monies, items lent, walking partners, health treatments. I was supported mentally: constant interest in the trip; encouragement; requests to write, to speak, and to be interviewed upon my return. I was supported in spiritual ways with information from intuitive friends and those who work with energies. Plus, I felt divinely supported, and I felt grateful for the generosity, for the prayers, and for the good wishes.

Friday, 4-8-11, Journal

I haven't written journal pages much at all lately. Perhaps that's why I am so off-center. My feet hurt when I wear the boots. [In the end I needed the heel lifts taken out and got additional arch supports.] *And, although I leave for the Camino on Monday—in three days—between the foot pain and the travel days, I won't be walking for the next week.*

Dad is in the hospital. No one is answering the phone. And where is the book I ordered online about the funny Camino pilgrim? I desperately need a laugh! I'm crying a lot. My frequent-traveler friends say this stuff happens before a big journey; that all sorts of roadblocks/difficulties come up. Or, is it just that things feel more difficult because of the approaching departure date? I want my feet to feel healthy before I go, or at least before I begin to walk. And, if they don't feel well, I will begin anyway and hope to ease into the Camino. People are calling to see me one more time before I leave. I still have so much to do, but it will be done in some fashion.

As for Dad's health, I pray for him to be fine, to have no big, or even small, health issues, maybe to learn some relaxation techniques. Is he stressing about me being gone for so long? Yes, I'm sure that's part of it. I suspect he is worrying that I will be "in danger." Danger is not my worry. I'm sure I will be safe. I am worried about my physical abilities. Please God; help me to be able to do this Camino. My head, heart, and spirit are all willing and desperately want to do this. My physical body is saying, "Hey, you don't use me much for years and now you want to do what?!"

Here, I thought to try the direct writing technique to "speak" with my physical self, my body. It seemed an appropriate time for us to have a "chat."

Me: *Physical Body, how can I persuade you to relax into this? You will eventually feel so good because of all this exercise. You will be healthy and able for years to come because of the good habits begun here. You will feel a quality of physical well-being and joy you haven't felt for years! We will be a wonderful team: you, the physical body, and me, the emotional, joy-filled, and compassionate being* *who resides here within you. Please be enthusiastically on board with this plan. Remember two weeks ago when we hiked the park with Sandy? Remember how good it felt to do the same distance as two weeks earlier, this time wearing the backpack, and to not be exhausted at the end? You were elated (or, you felt good, and I was elated). We were both on the home team and winning! What do you need to be able to do this?*

Physical Body: *Time.*

Me: *Is a week enough time?*

Physical Body: *Yes. What I want is a promise of me as top priority.*

Me: *You have that. I can't move into what's next without you. How does "top priority" look to you?*

Physical Body: *You would walk daily, but stop to rest hourly. Take off the boots, rub your feet, and stretch. Drink lots of water. Keep food with you and keep eating, nibbling all day. Wash me daily. Trust your gut (literally).*

Me: *How do I make you a "top priority" where food is concerned?*

Physical Body: *Eat whatever you want, but avoid greasy and gluten.*

Me: *What about sleep?*

Physical Body: *You will sleep and it will heal you. Buen Camino...Have a good Camino. Blessings on the spiritual side of your trip.*

Now, what about Dad? Can I be of help to him? Talk with him. Spend time. Convince him that I am not in danger. Let him know I will call or e-mail at least once per week. Yes, can do.

Saturday, 4-9-11, Journal

I got lots done yesterday and will again today. Dad is okay, coming home from the hospital today. It was stress. Thank you, God! I woke with a new song track in my head: "Today while the blossom still clings to the vine…" I printed out the lyrics and they are perfect! They speak of appreciating everything today and being open to the joys to come. I love it. I will adopt the lyrics as a mantra.

I am so scared and yet, I am excited, too. I am eager to see what will come. I want to be walking and feeling strong in the now, to be meeting new friends, hearing their stories, and to be on an adventure. What's that quote?

"Adventures don't begin until you get into the forest.
That first step is an act of faith."

— Mickey Hart, drummer with The Grateful Dead

I am taking a conscious leap of faith, literally into the forest, into the unknown. I am eager to leave fear far behind.

Time to get ready to deliver the completed framing. Oh! I get it: my customer's last name is Blossom. That's what may have brought the song to mind: "Today while the blossom still clings to the vine…"

E-mail sent to 230 Family and Friends on April 10, 2011

Hello Family and Friends,

I leave tomorrow, and I guess it's normal, but I am feeling quite anxious. Things keep breaking and going wrong, and I find myself looking deeply for the lessons in this last-minute stress. For me, one sign of anxiety is to get a song stuck in my head. I have had my own personal "sound track" running for about two weeks now. Finally a breakthrough yesterday morning: I awoke with a new song! I always check out the lyrics online to see if there is a message. The song was "Today," sung in the 1960s by The New Christy Minstrels and by John Denver. I printed out the lyrics and cut them to fit inside my travel journal. I spent the rest of the day singing them, as it brought me much joy, except when I'd get to the line "...who knows what tomorrow might bring?" At that part I would become teary and fearful. Last night I looked at the lyrics again and to my surprise I'd had been singing them wrong. The correct line is "...who cares what tomorrow will bring?" What a profound shift for me. I am told to be open and lighthearted. I am so grateful for this shift, for this lesson.

Again, I want to thank everyone who has helped me: with loans and gifts, pledges, kind words, advice, walking with me, keeping me healthy, and with prayers! This has been a huge awakening for me, with lots more to come. Please keep praying for me, for my strength, good health, stamina, courage, and for divinely guided luck, serendipity, and synchronicity. I will be praying for you as I walk, praying for all of us. See you in June.

Love and blessings,

Deborah

PART TWO:
On the Camino

"Who cares what the morrow shall bring?"

from Today, composed by Randy Sparks

CHAPTER TEN:
Feet on the Ground

"Courage is fear that has said its prayers."

Dorothy Bernard

"Unless you leave room for serendipity, how can the divine enter in? The beginning of the adventure of finding yourself is to lose your way."

Joseph Campbell

Monday, 4-11-11, Journal

Thoughts as I set out…

I've never thought of myself as the adventurous type. Yes, I've lived in lots of places, but that's because I was willing to follow my husbands' desires, not because of my own joy in adventuring. And, while white water rafting has been on my bucket list since I was in my twenties and still sounds exciting and fun, I'm almost sixty, and it hasn't happened for me yet. Between running my own business, child rearing, and my low income, I've been firmly tied down and have had few recent opportunities for adventure.

How is it I am choosing to act on this, of all adventures? Me, the former good little Jewish girl is setting out to walk an ancient Catholic pilgrimage trail. And since when have I been a hiker? Never. I've walked—for exercise, to enjoy nature, as moving meditation, to walk off anger and think myself back to sane. I can see the beauty in fast-walking and mentally reviewing my upset as I huff and puff. Once my angry adrenaline has been walked away, the root cause of my anger is clear to me. So, walking works for me on many levels, but hiking? Hiking boots, rocky trails, way-marker signs? I've never hiked, never backpacked, never even owned a backpack. And, I've certainly never walked twelve to fifteen miles per day carrying my "home" on my back. I will have six weeks of this in front of me. What am I thinking?

I have often wondered about my Camino compulsion. So much of this Camino desire and planning has felt illogical. Magical? Predestined? Divinely guided and supported? "Yes" to these. Definitely "no" to logical.

And, the desire to go alone? And, to be there walking within the crazy-short three-month prep period I set for myself? I've had just barely enough time to get prepared: to raise the funds for the trip and to cover my home bills while I'm gone, to attempt to get my body strong, to get my first ever, new hiking boots broken in! Thank God there was enough time to go back to the specialty shoe store and have the arch supports adjusted multiple times. My arch-deprived feet may be able to cope now.

Erin delivered me to the Megabus pick-up area early on the morning of my departure from St. Louis. We hugged. I tried not to cry, although I'm sure the redness of my nose was all that Erin needed to see to know I was feeling teary. I loaded my full backpack, with the collapsible walking sticks tied to its front, into the luggage compartment of the bus. Another hug and I got on board. I was wearing my cross over-the-body Baggallini streamlined purse, holding only the barest essentials: Kleenex, lip moisturizer, passport, thin travel wallet, Camino guidebook and travel-sized Spanish-English dictionary. Eventually, after

I had read the instruction booklet for my borrowed camera, the camera too would be tucked in my purse where I could easily reach it.

I was carrying a cloth bag with a few extras: books, snacks, and a hairdryer which would be left at my brother's in Chicago— one last day of styled hair before I left the U.S. Then, I would have "natural" hair and no makeup, whether I looked attractive or not, for the entire Camino. I was wearing my hiking boots and my quick-drying hiking clothes. I was as prepared as I could be.

Tuesday 4-12-11, Camino Journal
Chicago to Paris to Bordeaux

Arrived in Chicago yesterday. Had a pleasant time with my brother, Mick. Spent lots of energy on being anxious. This morning I cried saying "goodbye" to Mick's dog. Awkwardly carrying my full backpack, Mick and I took mass transit to his Rotary Club luncheon meeting at the Union League Club in downtown Chicago. At lunch I met lots of Mick's friends, most very interested in the Camino. I think Mick was enjoying showing off his adventurous sister. Had a nice chat with Pablo—he and his wife had walked the Camino in segments over the course of a few years—and with Pancho, a Spanish doctor. Mick and the Rotarians were easy to talk with and mostly kept my anxiety at bay. When it was time for me to head out to the airport, we collected my backpack from the coat check ladies and hopped on the "L." Mick, a wonderful and gracious host, made sure I got where I needed to be on time and safely.

I'm now on the plane to Paris, about two hours into the flight. My seat-mate has moved to an open seat to stretch his long legs. My not quite as long legs are welcoming the additional space to spread out. I was wondering how my feet would do cramped into hiking boots for seven hours. My boots are feeling better, broken in again after the new arch supports. I have renewed hope!

To pass the time I am reading the instruction booklet for my borrowed camera. I am trying to save the funny Camino book I brought with me, not gobble it up in one long reading session on the plane. I found an airline magazine with an article about the Camino written in Spanish and spent an hour or more pouring over it with my Spanish/English pocket dictionary, trying to translate it. One funny translation was the word "peregrino" [pilgrim]. According to the dictionary, when used as an adjective as in "ideas peregrinas" it translates as "crazy ideas." Good thing I didn't read this until I was already on the plane! Am I crazy? Maybe. I find myself reaching for the rune pendant that Natalie gave me. [Runes are an ancient alphabet of Viking origin, used for divination.] *This rune is the symbol for courage. I must be courageous 'cause I am scared to death and I'm doing it anyway.*

Wednesday, 4-13-11, Camino Journal
Arrived in Paris, later took train to Bordeaux

View from my Bordeaux hotel room window.

I am exhausted! Didn't sleep on the plane. When I finally would get comfy and start to doze, the baby on board would begin to cry.

I yawned for three to four hours at the Paris airport, waiting for my train to Bordeaux. Met a young French woman with a Trader Joe's shopping bag. She had been in the States to visit her dad, a pastry chef, in Washington, D.C. We spoke a bit. She watched my bag while I found the toilet. Paid half a euro to pee. They did have a lovely bidet-like feature!

I sat with an older gentleman on the train to Bordeaux. Richard was escorting his 10- and 12-year-old third cousins from Paris to Bordeaux to see family. Had a good chat with Richard about money and about the book he's writing on preparing for retirement. He explained to me the "altruism-to-materialism continuum." We talked politics, fuels, lots of topics. I think I may have spotted another pilgrim on the train (noting his backpack, boots, and quick dry pants). Will keep alert. A future friend?

Thursday, 4-14-11, Camino Journal
Bordeaux to St. Jean Pied de Port

I am sitting in front of the Gare Bordeaux [Bordeaux Train Station] *waiting for the train to St. Jean Pied de Port. A heavenly day. Sunny and mild. Sat on the edge of a decorative fountain/pool until I saw what looked like an eel swimming there. It kept swimming near me and I moved, fearing it might attack. I wonder if people feed it?*

Now, I am sitting on the steps of the train station enjoying the mild breeze. I am reading I'm Off Then, *the humorous Camino book by German comedian, Hape Kerkeling, that finally arrived just in time for me to take it with me. In it Kerkeling quotes the Dalai Lama about dropping a negative thought, not holding onto it and chewing on it. I love that concept! The rest of the book, while funny, is actually making me anxious. Perhaps I should just "drop" his comments about his Camino experience from my thoughts: crazy and predatory people, filthy albergues, and revolting food.*

So far, in Bordeaux, my food has been revolting, at least dinner last night was: a greasy falafel sandwich with too many raw onions and French fries, or, as they call them: chips. I ate one falafel, a little lettuce and tomato, and a few chips. Then I threw the rest away. I had a nice breakfast at the hotel: yogurt, applesauce, OJ, and a small café au lait. I took a tiny wedge of pre-packaged cheese for later. Of all the foods I don't eat, so many are basic fare here: breads, fish, meats, and caffeinated beverages. I can imagine drinking a small coffee with milk in the morning... maybe a teeny bit of caffeine will be OK? I can eat eggs, cheeses, and yogurts for protein. Then, I will pray for fresh fruits, veggies, and nuts to always be available.

I will board the train in about forty-five minutes, get clear on where I should go, what part of the ticket to punch into the machine, make sure I know what I'm to do. Meanwhile, it is a stunningly beautiful day and perhaps my last chance to sit in the sun with no miles to walk, so I will enjoy! I really have no idea what I am entering into, what this will be, who I will be at the end. I am reminded of my friend Kathi's intuitive reading. She saw me in a past life, as a pilgrim who died on the Camino. She sees me now as ready to complete my past Camino. The idea resonates with me. What also feels right to me is that I still have something to learn that I would have learned in that earlier life. Part of me wishes for a guide and part of me knows that there will be guides, as I need them. I know the Camino is about stepping up to a big new commitment to myself. Perhaps sending out the Camino letter requesting help was just the first of many personal challenges. There will surely be other challenges on the Camino, like finding my way, or staying calm when I've lost my way...ugh! By this summer when I return I will be in a different mental state! I am definitely "stepping into the forest" and this first step is all about having faith and trust. I am courageous!

Thursday, 4-14-11, evening in St. Jean Pied de Port

The train to St. Jean was full of pilgrims. We all looked the same, decked out in our easy-to-wash/quick-dry clothes, hiking boots, carrying backpacks and walking sticks. I heard multiple languages spoken all around me. The views from the train were stunning! Mostly hillside covered with enormous trees, green ground cover, all very ancient and beautiful. Although I have no way of knowing what is to come, I've had a few hints. Multiple intuitive friends back home told me that I will make wonderful friends here and will travel with them. Because of this, I found myself eager to connect with the English-speakers I had heard in back of me. As we exited the train at St. Jean, I asked a very lovely Australian woman if she knew where we were to go. She introduced herself as Charmaine—a good sign— as I already have a friend named Charmaine, making my first new friend's name easy to remember! She introduced me to her hubby, Angelo (Italian/Australian) and their friend, Vince. Charmaine and I chatted as we walked up the cobblestone path (really up!) into St. Jean. She knew where the Pilgrims' Office was as she and Angelo had begun the Camino there the previous year with their daughter. Their daughter had fallen on the trek down the Pyrenees, broken a bone, and they had to pack it up for 2010. Charmaine and Angelo were back to try again. No interest from their daughter, but friend Vince, a recent widower, had joined them.

We went to the Pilgrims' Office where we got our "credentials," our passports. The pilgrim's passport is not a government-issued passport, but one must have it to stay in the albergues, the hostels for pilgrims found all along the Camino. At the Pilgrims' Office we declared our countries of origin, gave our home addresses, and showed our legal passports. Apparently, they keep records of who's on the Camino for just-in-case situations. I also got to choose my scallop shell, the traditional symbol of the pilgrim. It is worn on the backpack or the body to denote that one is on pilgrimage. I attached mine to a loop on my backpack so it can be seen when I walk. And I made my reservation for tomorrow night at the Orisson albergue, about halfway up the Pyrenees. I will be doing the short walk tomorrow. I have been warned not to take on too much the first day. As per my Camino guidebook, what comes next, after the "credentials" and the scallop shell will be the traditional blessing, a meal, and then the walk. I love that. It feels so right to me. I must have had a past life as a pilgrim. A Celtic pilgrim? Did I start out from somewhere in Ireland or, perhaps, from the tiny island of Iona? Was I a scribe who worked on the Book of Kells? I feel a strong draw to certain parts of European history. Did I continue past Santiago de Compostela to Finisterre? I can see myself as a seeker in another lifetime, walking to learn. I am ready to revisit my past. Ready to re-learn. It is time.

Charmaine, Angelo, and Vince found a suitable albergue a few doors down from the Pilgrims' Office while I completed my sign-in. They came back and fetched me, and I signed in at the albergue. The albergue owner, Christienne, was wonderful, warm, and welcoming. The albergue, also her home, was chock full of art, cats, and dogs. Fortunately for me, she keeps the doors to the dormitory rooms closed, so I should have no dog and cat allergy issues, no sneezing and runny-nosing away my first night's sleep on the Camino. Then Charmaine, Angelo, Vince, and I went out to tour the town, to search for the church that would hold our first pilgrims' mass and to find a place to eat our first pilgrims' meal together after the mass. Yes! My first Camino friends!

St. Jean is an unbelievably old town: cobblestone streets, one main drag, and a wall surrounding the entire town. The pilgrims' mass was in a much larger church than was needed for the local population. Attending were a few rows of town folk and about as many pilgrims. The service was in French, a language I have never studied, but I enjoyed listening intently for the few words I could decipher. At one point, the priest read a list of all the countries that we, the new pilgrims of this day, had come from. And he prayed for our safe journeys. I found the service very moving. Even though I was not brought up a Catholic, I felt cared for. And I was proud to be part of such a diverse group.

Charmaine, Angelo, Vince, and I strolled the town until we located a restaurant that offered a pilgrims' menu. This evening: chicken broth soup, pommes frites, either chicken or lamb, and a galette for dessert. No vegetarian options. I can't say I was surprised. I knew being a vegetarian in France and in Spain would be a challenge. I ordered a Salade Niçoise and "fished" around in it to avoid the tuna, though eating some. My new friends are all concerned about my lower protein consumption. They are very sweet. I do hope I will get to travel with them some more. They are planning to do the whole Pyrenees climb tomorrow, up and over in one day, but they will be taking off for Good Friday at the end of the next week, so there's a chance I may be able to catch up with them then. I loved our dinner discussion of world religions. We lingered after our meal, enjoying the wine that came with the dinner. Although I'm not much of a drinker, I enjoyed their company, the conversation, and the night air. We are all accepting of one another's beliefs, of each one's personal path. Good folks! When we were done with our meal, we strolled the cobblestone main drag, noticing where the village fountain was located. That's where we will fill our water bottles on the way out of St. Jean in the morning.

Back at the albergue, I showered and washed my socks and underwear in the bathroom sink. Christienne hung my clothes on the line in her backyard for me, not wanting pilgrims to go out to her backyard and disturb her dogs.

Met all these lovely people today: Solveig from Sweden; Angelo, Charmaine, and Vince from Brisbane, Australia; Christienne, our inn-keeper/private albergue owner from St. Jean Pied de Port, France; two girls from Brazil; Meagan, James, and Detty (short for Bernadette) from where (?); and a girl from Seattle. It's now 10 p.m. Lights out in the albergue.

Friday, 4-15-11, Camino Journal
St. Jean Pied de Port to Orisson

I am in Orisson! I'm at the albergue after a climb I was not prepared for on so many levels: needed more practice, more oxygen, less stuff. Some of the extra I am toting is food from home and food items purchased in St. Jean. The English speaker working at the albergue here in Orisson tells me that the climb from St. Jean to Orisson is the worst part of the Camino: ten kilometers long (six plus miles) and about seven hundred fifty meters up. From looking at my guidebook map, I think the gentleman was only being kind in telling me I'd already done the worst leg. I must look awful. What shade of red am I? A perfect stranger just asked if I was okay. The road here was mainly uphill, part paved, part dirt, part uneven rock, all at a steep enough grade that I am glad I elected to do only the short route today.

Ascending the Pyrenees

Just went to the bathroom and saw myself in the mirror... my lips are white...oxygen deprived? Anyway, it is 11:45 a.m. I got up at 6:15 today, packed, washed up, and dressed. The albergue in St. Jean was lovely, but I was too wound up to fall asleep right away, and the snorers fell asleep before me. It got loud! I don't think I slept much. I brought earplugs with me, and I used them, but I think I needed some more powerful ones, perhaps like what the folks wear to guide jet airplanes on the runway!

Between lack of sleep, lack of oxygen, and lack of enough pre-prep, I think I did well today to walk as far as I did.

I had to stop often to rest, to breathe, and to let my heart rate settle back to somewhat normal. There was a period where I could only walk ten steps, then rest...walk ten more...but I am in Orisson! I think the name must mean "horizon" in the sense of the view, of seeing off into the horizon. Phonetically similar? Same root word? No matter...the view is breathtaking! I hope my foggy photo will show it well. I've never been up this high in my life!

Orisson, later, 4-15-11, continued

After the albergue rooms were ready, I went to my room with the intent to wash my body and clothing and rest a bit before our communal evening meal. I learned that the showers are coin operated. Really? I was given a "token" for the shower, told the shower would then give four or five shots of water, each about one minute long. I could press the button to control when the water would begin. I have now showered. Surprisingly, the shots of water worked. I washed some clothes in the sink and am now attempting to dry them in a coin-operated dryer. I don't think the dryer is heating. My clothes are not getting dry. No problem. I will hang items on the ends of my bunk bed and hope they will be dry enough to pack in the morning. If not, I have safety pins. I read somewhere to bring safety pins along for pinning damp clothing to the outside of the backpack, to dry while walking in the sun.

We are six pilgrims to a room. They have tent camping outside too. Glad I'm in here. It will get cold out tonight. My roomies so far are: Kim from Korea, Marion from Germany, Carmel and Terry from Australia. Now to read, relax, and rest a while.

Later still

Dinner was awesome! We are about thirty pilgrims total here in the albergue. Married couples, friends, individuals like me. We went around the long table and took turns saying where we were from and why we had decided to walk the Camino. There were Aussies, Koreans, Japanese... folks from everywhere... here for every reason: exercise, vacation, spiritual, religious, to honor a loved one. The meal was filled with laughter and delight! I feel so blessed to be a part of this community!

Saturday, 4-16-11, Camino Journal
Orisson, France to Roncesvalles, Spain

I met so many people today! Gaby and Judy. I saw Carmel and Terry from Australia again and their friend from Ireland. Spoke with Etta-Maria (she's from both Denmark and Spain). She gave me lots of good walking advice. Carmel also gave me good tips about using my walking sticks: L hand/R foot... R hand/L foot...and, she told me about her Aussie six-week paid leave from work! Marie Yvonne (probably in her 70s, this is not her first Camino) told me to walk slowly and to walk on the grass where I could. She says it's softer than the paved path, easier on the feet. Judy suggested I wait and ask someone if I'm not sure where to go, rather than to backtrack, which is too hard and damaging. She's absolutely right. Terry says I need to adjust my backpack. He's right too. It felt awful today. I am again assured that this is the worst part of the Camino, up and over the Pyrenees. I read somewhere that O'Cebreiro, towards the end, is worse but at least I'll be in better shape by the time I get there.

The day began well. I had a pretty good pace going up from Orisson towards the top of the Pyrenees until I mistakenly followed folks going up on the high ridge. It looked like a scene from "Heidi."

I really felt like I was on top of the world and that was exhilarating, until I picked up on the first clue that I might be going the wrong way: I seemed to be heading away from the city visible below. I asked a Spanish couple strolling towards me if this was the Camino, "Está el Camino de Santiago aquí?" (Is this the Camino de Santiago here?) Pidgin Spanish, but they understood me. They said "no" and

ushered me back to the correct path, but not before I had gone a kilometer or two out of my way, in good part uphill. The Spanish couple
was so sweet. We chatted a bit. He spoke some English. I attempted
some very basic Spanish to include his wife in the conversation. Then
they pointed out the marked path I had missed, and directed me
towards the easier of the two downhill paths. I was doing better than
the day before, starting to acclimate to the oxygen levels, or actually
getting stronger, but I was very tired at this point, and ready for the
shortest route, so I chose the more difficult, but most well-marked
path, the one that was mostly straight downhill through the woods.
After one grand adventure, my first "getting lost," the easier-to-follow
path was the one I wanted.

Deb walking a relatively flat part of the swirling Camino path...
easy to recognize from behind by her orange neck pillow.

It was a beautiful, though rugged path. I walked under a canopy of elderly and enormous trees. At one point I had to stop and sit on a rocky ledge next to the road, take off my boots, and massage my feet. I watched folks moving much slower than I, and some, much faster. I had walked earlier with a young man from England who had come to do the Camino with his "mum." He had been way ahead of her at the point when he and I were chatting. I'm sure it was this same young man I later saw running down the hill wearing running shoes, not hiking boots! I was astonished! I had been walking so slowly and deliberately and using my walking sticks for balance on the deeply uneven, rocky, and steeply descending path. I was praying for him to reach the bottom of the hill safely. Later in Roncesvalles I heard no reports of "downed hikers," so I guess he did fine.

When I finally reached the bottom of the hill I turned (the correct way this time!) towards the city of Roncesvalles. I reached a picnic table at the base of the city and was suddenly overcome with exhaustion. I pulled out some snack food and chocolate, ate, and rested a few minutes before I had the energy to walk the last few hundred yards into the city. When I arrived I was met by Carmel and friends who were sitting outside the restaurant, La Posada (The Inn). Carmel directed me where to pay in advance for my dinner and pointed me towards the new, modern, state-of-the-art albergue.

The albergue was formerly a convent. The original courtyard walls and church exterior remain as they have looked for centuries. Only the interior has been re-done. The facility now boasts individual berths for sleeping; clean, well-lit rest rooms; and showers with unlimited hot water! I checked in, showered, washed a few clothes by hand, and attempted to dry them with the bathroom hand-dryer.

I gave up after a while and hung them at the end of my berth, hopefully to dry before morning. [The reason for the daily washing of clothes is that, in order to keep the weight of my backpack as light as possible, I had brought only two sets of clothes: one to wear and one to wash. From the research I had done, this seemed the common pilgrim practice].

Had dinner at La Posada. They offered a vegetarian menu! Pasta without meat, though I couldn't eat it because of the gluten, so I shared it, salad, a tortilla (a Spanish egg and potato quiche-like dish with no crust), and yogurt for dessert. Sat with a new crew at dinner: Etta-Maria, who speaks multiple languages; Terry, the Aussie; and a number of Germans. It's exciting and yet draining to hear so many words I don't understand and to try to make sense of the conversation. Etta-Maria translated some for me. Very much appreciated.

After dinner I was directed to the computer room in the albergue. I got to e-mail home! They know I'm safe! I can feel a bit of the worry from home lifted off me. Yay! It has been a wonderful day. I am in Spain. I am a pilgrim, una peregrina. I have no clue what tomorrow will bring, only that I am excited to be here. Finally I am feeling more excitement than fear. Yes! Now, to see what I did wrong with the camera. Could take no pictures today. And, I wanted some of the route down the Pyrenees. Guess I'll have to come back.

CHAPTER ELEVEN

Camino friends

"There are no days in life so memorable as those which
vibrated to some stroke of the imagination."

Ralph Waldo Emerson

My friends from home were right. So much became easier once I was finally there, finally on the Camino. For starters, even though I had no idea what each next segment of the path would bring, I was doing it! Instead of imagining the best (new friends, a feeling of comfort in adventuring, spiritual insights) and the worst (pain and getting lost, aargh!), I was living it! Every day would bring new delights and new challenges. My trust in my own abilities grew, and my self-esteem was buoyed by living through the challenges and learning the lessons of each day. Most importantly, I was learning how to find and follow the way-marker signs!

Sunday, 4-17-2011, Camino Journal
Roncesvalles to Zubiri

A long day. Lots of ups and downs. This morning I re-did my backpack and left my cloth bag on a bed at the Roncesvalles albergue. There was just no good way to attach the bag to my pack or to carry it. It kept pulling off to one side, pulling me off balance. Two Spanish men chased me down as I left the albergue in an effort to return the bag to me. I told them I was choosing to leave it. They shook their heads, probably wondering, "What gives with these crazy Americanas?"

The Roncesvalles albergue was great. I got some sleep last night and felt ready to roll in the morning. Also fortunate: a few kilometers outside of Roncesvalles, in Burguete, I stopped for a morning té con leche caliente (tea with hot milk) and ran into Emma and Lorne, a couple of pilgrims in my age range. Emma is petite with straight, dark hair, and a motherly, welcoming nature. Lorne is a sturdy looking gentleman, very kind, but more reserved. I heard them at their table speaking English and asked if I could join them. I ended up walking with them for the rest of the day. We are all moving slowly and in less than tip-top shape, so our pace is pretty even.

Today was a long, hard day: up and over Alto de Erro. The dictionary says "alto" means "tall" or "high." This should have been a clue. We were all very tired and decided to stop in Zubiri, the city before Larrasoaña, our original destination. We arrived in Zubiri late in the day, and I found my thoughts leaning towards a prayer for "room at the inn." That's pretty much what we got. We had to go to three albergues before we found one with overflow sleeping space available: mattresses on the concrete floor of an old school gymnasium, the ceiling festooned with garlands of drooping spider webs.

The Zubiri albergue was a bare-bones setup with very basic shower facilities, the mattresses, and extra heavy blankets as the major amenities. Emma, Lorne, and I did our washing, and then set out to find a restaurant with a pilgrims' menu for our dinner. Given the lack of great vegetarian options on the pilgrims' menu, I sucked all the possible protein from a huge bowl of green beans, ate a salad, and had ice cream for dessert. We went back to our giant sleeping space and were getting comfy in our "beds," when I noticed a young man in his sleeping bag near the entrance door. His sleeping bag lay directly on the concrete floor, and he was shivering.

Because this is Semana Santa, Holy Week, the week leading up to Easter, the Camino is especially crowded, filled to the brim with Spanish pilgrims taking a vacation week to walk a Camino segment. Hence the need for the overflow housing facility. This young man was the last to arrive. They had no more mattresses to offer, but they didn't want to turn him away either. I was feeling bad for him, wondering if there was something I or anyone else could do, when I witnessed another young man offering his mattress. He and his girlfriend would share, he said. I am happy to have a home for the night, and I am happy that everyone will sleep in relative comfort. We are all being provided for. Time for rest and recuperation.

Monday, 4-18-11, Camino Journal
Zubiri to Trinadad de Arre

Another hard day with lots of ups and downs. Emma, Lorne, and I stopped for breakfast at a small café/grocery store. The owner had decorated the business with her framed art collection, including a pop art print of Twiggy, the original supermodel from the 1960s. The café owner appreciated my attempt to speak in Spanish to compliment her on her art collection. My problem is that if I communicate just one sentence effectively, one I've worked on with the help of my Spanish dictionary, they think I can speak their language. Then I get a detailed response in Spanish, spoken at breakneck speed. Sorry! I don't understand!

There are people here of every nationality: Terry, Carmel, Tony, and friends from Australia…Susan and Pon from Japan, Lorne from Canada, Emma from England, Kim from Korea, Nadeem from the United Arab Emirates, and so many more. I've only met one other American, the girl from Portland who was in my albergue room back in St. Jean Pied de Port. And, of course, there are lots of Spaniards.

Emma, Lorne, and I took a lunch break next to the centuries' old stone bridge across the Río Arga. It was a wonderful rest spot:

sitting on the riverbank under shade trees on a gorgeous spring day. We shared the fruits, nuts, and cheeses we had purchased at the café/grocery that morning. We chatted with other pilgrims as they made their way to the bridge. We even took off our boots and socks and dipped our toes in the water. Delightful! My pack is still too heavy, and my shoulders are tired, but much less so than yesterday. I am learning to pad the shoulder straps of my backpack with socks. It looks odd, but feels lots better.

On the path today we walked past all types of wildflowers. With the camera (or the camera's operator) now working, I stopped to take photos of what I thought might be wild orchids. When I squatted down to get the angle I wanted for my photo, I almost couldn't stand back up. A heavy backpack plus a non-normal center of gravity is a graceless combination! I have been hoping to create a purple wildflower photo collection to gift a dear friend who favors purples and connects deeply with the floral world. Either I'm going to have to go after other angles or get stronger thighs!

Tonight we are blessed with a sparsely beautiful and yet splendid accommodation in the Basilica de la Trinadad de Arre that was once the priest's residence. The attached church is still in use and has quite an art and religious history collection in an adjoining section of the building. We will sleep in the second floor dormitory, one room filled with twenty bunk beds.

I am currently sitting in the sunny courtyard here at Trinadad de Arre, waiting for my clothes from last night's wash to line-dry so I'll have clean clothes to put on after I shower. The courtyard wall is of stone about twenty feet high on one side, but only eight feet on the other side where it has crumbled. It surrounds a small flower and vegetable garden, lots of trees and bushes, tables and chairs, and the clothesline. The dormitory is also made of stone, with sturdy looking wooden beams at the ceiling.

Albergue courtyard in Trinadad de Arre

It is 5:45 p.m. Time to shower and prepare for dinner. Just to sit and write has been restorative, but it's toilet time and my body has been "rode hard and put away wet." I shared that line with Terry from Australia at dinner the other night. He laughed, said he enjoyed my Western analogy, that it brought back memories from his favorite childhood TV shows—"Pancho and the Cisco Kid" and "The Lone Ranger." I've also quoted Chief Seattle here, about making decisions by considering their effects out to seven generations. Who knew I was such a Western buff?! Who knew that the world was so connected?!

Monday, 4-18-11, Trinadad de Arre, after dinner
After a walk around the tiny town of Trinadad de Arre, asking the locals to direct us to a restaurant that offered a pilgrim's menu (and not understanding the directions given), we finally located the out-of-the-way place the locals were describing. Lorne, Emma, and I shared dinner tonight with Stephan from Ireland and two young

brothers from South Korea. Stephan has only a week off from work to do a stage of the Camino in memory of his late mother. The Korean brothers are both unhappy and ready to go home, one to do his mandatory military service. I'm not totally clear on why they want to leave now. Perhaps they are tired, achy, not making friends, and just not having the fun trip they had hoped for. Unbelievably, we all communicated fairly well as one of the Korean brothers knew a smattering of English. Stephan has walked close to forty kilometers today (twenty-four miles) and with a too heavy backpack. After dinner he invited us all back to the sitting room of the albergue to share some Irish whiskey. This is what makes his backpack so heavy—an enormous bottle of whiskey! He proceeded to get the Korean brothers drunk. Fortunately for us all, "lights out" at ten o'clock is mandatory, so the party has ended.

I have gratitude for our safe arrival, for this lovely albergue, and for Emma, Lorne, and all my new friends. And now, to sleep! Tomorrow: Pamplona!

Tuesday, 4-19-2011, Camino Journal
Trinadad de Arre to Pamplona

As we walked out of Trinadad de Arre we spotted giant birds' nests perched high atop church steeples: storks' nests! And the storks could be seen flying to and from their nests. This fascinates me, like something out of fairy tales. Sure, I knew that storks existed, that they were real, but, like the cuckoo birds which I heard on the walk yesterday, they have remained fantasy creatures in my mind until now. Finally, I have come to their part of the world and gained first-hand knowledge.

Each day we have stopped in to see the small churches that dot the Spanish countryside. I am in love with the feeling of antiquity, of time having stood still. I am not happy to see all the wealth that the church has acquired over the years. It's not just the Catholic Church here in Spain I know…all religious institutions accrue wealth and collect beautiful objets d'art. And I understand the concept of "wowing" the people with a display of what heaven will be like. What I don't understand is why the wealth is sitting here in the form of gilt statuary, stained glass, and valuable paintings in elaborately hand-carved frames when people are doing without. We saw a Spanish beggar in front of one church today. I didn't understand all he said, but it was something about having become handicapped on the Camino. Where is his church? Why must he beg to eat? Okay. Enough ranting.

Emma, Lorne, and I have arrived in Pamplona. Walking into this huge, old, walled city, walking up the path and through the city gates, felt like entering a fairy tale, a magical land untouched by modern time. Our walk was fairly short, maybe five or six miles. We arrived mid-morning, found a café, had breakfast, and drank tea for a long while, luxuriating in the lazy feel. Next, we checked into the municipal albergue. It took a bit to find it, but the local folks wanted to help when we asked for directions.

The municipal albergue is clean, newly re-done, and has glass floors! We're on the first floor. We can look up and see the dormitory upstairs through the ceiling/floor. We met a man who is installing foot massage machines in the front lobby, and he gave me a free trial massage. Interesting, but not my thing. Seems to pinch at my sensitive feet. He says he is installing computers in many albergues across Spain. E-mail…yes!

After checking into the albergue and leaving our backpacks (what freedom!), Emma, Lorne, and I walked around and saw a bit of Pamplona. We took photos of the main square, and then found a barbershop for Lorne to get a haircut. Emma and I explored some side streets while Lorne was getting prettied up. Eventually we went back, sat in the shop, and kibitzed as best we could with the barbers. "Bueno. Muy guapo!" "Good. Very handsome!" Our best barber compliments. We visited a market, looked in shop windows: butcher shop windows decorated with hanging meats, shops full of electronic gadgets. Everything is available in Pamplona! Perhaps it is only a medieval city on the outside...with a juicy twenty-first century center. While here in this good-sized city, I had planned to buy a European SIM card to use in my borrowed international cell phone. But after further thought, I have decided to skip it, to e-mail my family regularly, and to keep my Camino experience free from unwanted telephone interruptions.

Emma, Lorne, and I walked to the edge of Pamplona, high atop the city wall. We enjoyed the expansive view of the surrounding countryside and took more photos. Next we found the plaza where the bullfights take place. The Plaza del Toros was locked up tight, but we walked around the outside and imagined the bulls running through Pamplona's streets come July. In short, we were tourists, and we loved it!

Later, back at the albergue, we took in the art show on display in the albergue's lobby. A scenic photo of the Camino had been taken with a panoramic lens. After the photo was printed, it was cut into equal vertical slices. The vertical segments were given to individual artists, each of whom then created one section of the panorama on canvas in their own style, using whatever medium they desired. In the exhibit all the pieces of art are being displayed in the correct visual order. A very clever idea! I love this concept!

View from top of the Pamplona city walls, looking out onto the countryside.

Wednesday, 4-20-11, Camino Journal
Pamplona to Obanos

Had to laugh. Our albergue last night in Pamplona had some of the worst acoustics ever for communal sleeping. With all the hard surfaces (glass floors, concrete walls) you could clearly hear every sound ping-ponging from each of the floors. All of humanity's night sounds: snoring, hiccuping, groaning, coughing, farting. I could hear them all clearly.

This morning Emma, Lorne, and I left Pamplona, stopping multiple times for food, snacks, toilet breaks, and to breathe. Another tough day. We walked twenty-one and a half kilometers, about fourteen miles. Much of the walk was up and down hills. I did have moments of pain, of pain going away, of extreme tiredness, and of extreme self-satisfaction. We went up and over the Alto del Perdón today, the Hill of Pardon. It was a huge physical challenge, a difficult climb. I can understand why it got that name.

On the way to the top I was thinking that any of my unresolved sins have now been erased from the books! From my map the climb appears to have been at almost a forty-degree angle. Lots of twisty and turny parts. Some really rugged roads. When we reached the top we saw the sculptural metal cut-out statuary, silhouettes representing pilgrims of old, on foot and on horseback. They are larger than life-sized, a touching remembrance of those who have come before us. Today I thought about those pilgrims of an earlier age who would have had to climb up the Alto del Perdón, continue on to Santiago, and then turn around and retrace their steps to get home! I think I would have lost faith at that point. It's probably better not to know what's ahead on some level. Ugh!

Emma, Lorne, and I took turns walking the lead, looking ahead for the way-marker signs: a clamshell logo in bright yellow set against a bright blue background; or the abbreviation "C de S. Iago"; or a bright yellow arrow painted on a rock, on a tree trunk, on anything. We stopped to wait for whoever fell behind. We adjusted each other's backpack straps, secured water bottles for each other, shared foods and treats. Emma shared with me the finer points of peeing in the woods. It's been a very long time since I was a Girl Scout, and I needed some remedial tutoring. We walked alone some and together some. I've learned lots about both Emma and Lorne. When I first met them, I thought they were a couple, but quickly was informed that they had only just met going up and over the Pyrenees the day before they met me. They had been walking and chatting, sharing about their lives back home in England and in Canada. Both were concerned about their ability to do the walks and the climbs, so they had decided to team up, to each make sure the other was being "watched over properly." And they have been generous to include me in the team.

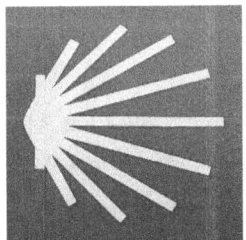

Camino way-marker sign: yellow "shell" against blue background

A plus from today's walk: at day's end, when we reached Obanos, we were able to turn around and see the wind turbines at the top of the Alto del Perdón, to see exactly where we'd been. To know I'd actually been up that high, that I was doing the climb, was quite satisfying! Go me! We had planned to head for Puente La Reina

[Bridge of the Queen, named for Queen Doña Mayor who, centuries ago, had the bridge built for the use of the pilgrims], *but I was too tired. We'll cross it on our walk tomorrow.*

Had a wonderful pilgrims' meal with lots of new faces: Gunther, two other German fellows, and some people from Italy. The Germans speak English well. The waitress was great. She was trying her best to explain the menu options to our Spanish-challenged table. Talk about going all out... she ended up making the appropriate animal noises to explain the meat options! My rudimentary Spanish is occasionally helpful, but I need to build my vocabulary big time.

Thursday, 4-21-2011, Camino Journal
Obanos to Estella

Left Obanos this morning and made it to Estella after 6 p.m. We walked almost twenty-five kilometers today, close to fifteen miles. We walked for more than ten hours! I am exhausted! Hope to have time to relax, wash clothes, send e-mail, and just get strong for tomorrow.

On the way we crossed Puente la Reina, a spectacular stone bridge supported by multiple stone arches. The reflection in the river is gorgeous! Lorne, Emma, and I walked past many huge, old fig trees with figs ripening, though not yet ripe. I would love to be able to eat a ripe fig straight off a tree while I am here in Spain. Lorne got a tour of a local power plant, housed in a building the size of a small two-story home. He was involved in that work before retirement and was tickled to get to see what type of system is in use here. We walked past vineyards and also on some stretches of two-thousand-year-old Roman road. The surface is difficult to walk on, as it is not worn even and smooth as one would guess— the individual stone blocks stick out at odd tangents. It's like walking where the sidewalks have been lifted to varying angles by hundreds of tree roots. Emma has clued me in that the red way-marker signs mean we are walking the Route de

Napoleon, the way Napoleon led his troops into Spain, following the centuries' old paths of shepherds and pilgrims.

I will say that the locals in Estella could not have been more welcoming. We were standing at a corner, checking our guidebook maps, trying to figure out where the albergue was when people came over to direct us. They can see that we're pilgrims from our backpacks and scallop shells, but they didn't even wait for us to ask for directions. They just came up and pointed out the way. This happened multiple times. It makes me feel cared for.

Puente la Reina

We are being housed in a large church. This is another overflow housing situation. Our room is right next door to the church's Teen Computer and Game Room. I hope the teens get quiet or get kicked out early! A mass is going on downstairs now. Many parishioners are attending. The actual church-sponsored albergue is across the street, but it is packed full, so we are being put up in the church proper. We have to shower at the albergue and then walk across the street and a block or so over to our sleeping quarters to put our washing away. Then back to the albergue for our meal and then back to the church to sleep. I am so tired! The bunk beds look rickety, so we have elected to pull the mattresses onto the floor.

This albergue is free but accepts donations. I gave a ten euro donation. It is staffed by volunteers: friendly and gracious people. I can imagine coming back to walk another Camino someday and volunteering at an albergue for part of the time. Dinner and break-fast are included with the washing and sleeping facilities provided here. Dinner (which was pretty awful) was a common pot of rice, with lettuce, onion, and hard-boiled eggs. I saw them cutting up the eggs to put in, but I couldn't see any egg in the finished product. There was also some odd, meat-colored, flavorless vegetable. I ate because I was hungry. Emma and I ended up sharing a not-very-fine-dining experience in the albergue's check-in room. Everyone else was sitting at a communal table outside, laughing, but cold! Emma and I were exhausted, but warm and content where we were. Sometimes you have to take responsibility for your own comfort.

CHAPTER TWELVE

The United Nations of the Camino

"Draw doors where there are none and open them and pass through into new ways and new lives."

Clarissa Pinkola Estes

One of the real joys of my Camino experience was the opportunity to meet so many folks from all over the world. I knew that most would be friends for the Camino, or friends for the day, or for the conversation. I was hoping to meet the "friends for life" (FFL) that my psychic friends back home had told me about. But when first meeting so many new people, it was difficult to sort out the ones who would become FFL from the ones who would become only delightful footnotes in my long-term memories. Every person I met had FFL potential. After all, we were enjoying an extreme bonding experience with each day's walk.

Some of the folks mentioned here remain sweet vignettes in my Camino memories: these were the folks I met just once or twice; we never engaged in a serious conversation. Perhaps we ran across each other somewhere farther along the way. Even among those who did not become regular walking partners—my "Camino Family"—it was always a huge delight to recognize someone I had met on an earlier walk. These brief re-acquaintances held the feel of greeting a long-lost friend. We were always thrilled to see each other. And we always had more to talk about: our experiences on the trail since our last meeting. That said, there were occasionally potential friends who didn't make the cut... whom I didn't choose to take on as a friend.

I was on the lookout for my "friends for life," the friends I would eat with, walk with, wash clothes with, and bunk down with... we would plan our next day's route together, and as we walked, we would share our life stories. I saw us baring our souls to each other. We would learn the Camino necessaries together: how to spot the way-marker signs, find the café-bars, and the albergues. And we would laugh together, delighting in our shared experiences. At this stage I was exploring potential friendship opportunities with each person I met. I did not want to risk missing out on meeting my "Camino Friends For Life"!

Friday, 4-22-11, Camino Journal
Good Friday, 2nd night in Estella

Emma, Lorne, and I had been the lucky recipients of three of the last four available beds in the church's overflow pilgrim housing last night. I was so grateful. I could not have walked another step. Had an OK night's sleep. The teen game room was blissfully quiet. Yesterday we started at about 8 a.m. and walked a full day, taking breaks as needed. Lorne was doing well with his walking, feeling strong. Emma and I would have been content to stop about eight kilometers earlier at the albergue in Lorca, but we had plodded on because Lorne has a deadline. He has to keep to a certain pace or he will not be done with his Camino in time for his plane reservations to go back home. Also, Emma's hubby, Leo, is to meet up with her today here in Estella, so we had to push on. A little too much push for me. My body is sore, my left foot is achy, my back is tired, and I need an entire night of solid sleep to feel completely restored.

All of that aside, I am becoming more and more happy with having come. The people and the joy of the camaraderie are superb! I have especially enjoyed the opportunity to have in-depth conversations, while walking, with Abby from England and Meg from Australia. I am learning what these young folks (twenty-somethings) are doing out in the world. They are finding ways to travel while earning a living: nursing, providing childcare, teaching English… They find out about an opportunity, and they go. They don't feel tethered to home, but are able to move around the globe. I would love for my trip to inspire my adult kids to try some in-depth travels, to get out and have experiences while they are young and relatively free of responsibilities. There definitely must be an adventurer gene. I don't have it in a big way.…in a small way, yes. I hope my kids' adventurer genes will surface and delight them!

Lorne has decided to walk on ahead. We have exchanged e-mail addresses and promised to forward photos when we hit home. Meanwhile, Emma and I found the train station and connected up with her husband, Leo, who will join her (us?) for his vacation week. They are so sweet together. Leo, a friendly fellow, is a lawyer who does advocacy work. Emma works in a program that offers rich play experiences to special needs children. They have been married for almost thirty years.

We are in a new albergue in Estella. The rule is that one cannot stay two nights in a row in the same albergue, so we have moved. Most of these pilgrims must be Spanish, here for Holy Week. I hear no English. Had a nap, a short walk, and dinner out at a restaurant with Emma and Leo. Food was odd, not tasty. Had a salad of lettuce, with a mayo and vinegar-laden potato-y mixed veggie lump on top. Feeling a bit desperate, I tried the fish. It was greasy, flavorless, and just awful. Had yogurt for dessert. Thank God for yogurt!

Emma, Leo, and I have decided to attempt an earlier departure time for the mornings: 7:30ish. We will stop walking around 1 p.m. when the albergues open. That way, we'll walk less per day and not wear out. If we can, we will opt for small town albergues over the bigger city ones. Emma needs to be home by the end of May, so it's possible we could travel the whole way together and then I could leave for Madrid. That sounds perfect. I just checked the guidebook. We'll have to do fifteen to twenty kilometers per day (nine to ten miles) to make that happen, or have a few rides! Surprisingly, I'm okay with that idea, though that may change later.

Note to self: After returning to the US, I want to go back to dance class. I'll paint from my Camino photos, and I'll need a gallery for my Spain show! Shorter hair-do, wear more scarves/headbands, build a stone wall across the back of the yard, and add lots of bushes and trees. Maybe I'll get tattooed eyeliner, easier to look good on the trail!

Saturday, 4-23-11, Camino Journal
Estella to Los Arcos

Walked about twenty kilometers/twelve miles today. Left Estella early, at 7:30 a.m. and only made one stop. Had a good breakfast: tea with hot milk and a wedge of egg, potato, and cheese "tortilla." Filling and healthy! Today we walked past more vineyards with new green growth just beginning to leaf out. The sun remained hidden. There were trees with deep purple leaves set against a background of bright spring green trees further off in the distance, and all backed by the deep steel-blue sky. What a colorful and delightful part of the world! We walked about seven hours and arrived at the Austrian Association Albergue in Los Arcos at mid-afternoon. Our first really good day! I'm tired and my feet hurt, but I am washed, my laundry is being done for me... yay! I'm now sitting on the back patio/courtyard. The clouds have cleared, my sore feet are open to the sun and *"free at last!" It's about three hours 'til dinner, and I'd better quit eating prunes!*

Many of the pilgrims at this albergue are from German-speaking countries. Emma already knew Elsa (German, multi-time pilgrim, in her 70s). On her first day of walking as a pilgrim, Emma had been sick, and Elsa had taken care of her. Elsa told Emma about this albergue saying, "Stop here and see me again. I will be volunteering." And so we are here with the mainly German-speaking group. One young man here has such bad blisters on his feet that you can see almost through to the bone (so I am told...I did not want to see for myself). They are calling a doctor for him. I don't know if he will be able to continue his walk. I will say a prayer for him.

The entryway of this albergue is decorated with favorite sayings of pilgrims who have stayed here, all written on the walls with marker. One quote, of the ones in English, really appealed to me, and I hope to remember to copy it down later when I tire of the sun and head back inside. [I did not remember...a good excuse to go back!] *For now, my feet and legs are quite happy to be enjoying this sunbath.*

This is neither the prettiest, nor the plainest albergue I've seen, but all the people running it, including the volunteers, are wonderful! When we arrived a young man carried our backpacks upstairs for us—like hotel room service! Another volunteer is doing our washing and drying, and Elsa is baking bread for Easter breakfast. I will have some of that, gluten or no.

This building is cobbled together, an old stone wall between two newer structures. If I were going to volunteer here I'd want to set them up with a real garden. Maybe some flowers for decoration? Maybe some veggies to serve to hungry pilgrims?

As I've been sitting here writing, a pilgrim couple and their dog have arrived. They are being allowed to set up a tent for the dog to overnight within the courtyard walls. I wonder if this is the origin of the term "pup tent"? Gotta' laugh…

Sunday, 4-24-11 Easter Sunday, Camino Journal
Los Arcos to Viana

The Easter breakfast at the Austrian Association Albergue was wonderful! They offered us a dense homemade German brown bread, dyed hard-boiled Easter eggs, and lots of butter, jam, coffee, and tea. I did not pig out on the bread, though I wanted to. I've been gluten-free for about a year, testing to see if it would help my thyroid. I have today reintroduced wheat and rye. I want to see what effect, if any, this will have. I want it to be only a minor effect if I am to have any bad response. So far, no problem. I have felt no difference! I may include some breads now, as my diet here has been so restricted. The Spanish are very meat-centric in their eating. At one meal I had ordered a bean soup and had to eat around a few hunks of meat. I've been more careful since then. I've even learned to order my "ensalada mixta" (mixed salad) "sin atún" (without tuna), as tuna in the salad is standard fare.

Easter or no, we walked from Los Arcos to Viana today: twenty kilometers (twelve miles) or a bit less. It felt like more. The walk was our first in rain. Not too bad. It was a light rain, and at one point there was a rainbow! The temps were in the 50s. Very pleasant. I ended up walking alone for most of the last half. That was actually great. I found my own rhythm, and even though I walk slowly, my pace is steady. I was very happy walking alone, listening to bird song. I heard my second real cuckoo bird. For part of the time I attempted to pray and to quiet my thoughts.

My young friend from England, Abby, walked with me for a few kilometers, but my attempt to converse about past lives may have pushed her away. Or, it's possible that she just wanted time by herself. All good. I did have an unpleasant realization that the German man I walked with for a short bit today was not on the up-and-up with me. I was trying my best to communicate with him in my limited Spanish, as he seemed to speak Spanish well. I do not speak German at all, and he indicated that he did not speak English. Finally, having difficulty communicating, we parted ways. Later I overheard him, speaking in perfect English to a male companion, and saying ugly things about his wife. Seems he was doing the Camino with his wife, but was avoiding walking with her. I now know to steer clear of him. The Camino is no different from regular life in this respect. There are people I'd like to develop friendships with, and those I would rather not. I can comfortably choose to winnow away this potential friendship! That said, I am open to seeing what comes. A wonderful Easter spent walking the spiritual path!

It's now 9:25 p.m. I took photos of the remains of a ruined church right out in front of this albergue in Viana. The former church has no ceiling and only partial walls. Was it destroyed in a bombing raid in some twentieth-century war? Looks that way.

The Church of San Pedro was built in the 13th century and collapsed in 1844. It fascinates me that—instead of knocking down the remainder, as we probably would have done in the U.S., and rebuilding something new in its place—the ruins in Spain, complete with the frescoed walls and other architectural details, were left standing. I understand the reverence that the Spaniards must feel for this structure. Walking inside its remaining walls is peaceful.

Had dinner with Emma and Leo. We engaged in a good conversation about U.S., British, and world politics. Emma and Leo are off on their own couples' retreat. They are spending some hubby and wife time in a nice hotel close to this albergue. I will catch up with them, I hope, tomorrow.

Tonight, I am in a room with five others. So far I've met Michaela and Miroslav from the Czech Republic and Lucia from Italy. Very gentle people. Michaela doesn't look well. She says she and Miroslav have come here to pray for a miracle for her health. He is very tender, cuddling with her and bringing her food. Lucia says I am the first person from the States she has met. This surprises me. Maybe she's just speaking of folks she's met while on the Camino?

This bunk bed is awfully uncomfortable, but I will not complain. I am grateful to be on only the second tier of the three-tiered bunk bed. I must remember that I represent the U.S.A. here in some fashion. I need to be my kindest and most compassionate self for more than just my usual reasons—now for international relations!

Monday, 4-25-11, Camino Journal
Viana to Logroño and on to Navarette

Walked with Emma and Leo from Viana to Logroño this morning. An okay walk, mostly rural. On the way we stopped at Capilla N.S de las Cuevas, saying "Buenos Dias" to two men, very friendly fellows who were setting up for a community picnic. They gave us a tour of their chapel —they were so proud of its beauty. And they allowed us to use the toilets. Most appreciated! Their community picnic included Gypsy vendors, we were told.

I wasn't sure why these men felt the need to make the "Gypsy vendor" comment, but it seemed important to them. In researching this later I learned that the Spanish are proud of their treatment of Gypsy peoples, the lack of prejudice shown, the many educational and other opportunities given to those of Gypsy or Roma ethnicity, especially as compared to Roma prejudice and discrimination in other European countries.

When I set out on this journey I was woefully ignorant about Spanish history and European history generally. I was the typical insulated American tourist in so many ways. There was much about the Spanish political scene that I didn't know or understand. As a teenager, I had read a book on the horrors of WWII and could not stomach the violence and cruelty. After that I avoided learning and thinking about history, conflict, and warfare. On this walk I saw many Basque protest movement signs, graffiti painted in the interiors of tunnels and other out-of-the-way places. I tried to translate the signage and realized that there was a desire to break away from the existing government. Beyond that, I was clueless.

Our day's walk took us through the countryside, up and down hills, along the highway. We walked for a kilometer or so next to a chain-link fence that had been decorated by passing pilgrims. Twigs and grasses had been woven into the chain link at right angles to create a wall of crosses. Some creative types had added in other symbols: stars and peace signs.

Emma, Leo, and I walked on into Logroño, a huge city. We decided to stop for tea/coffee and ended up splitting an order of churros con chocolate. I had never eaten churros con chocolate, but since I was in "testing the waters mode" regarding gluten, I allowed myself to sample this Spanish delicacy. I thought it would be like hot cocoa with doughnuts to dip in, but the chocolate is thick like a pudding and so rich. It's almost hot fudgy. The doughnuts are long sticks of fried dough. Happy I tried it. Glad there were other folks to share it with. Eating it alone would have been a huge sugar and caffeine overload!

We sat at an outdoor table, rested our feet, enjoyed our sugary treat, and took in the feel of the plaza. Afterward, we walked the plaza peeking into little shops, mostly fruterías, sellers of dried fruits, nuts, and candies, looking to purchase good back-packing foods.

We then left, or tried to leave, Logroño. The city goes on forever! I have never walked through an entire big city and its suburban sprawl before. Lots of stop-and-go, heavy traffic, streets lined with bustling retail businesses much like small town America. The Camino signs were different—harder to spot—some literally embedded into the sidewalks. It took our combined three pairs of eyes, Emma's, Leo's, and mine, to find the way-marker signs. I was excited as I finally contributed to the "spotting" effort. I found a few before Emma and Leo! Finding our way out of Logroño was a team effort.

Before we could finally exit the city, we had a long walk through a large, well-used city park: dodging bicyclists, runners, and other walkers, mostly locals out for a stroll. We passed through a boring, forgettable area, and finally, up a hill (what else?!) into Navarette.

About this "up a hill (what else?!)" comment, this seemed to be the regular set-up: we would see our destination off in the distance, walk a few (or many) kilometers downhill, thinking we were almost there only to realize that, from where we'd first spied the city, we could not see the additional climb up that we would need to make to access it. Just when you thought you were almost there, you realized you weren't. Aargh!

Tuesday, 4-26-11, Camino Journal
Navarette to Nájera

Walked from Navarette to Nájera: fifteen kilometers—nine miles—by the book. But after we walked through the newer part of the city to reach this albergue (we had tried to find a different albergue and couldn't, so we came back to the first one), our walk was probably more like seventeen to nineteen kilometers. We all feel very sore, even more so than in days past. Now I'm sitting outside the Nájera albergue, on the concrete patio. I have showered. My clothes are drying on racks in the sun. It's 4:10 p.m. Nothing to do until we head out for dinner but snack, journal, and rest.

No great life revelations yet except for how lovely folks are the world over. A Spanish man wearing hearing aids has come to this albergue to sleep, and also to visit a dear old friend. He hears enough, and they are chatting happily. His friend is one of the hospitaleras here; she runs the albergue.

[In the middle ages, a pilgrim would overnight at a hospital... pronounced: os-pe-tal with the accent on the last syllable. A *hospitalera/hospitalero* (female/male) is one who works in a hospital. The meaning of hospital here is more closely related to hospice or a place of hospitality. The word *albergue* translates as hostel, shelter, or refuge. A synonym is *refugio*, a refuge, shelter, or protection.]

Emma is still feeling somewhat sick and it must have shown. When we first arrived here at the Nájera albergue, we were greeted by the sweetest hospitalera. This woman came out from behind the counter to give Emma a bear hug, rocking her back and forth for quite a while, like a mother comforting a fussy infant. Emma said she felt better after what we now call: "The Camino Hug." Emma asked the hospitalera, in jest, whether she and Leo could push two bunks together, like a double bed. In an effort to explain her request and to practice my Spanish, I looked up "double bed" in my pocket Spanish/English dictionary: "una cama de matrimonio"…a marriage bed! How funny!!!

While waiting for my laundry to dry, I had a wonderful chat with Bill, a temporarily laid off social studies teacher from Canada. Bill had decided to use his savings to travel to Israel/Palestine. There he took on a volunteer job as an observer at an Israeli checkpoint, making sure Palestinians were being treated fairly as they went through. He reported to a Christian group that reported to NATO. Bill says he loved Israel and will be encouraging all his Jewish friends to go. And now, he's on the Camino. I told Bill he could use me as a job-hunting reference. I said that he should tell the school principal that, "Deborah from the U.S.A. says that I will be a fabulous history teacher because of my world travel experiences." I'm sure my recommendation will make all the difference. Ha, ha! Anyway, Bill got a laugh out of it. But I meant it. I would love to have been taught by a history teacher with on-the-ground experience, with real-life stories. The studies would have been so much richer and more relevant than dates of battles in history books.

Before dinner, Emma, Leo, and I went shopping to find new shoes and socks for Leo. We were barely able to communicate with the shop owner, but he found just the perfect hiking boots for Leo and gave him a "pilgrim's discount". I, on the other hand, did not get a "pilgrim's discount" at the farmacia (pharmacy). A small tube of toothpaste, a tiny liquid soap, and SPF50 sunscreen: almost twenty euros! I'm sure a local would have known better where to shop. I probably should have bought a new deodorant, too. Between the "natural deodorant," I brought with me, my questionable plan to "go European" (not shave my armpits), and the physical exertion of each day, I can now smell myself. I wash each day and wash my clothes, too, but I know I need more. Fortunately, everyone here seems to be in the same boat regarding body odor, so I don't—at least I hope I don't—stand out in the crowd. Anyway, in the future I will be on the lookout for a cheaper place to purchase toiletries and only hit the farmacia for medicines.

After shopping, Emma, Leo, Teacher Bill, a friend of Bill's, and I all enjoyed dinner together at a tapas restaurant. I've been complaining bitterly to Emma and Leo about how disappointing the Spanish food is for a vegetarian. I've learned to say, "Yo soy vegetariana." (I am a vegetarian). Sometimes that is helpful. I get steered to my one possible food choice faster and have no meat "surprises." Emma and Leo love the Spanish food. This is part of the reason we went out for tapas. There's some blood sausage thing Leo is dying to have. This restaurant had it. He was a happy camper—new boots and blood sausage! Woohoo! I used my vegetarian line and ended up with "patatas bravas," a potato dish with some "heat"! Awesome! Everything else I've had to eat here has been really bland. I guess that's what happens when meat is the main flavoring, and then you leave out the meat. Anyway, great company at dinner. Fun conversations and laughs.

CHAPTER THIRTEEN:
Camino Normal

"... several stories in this book deal with protagonists who fall asleep in the middle of their adventure, or die a short-term death and cannot wake up until their innermost transformation is complete. When they open their eyes, they find a Prince hovering over them, which makes us think at first that the Prince's presence, or kiss, has saved them, but it's also possible that after their new consciousness has fully ripened, the time comes around for them to live with a higher sense of self, and so the Prince appears."

Joan Gould

I was learning to accept what is and to enjoy the heck out of it. Every day held surprises. And that's the part I remember the most: the delight, the joy, and the peace. Physical pains and discomforts are—like childbirth pains—not possible to truly remember in the body. Thank God! Emotional pain is another story, but here on the Camino, in what we all referred to as "time out of time," I was feeling no emotional pain. What I recall was a sameness to each day, punctuated with periods of delight, each day a new setting and new characters.

Every day had a similar structure: the rush of activity in the albergue began around 6a.m. (or, if earlier, thank God, I slept right through it). Because so many were trying to use the toileting facilities at once, I generally preferred to wait until the early crowd was out of the door. I got into the rhythm of preparing my backpack, to the degree I could, the night before. Then the next morning there was less to do. I eventually learned to fill my inside-the-backpack water bladder before going to bed, as that was a time-consuming chore. With daily practice I became more efficient at stuffing my extremely lightweight sleeping bag into its pouch, but at this stage there were mornings I had to pack, re-pack, and re-pack yet again until I got everything to fit. And never having backpacked before, it took me some weeks to learn to stow the heaviest items low and close to my body, close to my center of gravity, and to add the lighter items on top. The other trick I eventually learned: always to pack a layer of soft clothing directly against the back and spine.

Most albergues wanted us out of the door by 8 a.m. so they could clean and prepare for the next batch of incoming pilgrims. My new friends and I would generally walk to a pre-planned destination. A small icon on the guidebook map indicated where we would find a café/bar to eat our breakfast. Then more walking, in whatever conditions the route offered up, until we were at our planned destination—or wherever we ended that day. Once we were settled in our next albergue, we would have time to wash clothes, to wash ourselves, to journal, read, or e-mail, to socialize, and then to find a restaurant that offered a pilgrims' menu for dinner. After dinner, bed! Hopefully, the day would include a beautiful walk. This particular spring offered up perfect Spanish walking weather. Most days were pleasant temperature-wise. We needed only our light jackets and, only occasionally, our rain ponchos. Many days the sky was cloudy and overcast, but usually the rains held off until night when we were indoors, tucked into our bunk beds and, with luck, sound asleep. The scenery varied. My favorite walking venue was the narrow path through light woods. It is my conjecture that after many centuries of hundreds of thousands of pilgrim footsteps per year, some of these paths seemed to have been worn down to a lower level than the adjacent plant life. The trees growing on the higher section next to the path would overhang the winding path causing it to appear to spiral off into the distance. I loved this optical illusion! I couldn't get enough of it. I took multiple photos, had photos taken of me walking off into the spiral, into the Camino "magic."

Perhaps it was my romanticized imaginings of the Camino: walking alone for hours each day, through woods as old as time itself, perhaps this explained the Camino's appeal to me. I've always felt a call to "magic places." Since childhood I have been aware of personal resonances with certain areas in the world. For example, my family vacationed in the summers at a 1920s central Missouri resort. From a third-floor balcony of the old hotel building situated high on a bluff, overlooking a cornfield and masses of distant trees, my child self felt I could see "forever."

On a camping trip in my twenties, my fellow campers and I got lost on a winding country road at night. We pulled onto a quiet side road to turn around and were drawn to get out of the car and explore a millpond. With moon and stars reflecting on the pond's surface, we danced around the pond that night. There were surely elementals about: sprites, gnomes, leprechauns. Like *A Mid-Summer Night's Dream*, we were all beguiled and breathing fairy dust.

In my thirties I went with friends to a small, mostly uninhabited island off the coast of St. Petersburg, Florida. We explored the island, swam, collected shells and driftwood, and visited with the local Coast Guard staff, the island's only permanent residents. They invited us to tour the lighthouse and, after we climbed up many stairs, we looked down from this very elevated perch to see brown oval objects moving on the ground far below. We asked our hosts what we were seeing: giant tortoises, native to the island! After dark, we sat on the dock with our new Coast Guard friends and told stories well into the night. Sitting between sea and stars, we hunted for UFOs, and believed they were out there.

On my first visit to Ireland, as our airplane descended in preparation for landing, we saw the Irish coastline rising from the sea. We could see the depth of the land, how it meets the sea at cliff height, not beach level. Into my mind came a thought, the knowing that I was "coming home." It made me cry. I have learned to know truth exists when I am brought to tears by a thought. My response to the ruined Dunluce Castle in Northern Ireland surprised me greatly. I found myself running towards the sea and the castle remains, climbing as high into them as I could, and feeling I was in a familiar place, that I had been there before...when the castle was whole. All of Ireland was magical to me!

In short, the descriptions I had read of the Camino felt magical to me in a similar way and the thought of walking in ancient woods, walking into the past, called to me loudly. Although I never connected with the past-life me while on the Camino, I never felt alone. I was always surrounded by pilgrims past, present, and future. I had imagined I would have plenty of alone time, although I knew from my readings that the Camino is a very well-traveled trail. The statistic I held in mind was that more than one hundred thousand people per year walk the Camino. I knew there would be opportunities for quiet…and that others would be around if I needed help. Perfect!

Wednesday, 4-27-11, Camino Journal
Nájera to Santo Domingo de Calzada

A nice walk today, but I am not in tip-top shape. This afternoon after arriving at the albergue, we all waited in a long line to see the "foot doctor." I question whether he is an actual doctor as he saw us outdoors in the covered courtyard, a cigarette hanging out of his mouth the entire time. Waiting and watching as he treated those in line before me, I saw him sew needle and thread through blisters to drain them, and massage (very painfully) people's too tight muscles. Some were screaming out loud. I was getting an idea of what was in store for me.

When it was my turn, the "doctor" first examined my feet and asked a few questions: what hurts where, when, etc. Then he had me lie, facedown, on a mat on the floor, and did a calf muscle massage which was incredibly painful (akin to childbirth). But, in fairness, my calf was in a knot and needed help. He taped up both of my feet and my incredibly sore right calf, reconfigured the inserts in my left boot, and told me to walk so he could watch. I was limping in pain and he kept yelling, "Walk normally. Walk normally." I guess he decided that I passed muster, or that there was nothing more he could do for me, so it was on to the next patient/ victim. Reminds me of the time I was in physical therapy, thinking "physical terrorist" instead of physical therapist.

I went to dinner with Emma and Leo and new friends tonight: Suzanne and Emer from Ireland, a bunch more from Ireland and Australia, and James from London who is American and Irish, he holds dual-citizenship. We met James standing outside the albergue this afternoon. He is a handsome fellow of about 50 years, with a friendly smile and an engaging manner. James was wearing his newly acquired hot pink Crocs footwear. He had received them as a parting gift from Gunther who is ending his Camino tomorrow, going home to his family in Germany. James' feet were so sore and blistered that he could not bear to wear his hiking boots. When Gunther graciously offered up his Crocs (and they were incredibly comfy, "like walking on boxes of Kleenex" to quote James), James could not say no. The fact that the Crocs were ugly, a less than masculine color, and not really hiking gear was immaterial.

I love the joking salesman aspect of James. He's intelligent and loves to laugh. He asks good questions. I like that he found his last Camino (from the previous year) "both uplifting and encouraging with regard to humanity." I was tickled that he made a point of sending Suzanne and Emer to "rescue" me from some pilgrims whom he found odd. James told Suzanne and Emer to tell me that it was time to go to dinner. I'm so glad he did, because I thoroughly enjoyed everyone's company tonight!

Leo may need to take a day off tomorrow and rest his feet/ legs. He is also freshly bandaged after his foot doc treatment, with tape wound round both his calves. Emma and I may walk, or we may all take a taxi (James, too?) and just see where we want to go. My calf was so incredibly painful earlier, and my left foot, too. But maybe by morning I'll be ready for a light day. We'll see then.

I just had one of Emma's super-dooper Ibuprofens (600mg.) and have my foot up on a coffee table. I am sitting on an actual comfy sofa in the lounge of this albergue in Santo Domingo de Calzada. I just shared with Jenny from New Zealand the story of my mistaken lyrics to "Today," [p.68 and 69] and she lent me her copy of the poem, "Desiderata" [p. 178] to copy into the back of my journal. Some parts of "Desiderata" feel extremely meaningful to me: "You are a child of the universe, no less than the trees and the stars." I promised Jenny I'd e-mail her the "17th Century Nun's Prayer" [p. 250] when I got home. I just love the camaraderie and the goodness of all on the Camino!

Also, had a good walk and talk earlier today with Ernest from South Korea about his future in advertising. I had heard about Ernest and his Camino sello (stamp) from other pilgrims.

[At every stop along the Camino, the pilgrim gets his/her "passport" stamped. Each albergue and many of the restaurants along the way have their own distinctive stamps. Ernest had created his own personal stamp, complete with his image, and was stamping the passports of any pilgrims who asked.]

"Way to go!" I told Ernest. "Anyone who can self-promote so creatively can excel in advertising!" I think he got it. And he seemed pleased with my reasoning!

[In the coming days I had other opportunities to walk with Ernest, to share meals, to watch him eat. Ernest is in his mid-twenties and eats and drinks as only young men can. I enjoyed watching him absorb giant "Dagwood" sandwiches and throw back wine to wash them down. He is so funny! One night, Ernest set out to convince two women who had just met him that he was from North Korea rather than South Korea and that he was the nephew of the "Supreme Leader." I knew better, that he was actually the son of a South Korean teacher and that he was named after the writer, Ernest Hemingway. He is a delight!]

Thursday, 4-28-11, Camino Journal
Santo Domingo de Calzada to Belorado and on to Villafranca Montes de Oca

We cheated and took the bus to Belorado. Actually, it's now 8:05 a.m. and I'm waiting in the lounge at Emma and Leo's pension. Emma is not well and has decided to wait for the Imodium to kick in and then take the bus to Burgos. In another show of our pilgrim bonds we easily swap medications: "I'll give you some Imodium. May I have some of your Ibuprofen?"

I offered to stay with Emma. It's her call. I really am okay either way. I could walk with Leo and James for fifteen kilometers and then take the bus to Burgos, or wait with Emma. Part of me feels bad not to walk. Part of me is afraid? Of walking and of being in pain again, of being damaged. The Meseta (the plains, flat lands) comes after Burgos. I would find that easier. No hills, just peaceful forward time to be meditative, to think—or not.

I rested well last night. Had a strange dream about my brothers coming to see me on the Camino. That morphed into one brother becoming Michael Landon (the actor from the 1960s TV show, "Bonanza"). The dream became a TV show. Michael Landon is in the water and sharks are coming to attack him. Dolphins appear to try to save him. The dream/TV drama ended, and I guess I'll have to "tune in next week" to find out if the dolphins are successful.

So, it is decided. Leo will wait with Emma. James and I will walk and meet them in Burgos. That will be a good test for my feet. It appears that I am supposed to walk.

Friday, 4-29-11, Camino Journal
Villafranca Montes de Oca to Burgos

Yesterday James and I walked from Belorado to Villafranca Montes de Oca where we then caught the bus to Burgos. A very pleasant day. My feet hurt a little, and I am tired. We walked about fifteen kilometers. James and I talked all day. He is actively involved in a relationship, but thinks it may be ending because they live countries apart and neither wants to move to where the other lives. He is a wonderful walking partner, a great conversationalist. We talked about our favorite music, favorite movies, our life histories, our family stories, about everything.

James and I had a fun morning "pit stop" for coffee and tea at a café/bar along the way. We arrived just as the Royal Wedding pre-show (Prince William and soon-to-be-Princess Kate) was being screened on the TV in the café/bar. I tried to translate all that the Spanish broadcasters were saying. At that point, it was mainly about the clothing being worn by all the royals attending. They kept coming back to the beautiful wife of the Spanish Prince Felipe, Princess Letizia. They showed the same ten-second clip, her getting into a car and heading off to the ceremony, over and over. There was heavy coverage of who was wearing the horribly pricey red-soled footwear of designer Christian Louboutin. I had a great time watching. James was not very enthused, but he was good-natured about my "royal" curiosity. When a mom and her toddler son came into the café/bar which was run by the boy's grandmother, we both enjoyed visiting and trying to communicate with the little one. I had a small flashlight with me. I took it off my key ring and gave it to the boy who seemed amused by it.

We later met up with Emma and Leo in Burgos. The albergue in Burgos is fairly new. It has berth style beds, lots of wash-up sinks and plenty of toilets...a plus! We took a stroll around Burgos, a good-sized city, scoping out various eateries. Leo was excited to tell me he'd seen an actual vegetarian restaurant! He gave me walking directions; I headed over, and found it. Unfortunately, it was not open until later, after siesta, and we were hoping to eat sooner, but I was so pleased that he had spotted it for me. On my way back from the veggie restaurant, I passed a number of beggars sitting outside the church. I didn't give money, but sent prayers.

Leo finally got Emma to a doctor, and she's on antibiotics and bed rest for three days. James and I will walk ahead, and Emma will bus ahead to catch up with us after she has rested. We will keep in touch by texting.

Out of nowhere I had the thought today that I don't know what I want to do next in life. I feel like the best I can do right now is to be open, to just be blank and let time and thought be slow and fluid.

CHAPTER FOURTEEN:
Living the European Life Style

"Happiness is when what you think, what you say,
and what you do are in harmony."

Mahatma Gandhi

The Camino is a different life style: because it's the Camino—
time out of time—but also because the Spanish culture and many
other European cultures, as seen from an American perspective, are so much more relaxed, so focused on enjoyment of life
as opposed to meeting survival needs. The Spanish culture, from
what we pilgrims could see, was laser-focused on the family...
enjoyment of the family, love and appreciation of family, time with
extended family as a regular pleasure of life, with at least one multi-
generational family party per day! Is there sibling rivalry in Spain?
I wasn't making a formal study of the families there, but I saw none.
I saw no circumstance in which a family member, or even a pass-
ing-through pilgrim, would feel anything but completely loved.

Saturday, 4-30-11, Camino Journal
Burgos to Rabé de las Calzados

Fourteen kilometers, a relatively short walk. But first James and
I had a long "goodbye" breakfast with Emma and Leo. We will catch
up with Emma in a few days. At that point, Leo will have gone back
to London, his vacation ended. Leo hopes to return at the end of

May to rejoin us, so I am not saying "goodbye," only "see you later."
During our leisurely meal, Leo, Emma, James, and I discussed all
manner of American and British politics. I felt I held my own as the
defending American "champion." It seems these Brits are appalled
by the lack of a complete safety net for each U.S. citizen: health care,
unemployment, career counseling. They feel—and I have to agree—
that in the U.K. folks are generally cared for more completely and feel
more secure. As if to further illustrate how good they have it, Emma's
U.K. healthcare package had covered her visit to the Spanish doctor
in Burgos.

We went over all the negative images of Americans that the
group could throw at me. Bottom line: some of what they say rang
true. We are, as a nation, overweight and under exercised. Many
of us are not politically astute. We are easily led by fear. I pointed
out aspects of American life I felt proud of: institutions such as
the Peace Corps, tuition remission programs for those teaching
or practicing medicine in areas of need, and in my own commu-
nity: Nurses for Newborns, Parents as Teachers, and other not-for-
profits that make life better for many. Americans love to be of help!
There are good folks all over the world. James says they all find my
idealism "charming."

[In every world culture, in every country, there is national
pride. We each think our own system is the best. This is true for
the Brits, for the Spanish, and for us Americans. U.S. citizens may
avoid looking at other perspectives in favor of being "Proud Americans." In truth, our comfort level with all things American and
our discomfort with the unfamiliar keeps many of us from looking
beyond our borders for inventive ideas. I'm not speaking here of
right or wrong, not chastising anyone. Travel abroad is not for
everyone, and few of us will have the chance to live abroad. Many
would prefer to have their adventures in the United States...there

are wonderful things to do and to see in the U.S.A.! But given our "State-side" perspective, we are not likely to know how our lives compare to the rest of the world. Here on the Camino I was seeing from the perspective of my European friends. My findings: Europeans appeared to have a cultured and rich lifestyle. I was taking note of the differences, of ways I wanted to enrich my own life. I was being shown life through a broader lens. "Yes!" to travel!]

This morning I saw an English language newspaper, the first in days. Many tornados have touched down in the U.S., and a tornado killed three people in Missouri. I am anxious to e-mail home and to hear from family, to know that they are all well.

Besides e-mailing home, I would like very much to shower, wash socks, undies, etc., and to get a great night's sleep! The albergue in Burgos was new, very attractive, and well designed in many respects, except that the acoustics were perfect for snoring amplification! It finally came out in conversation this morning; Leo and James say that Emma and I both snore...gently. They were amused by the sounds of the two of us playing a soft snoring concert, a duet. Could be worse, a lot worse...I know! I've been wearing my earplugs at night and using my U-shaped neck pillow to cover my ears, and I still hear the other snorers.

The walk out of Burgos was delightfully decorative, very creative landscaping. I especially liked the large geometric topiary bushes and the tree branches trained to arch over the sidewalks. Today's walk was flat and easy, through the city's outskirts and into the countryside and small towns.

After checking into the albergue at Rabé de las Calzados and attending to personal hygiene, James and I went to the tiny town's single café/bar. When we arrived there we saw a young Japanese man, also a pilgrim, sitting on a bench outside. Friendly James tried to engage the fellow in conversation, but the young man remained quiet and internally focused. James and I went inside for a snack and were greeted by the owner who asked if we were pilgrims. When we said "yes" he handed us gifts: small metal pendants with an image of the "Virgen de los Milagros," the Virgin of Miracles. I was really touched. The brother of the café/bar owner had made his pilgrimage to Santiago, and to give thanks for his brother's safe Camino, the owner was giving the Mary pendants to all the pilgrims who came to his establishment. I love the kindness and the deep reverence of the Spanish people!

Burgos landscaping

Later, we watched as the town children paraded in for after-school treats. The grade-schoolers plopped down at a table (like they do every day?). The eldest took their treat orders and returned to the table with chips, baked products, and candies. James and I both love children, and we enjoyed watching them. How sweet they all were with each other: no fighting, the older ones helping the younger ones with homework.

James helped the little ones open their treat packages, and they all smiled for a photo. After siesta, we returned to the same café/bar for a small dinner. There was no other option in town, but, fortunately, we liked the place. Whole families with kids of all ages were arriving for a social hour. Adults had a glass of wine or a beer. Children drank a soda and were allowed the run of the place to play. Teenagers hugged their grandparents. Babies in strollers were part of the family atmosphere as well. All generations came together to socialize. I have seen this family-focused post-siesta gathering in a number of Spanish towns on this trip. I applaud the Spanish for having found such a wonderful balance of work, play, family, and social time!

Sunday, 5-1-11, Camino Journal
Rabé de las Calzados to Hontanas

Walked with James from Rabé de las Calzados to Hontanas today, about eighteen to twenty kilometers. It poured rain, and I ended up with some seriously muddied boots and pants. I wore a poncho so my upper body and backpack stayed dry. Eyeglasses were another story. All is washed now. The albergue has outdoor sinks on the second-floor balcony. I scraped thick mud off my boots with the butter knife I scavenged from the kitchen and rinsed off the rest of the mud in the outside sink. Now my boots, along with everyone else's, are stuffed with newspaper and parked in the hallway in front of the radiators to help them dry more quickly. I put my socks on the radiator to dry, beside the socks of many others. I will trust that all will be here when I return. So far, so good. All the pilgrims, as far as I've heard, have been very honest: a pilgrims' code? The only place I have "lost" anything was back at Viana about a week ago. The Viana albergue had a huge cloakroom where we were told to hang up our wet rain ponchos and store our boots before we went to our rooms. The poncho that my sweet friend Kristine had lent me, a very nice navy blue one, was hung in there. In the morning when I returned to fetch it, a similar poncho was hanging there, but not Kristine's. I choose to believe that this was a case of an accidental switch, not an evil-hearted, out and out theft.

Now my body is washed and I'm relaxing in my top bunk, writing, and hand-fluffing my hair to encourage it to dry semi-styled. Next, to find Internet service! Since two days ago when we read about the tornados in Missouri, I have not been able to e-mail. Also, it's been three days since I've been able to check in, to say that I am well. Will I have to wait another day? James says he may have seen a computer in the café downstairs.

I am so tired. I am in a small room, four bunk beds. All guys and me. That is a nice change of pace...I haven't been surrounded by men for a long time! Had a chat with Samuel from Brazil. He is here praying to win back his wife. He has shared an ancient tradition with me, a rite, prayer, a spell... using a fruit he calls a "roma." "You put nine seeds of the fruit in a glass of wine," Samuel explains, "three for each of the wise men. Then, you ask for health, peace, money, and love, and you drink your wine."

I think the fruit he was talking about was a pomegranate. In any case, I love learning customs from other cultures. Even the salutations before taking a drink are so varied and interesting. I learned, for example, that you must maintain eye contact when clinking wine glasses or you chance seven years of bad sex. Then there's a choice between: "To your health," "Salud," "L'chayim," "Skol," "Slainte," "Prost," "Kippis," "Chin chin." So many ways to celebrate!

Samuel, my new Brazilian friend, said the funniest thing. He was rooting around in the bottom of his backpack trying to find something when he made a comment about it being "like putting your hand inside a cow." At first, I wasn't sure I'd understood what he was saying given his thickly accented English, but he went on to explain that he works on a cattle ranch in Brazil and that there are times he has to put his arm literally inside the cow to feel for the baby calf, to know if it is in the correct position to be born. I am learning about things I would never have known had I remained in St. Louis!

CHAPTER FIFTEEN:
What I Want

*"Become so wrapped up in something
that you forget to be afraid."*

Lady Bird Johnson

Whether it was a result of the daily focus on my pre-Camino desires and the rousing success that had come from asking my family and friends for help to make my Camino trip, or because of the "Celebrating Men/Satisfying Women" class I had once taken where we women learned that men like to be told what women want, so that they can "hit the target" and please us… somewhere in there I had finally absorbed the life-changing notion that knowing what I wanted and asking for what I wanted would significantly up the odds of me getting what I wanted! Now, here in this new experimental life, I determined that I would practice speaking my desires.

I had spent most of the last almost sixty years attuned to the desires of others, attempting to please them, often at the expense of what was important to me. My own wants were too often put out to pasture. Now, here on the Camino, as an unknown quantity, a new friend with no preconceived traits, no history, I could practice this new-to-me life skill of noticing and speaking my wants with few, if any, negative repercussions. At worst, if I ticked someone off, there would be other new friends to practice with, allowing me to refine my technique. Later in my journey, I would expand into asking the Divine for what I wanted in the way of personal needs and desires for each day. That, it turned out, worked surprisingly well!

After dinner, Sunday, 5-1-11, Camino Journal
Rabé de las Calzados to Hontanas

I wonder what area of interest I will follow when I return home? Will I go back to life as usual or feel completely changed? Already I feel as if the entire world is open to me, whereas before, it was closed off by circumstances. Or by my closed-mindedness? I am so happy sharing this Camino experience with these new friends I already love so much. What else am I learning? The Camino is a perfect opportunity to explore what is both enticing and fear-producing. I hope to learn to overcome many fears as a part of my Camino experiences, and then to help others surmount their fears as well. This is also a wonderful chance to practice speaking what I want with James and everyone else. I first become conscious of what I want and then express it. I told James that my birthday is now only a few days off and that I will want a birthday party of sorts: all of us together, Emma too, and a gin and tonic. That will make me happy.

We may be caught up to Emma by mid-day tomorrow. Then, if we walk about twenty kilometers per day, we could be in Santiago by May 25 and have plenty of time to go to Finisterre. For me, the concern is money: will my funds stretch to cover the entire trip? Can I know at this point? No. Moving on…no dwelling on fears allowed!

I love meeting new Camino friends: Jacques from Belgium who jokes in English and will pray for us, Anna Marie, Cornelia, and James, all my dinner companions tonight. And I got to check e-mail! Everyone at home is fine. There was no tornado damage near my family and friends. As a plus, I received a darling e-mail from my just-turned-seven-year-old niece, Grace:

> *"Dear ant dube*
> *i hop you hav a good time ther. thak you for mi pensols theat wus swet of you.*
> *i know you miss us and we miss you to.*
> *love grace w"*

She is right. I miss her so much! I miss everyone, of course, but she is the one who will have changed the most in my absence. And, therefore, she is the one who tugs at my heartstrings, who calls up twinges of homesickness.

When I get back home, I will want to be more active, to keep myself in better physical shape. I could walk to Grace's house or to see friends. I want to get back to dance class. I am liking this slimmer-bodied me so much better. I don't see changing my eating habits so much as changing my movement lifestyle.

Monday, 5-2-11, Camino Journal
Hontanas to Itero de la Vega

Walked ten kilometers this morning with James. We met up with Emma in Castrojeriz. She had been there for two days, and the hospitalero had nursed her, bringing her food and letting her sleep instead of kicking her out in the morning with the other pilgrims. She seems weak, but on the mend. She's happy to see us! We had lunch in a local café/bar. It's actually a beautiful restaurant, complete with a stone rear exit, an exit tunnel! The waitress, with her dark, slicked-back hair and many facial piercings, was very proud of her Spanish heritage and of the Spanish food. The food at the restaurant was fine, but she and the place were gorgeous!

I am learning to accept what is: a new bed and bathroom setup each day, boring foods with little flavor, snoring and noise as normal, mud, smells, weather. I accept all that is beyond my control. But, that said, I have to laugh. Something is off in the Spanish psyche regarding toileting facilities. The beautiful ladies room in the restaurant was hooked up to a time-controlled light fixture. Once you turned the light on, it remained on for a prescribed amount of time and then it shut itself off. Yes, this is an elegant solution to the problem of people leaving the lights on in public restrooms and wasting electricity, but the light switch is beyond arm's reach when sitting on the toilet. Once it clicked off I could not turn it back on. Fortunately, there was a large frosted glass window in back of me, it was day time, and I was able to "finish my business" with enough light to find what I needed.

We are now another eleven kilometers past that. I have learned a valuable lesson today on where not to toilet. I had gone off the path to a private green area to "wee," as the Brits say. There was an old broken television lying in the grass—the perfect spot to "use the facilities" as I could set my backpack on top of the TV. Being new to both the European fauna and flora, I did not know I was squatting next to a stinging nettle plant. Ouch! I was left with a sore spot on my thigh as a reminder, but it could have been so much worse!

We walked all afternoon to Itero de la Vega, a tiny town. We were not able to stay in the nun-run albergue on the edge of town, as it was full. We saw Ernest from South Korea and many others, mostly young women, who were settling there for the night. A nun was preparing a wonderful smelling meal. Oh well. We were okay with missing out on this bit of rural paradise when we realized that the bathrooms were out back in separate quarters, not fun for a middle of the night emergency pee.

We walked on another kilometer or so, passing some very cute older Spanish men sitting together on an outdoor bench, swapping stories, and enjoying the mild spring weather. Emma and James both took the men's photos. We told them it was because they were "muy guapo!" (very handsome!). They were delightful, as are all the Spanish people we've met so far. Later we met another older Spanish gentleman who got out of his car and came up to greet us, basket of candy in hand. He was very proud to show us the pin on his hat that read: "Amigo del Camino" (Friend of the Camino). He is an official greeter!

We are now at the municipal albergue. It is charming, but dirty! This evening, of all evenings, we had decided to buy ingredients at the store and to fix our own meal. The meal was wonderful, but we had to wash all the dishes first so they felt safe to cook in and eat off of. The kitchen was a riot: we looked for spices…nothing but salt and multiple containers of paprika. We looked in cabinets for bowls and equipment and found one cabinet stuffed with meats, each in its own pre-sealed package, but not refrigerated. There was a pot of cooked potato pieces on the stove. No clue how long they'd been sitting there. We dined al fresco in the back courtyard. From our table we could see the occasional stork fly over and the church steeple where it nested.

This albergue was probably once a private residence. The upstairs where we will sleep has a few small dormitory rooms with the obligatory bunk beds. It is more private than many: only three bunks in our room, only three of us: James, Emma, and me. A bottom bunk for everyone. Hooray!

Emma is still healing, tired, in bed early. I am waiting for a turn in the teeny-tiny shower and then to get in bed too. My calves are very tight again after our last good-sized "mountain" before the Meseta, the plains. We will try to get going fairly early and walk only fifteen kilometers to Frómista tomorrow. I could do with a really good, cheap washer and dryer and good Internet, plus, a decent bed.

The sky was so beautiful today as we walked into Itero de la Vega: huge puffy clouds set against clear blue. Everything lush and green. It made me cry, wanting the sense of peace I was feeling to go out to all humankind! I wondered if the world would be a less violent place if everyone were blessed to have this type of natural beauty in their lives?

CHAPTER SIXTEEN:
From Bad Day to Birthday

"... a very powerful practice for abetting calcination is to refrain from trying to understand the reason for a misfortune. Look neither to the past for how it happened, nor to the future for why. Don't blame others. Don't blame yourself. Don't draw any lesson. Just experience the pain while allowing it to go entirely unexplained. It is unlikely that you'll be able to persist in this forever, especially around a major blow, since insights will eventually spring to mind unbidden. They'll probably be different from the conclusions you would have drawn had you been thinking about it on purpose."

Catherine MacCoun

For me, this period on the Camino was one of both joy—walking in stunningly beautiful landscapes, having an adventure with wonderful new friends—and of deep disappointment. More on this to come. When one is in pain and sleep-deprived, one is less able to cope with disappointments, to bounce back from perceived slights, or even to locate one's sense of humor. Mine had been temporarily misplaced, along with my travel towel and my toothbrush. I was in pain and becoming more sleep-deprived by the night. This, along with the alluded to "perceived slight," contributed to my feeling mentally and emotionally alone, separate, abandoned, untethered, and misunderstood.

Tuesday, 5-3-11, Camino Journal
Itero de la Vega to Frómista

Had a wonderful morning walk with a rest stop for an ice cream break and toileting at the beautiful albergue at Boadilla del Camino. This is the albergue of "Wooly Hat Man," as Emma has dubbed the sexy, touchy-feely ladies' man hospitalero/manager with Rasta dreadlocks tucked under his hat. We women loved how he gently took us by the elbow to guide us to our seating (or to the ladies' room…or anywhere!). The garden statuary here is nontraditional and so much fun. I took multiple photos of my favorites: the five foot-tall, upside-down, forked tree branches stuck into the ground, looking like two-legged "tree men" walking. Very clever! I have made a note in my guidebook to spend a night here on my next Camino.

For our break we sat on the patio, in the albergue's courtyard, enjoying the perfect spring weather. At a table across from us sat a darling older Spanish man, a local, not a pilgrim. He reminded me so much of my paternal grandfather that I wanted to take a photo of him. I held up my camera and pantomimed taking his photo, asking his permission with a look of question on my face. His response: pointing a finger to his cheek, saying with his gesture, "Yes, you can take my photo…for a kiss!" He got his kiss, and I got his photo to remember him and my grandfather. A good deal even if I had to endure the ribbing from Emma and James about my "boyfriend." We later met another older Spanish gentleman, who kindly attempted to give us directions, multiple times, until it became apparent that he was suffering from dementia. We gave our thanks and said our goodbyes. Although the beautiful crisp spring day was heavenly, this last gentleman seemed to be a harbinger of ill as the rest of the day was not as peaceful. We had an alligator scare.

Courtyard in the alberge at Boadilla del Camino

Boadilla del Camino tree-men walking

We were walking on the Meseta next to a peaceful canal, seeing the clouds both in the sky and reflected in the calm waters of the canal. I was totally immersed in the natural beauty: the rotund, spun cotton clouds, the kind I had loved to watch as a child, waiting to see what animal shapes they would take on next. Concurrently, I was checking the rocky path for unevenness, walking carefully so as not to step in an awkward way thereby making my feet even more sore and unhappy. Emma and James were walking about fifty yards ahead of me. I didn't even realize that they had stopped until I was right upon them.

"Did you see it?" Emma asked me.

"See what?" I responded.

"The alligator!" James almost jumped when the word "alligator" came out of his mouth. "It slipped back into the water before we could get a photo."

"You saw an alligator? How big?"

"It was huge!" Emma said. "Maybe ten to twelve feet long!"

We walked more cautiously by the side of the canal, discussing how a 'gator could be here in northern Spain. None of us had any reason to believe that alligators were native to Spain, although, just days before we had seen a couple of two-foot-long lizards run away from us to hide in the tall grass. We surmised that the big 'gator may have once been a pet baby alligator and that the well-meaning pet owners flushed it down the toilet when it grew large enough to be fierce-looking.

Peaceful canal along the Meseta

I was feeling quite concerned about our safety, walking so close to the canal. In my mind I was flashing back to Dunedin, Florida, on the Gulf Coast, where I had lived many years before. There, in a city park, in a large pond, lived an alligator. Parents were cautioned not to lose sight of their children, nor to let them play in the pond. Owners of small pets were told never to let them off their leashes. Although I had never personally seen the creature, attending art shows at the park and reading the signs saying "Beware of the Alligator" had left me with a strong and visceral memory. Now, walking next to the (formerly) peaceful Spanish canal, I was the one urging my friends to walk faster. In my head, I was figuring out how to let the authorities know. My very loose plan of action: to get somewhere and speak with someone in charge.

When we finally reached our albergue in Frómista, a few kilometers down the road, I had my "pidgin" Spanish sentence formulated and was ready to share the information with our hospitalera. I had looked up "alligator" in my Spanish/English dictionary. "Está un caimán en el canal." To my knowledge, I was saying, "There is an alligator in the canal."

For some reason, Emma and James found this hysterically funny, perhaps because to them the Spanish "caimán" sounded like the word for ham: "jamón"…pronounced "hamon," both words with the accent on the second syllable. Jamón…caimán. They kept laughing and telling me that the hospitalera wouldn't believe me, that she would think I was crazy. And, indeed, she looked at me in a very odd way. Perhaps I had said something to her that made no sense: "…a ham in the canal?"

We had dinner with two pilgrim friends from South Korea, Hu and Kim. As I was telling them about the 'gator sighting, I had a mental flash. I remembered a photo I had seen in a tourist pamphlet on the Spanish architect, Antonio Gaudí. "Wait a minute,"

I said, as I rummaged through my purse for the pamphlet. "Here it is!" The photo's caption read, "San Jorge" (St. George). I showed Hu, Kim, Emma, and James the photo: a sculpture of a medieval knight stabbing a dragon with his sword, but the dragon pictured was an alligator!

The photo proved to me that alligators had, at some point, been a part of the Spanish landscape. Hu and Kim had no response. "Okay," I thought. "Maybe they aren't understanding me either." What I had failed to see, being so engrossed in flipping through the Gaudí pamphlet looking for the photo, was James and Emma gesturing silently to Hu and Kim that I was crazy.

Wednesday, 5-4-11, Camino Journal
Frómista to Carrión de los Condes

I am having a bad day! Very tired and off from the schedule I would prefer. My body would like to walk earlier, to continue on without stopping for a long lunch break, and later to have an entire afternoon to recoup. But there's more than that. I have been feeling fragile, over-tired after many nights of trying to fall asleep in rooms filled with loud snorers, in pain from foot, ankle, knee, and hip. Then, this afternoon I bruised a rib climbing down from my metal bunk bed, I lost my travel towel, sat on a toilet with no seat, and lost my tooth brush. I am having the adult pilgrim version of the kids' book "Alexander and the Terrible, Horrible, No Good, Very Bad Day."

To compound my terrible day, Emma and James finally came clean. There was no alligator. It was a hoax, a practical joke. And I, as the world's most gullible person, fell for it. My first response was to feel hurt, and then, anger. With new friendships, even with those as intense as ours of only a few weeks we have lots to learn about each other. In my case, what Emma and James don't know is that pulling the wool over my eyes is as easy as choosing chocolate for dessert. But, mostly, because I am new to these friendships

I wasn't expecting what feels like a breech of trust. My feelings are hurt.

What I have since learned about Emma and James is:

A. They are both gifted actors.

B. They both have soft hearts.

C. They were crushed that my response was not amusement to be shared as part of the group.

Emma came up with a plan in which she and I could "pull one over on James." She would pretend to be drawn into a life in the convent. And although I can see her playing that role brilliantly, I don't have the heart or the energy to participate. I know that the suggestion was Emma's way of saying to me, "I love you, and I want you to be part of the fun, too."

James has apologized profusely. He said they had actually been surprised when I fell for the story and had planned to tell me the truth at once, but I kept pushing the story forward, telling people, finding evidence. And that is exactly what I did. I accept James' apology and Emma's show of love. It is obvious that neither one has any desire to hurt me or cause me pain, and yet, I am still upset.

My job now is to move past this, to drop it, and refuse to pick it back up and "chew on it." This reminds me of the story Hape Kerkeling shared in his funny Camino book, "I'm Off Then," of the two Buddhist monks and the woman who needed help to cross a vigorous stream. One monk picked up the woman and carried her safely across to the other side. After, as the monks continued on their way, the monk who had watched his fellow carry the woman finally spoke. He said he was surprised that his friend would do that, touch the woman, considering he had taken a vow of chastity. The monk who had done the carrying responded "Yes, but on the other side I put her down. You are still carrying her." Okay,

I know what I want to do: drop my upset, put it down. I hope to let this go gracefully. On to the rest of the day...

My pain and sleep deprivation were doing me in. I was not able to bounce back from the "joke" as I wished to. I know that, even in the most loving of families, feelings can get hurt. I am hypervigilant about peoples' feelings. This is a learned skill, which was useful in my childhood to keep from upsetting my sensitive mother. It was one of the gifts of my upbringing that took me years to appreciate. Being subjected to Mom's mood swings taught me to be always on alert for changes in her emotional state. She could go from screaming to, seconds later, calmly picking up the phone...her emotions swung both ways. As a youngster, I learned when to back down—when to head off to my own bedroom—where I may also have slammed the door and sobbed loudly.

Being exquisitely sensitive to another's upcoming breaking point may have, conversely, given me more skill at knowing just where to aim and when to fire. My child/teenaged self did not handle feelings of unjustness in a saintly fashion! But, for all my mother's exaggerated responses, from her zero-to-sixty ability to fly off the handle, from her lack of personal control, I had learned to pay attention to emotional clues. With most folks I grew to feel comfortable "reading" their emotions. I would listen to someone tell a personal story, and I would feel their feelings, sometimes being more clear on their emotional state than they were. I grew to appreciate this gift of empathy as it allowed me to understand others: family, friends, and business relations.

Bottom line, because I am so aware of others' feelings, my adult self is careful to not overstep, and because this seems "normal" to me, I forget that not everyone is perceptive in this way. People often misjudge the fears, worries, and sensitivities of others. Most often, they just fail to collect enough info on the person and plunge into what turns out to be a hurtful event. They are innocent of any ill intention.

Even though I was aware that no harm or ill will was directed my way, the alligator practical joke had an exaggerated negative effect on me, mostly due to my low energy reserves. I appeared to recover and move on, but something inside of me felt "off." Not until my return home from the Camino was I finally able to make peace with this incident, to fully forgive and love my Camino friends wholeheartedly again. Back at home, when I sat down to write this event as a complete story, the correct ending presented itself and offered me the healing I needed. (p. 256)

Wednesday, May 4, 2011 Camino Journal, continued

The real delight of today was the rest break we took at the teepee albergue at Villarmentero de Campos. It seems that the parts of the American experience that have oozed out into the world are often related to Native American lore and to drug culture. This albergue literally has Native American-style teepees to sleep in. I remember years ago, on a trip to Ireland, breakfasting in a Native American-themed café in Dublin. The walls were decorated with the words from famous Native Americans, like Chief Seattle's "…unto the seventh generation" quote.

The teepee albergue was being run, we surmised, by some former druggie-folk who loud-speakered Bob Marley's reggae music into the courtyard and decorated with lots of pot-related poster art. The place had a distinctive vibe! My favorite part of this rest stop was that I got to enjoy a real "feet up" rest in a hammock. Emma took a photo of me naturally "blissed out" that she promises to send me when she gets home.

I told Emma and James what I want: to be done early enough in the day to sit and enjoy the afternoon. We will do that tomorrow.

I have to laugh at myself. I felt so terrible today, physically, mentally, and emotionally, that I am planning to remember this town, Carrión de los Condes, as I wish to translate the name: Carrion of the Condor…basically saying that I feel like leftover, rotting dead flesh. Okay, I will choose to laugh at how funny I am, and not wallow in self-pity. My body is hurting, but it is doing what I ask of it. Go Body!

P.S. Met Julie from Chicago today, one of only a very few U.S. citizens I've met on the Camino. She's between jobs. That seems to be a "theme" of this Camino. Emma is between jobs. James is "waiting for a phone call." Ernest is "looking." Quite a few others are in the same boat.

Thursday, 5-5-11, Camino Journal
Carrión de los Condes to Sahagún

James, Emma, and I took the bus today from Carrión de los Condes to Sahagún, about thirty-five kilometers, in order to connect with Emma's son Jack who will vacation/walk with us for some days. Jack is in his mid-twenties, a designer who has just completed a large commercial project. Jack graduated from the school in Scotland where one of my creative heroes, Charles Rennie Mackintosh, painted and designed. Jack has seen the famous Willow Tea Rooms in Glasgow that Mackintosh designed from floor to ceiling, walls, windows and furnishings, too. I am so jealous! God, please get me to Scotland for my next big trip! Also, we decided the bus ride was important because we still need to rest our very sore feet. The bandages and massage from the "foot doctor" have helped, but my left foot seems to be changing shape slightly, taking on more of the look of my elderly great aunt's feet: horrible bunions, feet that don't fit into shoes well at all.

We didn't end up doing much today, only meeting up with Jack, and then a bit of exploring Sahagún. We walked down one street, and I happened to look up in time to catch a trompe l'oeil scene painted onto an upstairs apartment window: "hanging meats" like the window of the butcher shop in Pamplona. Ha!

We strolled a bit and then headed back to the albergue. I was in the lead, thinking I knew where I was going, but I was totally turned around. James, Emma, and Jack hadn't said anything at first because they thought I had some clue of where I was heading. They said I was walking so confidently! When they finally said something (gently) to me like, "Do you know where you're going?" I realized I had missed some landmarks. Good thing I'm not traveling all by myself! Our little band of friends now has a new acronym to put on a button, bumper sticker, or a t-shirt: SCEWC: "Self-Confident Even When Clueless." This time I can easily laugh at myself!

Our lodging for tonight, the municipal albergue of Sahagún, was once a church. The original roof is gone, perhaps destroyed by a bomb—that kind of gone. The walls of the original structure end unevenly and the cap of a roof rests on top of the broken-looking upper walls. The bunk beds are spacious, built-in wooden berths. I am on the bottom bunk and there's space to sit up and write! There's so much wood in here that the acoustics may be good for absorbing snores. Let's hope! The shower rooms and bathrooms are co-ed, but at least they have individual stalls. There is enough privacy, though just barely. This must be culture shock for poor Jack. I wonder if he was expecting nice hotels, or, at least, a private room. There are multiple pilgrim cooks sharing the albergue's kitchen and a whole gob of folks in the common area eating, playing guitar, and singing. There are quite a few familiar faces here. Haven't seen Terry from Australia for a while. Good to catch up with him.

Original walls meet new roof, Sahagún albergue

I've taken my shower. My hair is almost dry. Our breakfast café is mapped out for the morning. Tomorrow is my sixtieth birthday. Here's how I would like the day to look: be up and out by about 8 a.m., eat a healthy breakfast, good "toileting," decent-looking hair, clean-smelling clothes, and no leaks in either my water bottle or my water bladder (the one inside my backpack). I would like an easy walk of about three hours/ fifteen kilometers, and to feel good while walking. I'd like to find a wonderful albergue with great servicios (bathroom facil- ities) and Internet, either in Calzadilla de los Hermanillos or El Burgo Ranero. I want to enjoy good company at dinner, treat myself to a gin and tonic, and get a good night's sleep! Why was I so tired earlier? Now I would be happy to stay up and read...if I had something to read. I suppose I could try to translate more of the pamphlet on architect Antonio Gaudí.

Friday, 5-6-11, Camino Journal, My Birthday!
Sahagún to El Burgo Ranero

My sixtieth birthday! The morning started out well. Emma, Jack, James, and I sat in the café, a block down from the Sahagún albergue, and breakfasted. There we met Ignacio, the kindest, friendliest Spanish man...muy guapo! He joined us for breakfast and then asked if he could walk with us. Emma and Jack have decided to walk on together and have mom/son catch up time, so that left me walking with James and Ignacio.

James is a huge people person. I am more introverted, so it is fun for me to watch him, to see what an extrovert does. James and Ignacio were enjoying comparing notes on all their favorite movies. They found they had a bunch of top picks in common. I was enjoying listening. The conversation eventually came round to what we all did for a living. Ignacio told us he is a lawyer in international business. James was all over that! He was positively beaming with pleasure for having scored such an interesting new companion... until Ignacio added that he would be "...giving up law to pursue the priesthood."

I tried to stifle my laughter. James is not into organized religion, Catholicism in particular. I understand that, as I'm not drawn to organized religion, either. I'm happy to be the creator of my own personal religion/spirituality. Anyway, I could see James's jaw hit the ground. He was stunned into silence. I had to pick up the ball and say, "That's wonderful, Ignacio!" and to ask more questions. This gave James time to recover and to take in his first "Camino Lesson" of the trip: to be respectful, perhaps even to open his mind a bit, to see that organized religion can be okay...good...important, even to someone as interesting and worldly as Ignacio. We later said "adiós y buen Camino" (goodbye and good Camino) to Ignacio at a town along the way. He plans to walk the rest of his Camino with priest friends.

The walk and talk with Ignacio had been a fun scene to watch. It was especially humorous because James and I had just been talking, wondering if we would have any Camino lessons. Have I had any Camino lessons yet? Yes, about how wonderful the people are here, how much I appreciate them all, and that they appreciate me, as well.

We ended our day's walk in El Burgo Ranero, a flat, modest town, larger than some, with more than one main drag. We found room at the second albergue. The first one was packed full. In El Burgo Ranero, we met up again with Emma and Jack. The four of us found a small restaurant for my birthday dinner. The poor waitress was having so much trouble with us. We just could not understand her explanation of the menu options. There was one entrée that we were especially clueless about: conejo. She said it slowly, over and over. She tried hand gestures, forefingers up at her temples…a bull? She did not try the "sounds like" trick. She finally went to the kitchen and brought it out on a plate. It looked like a chicken leg. Somehow, I got enough of a sound clue to look it up in the dictionary: rabbit! But by this time, our poor waitress was so frustrated that she left and got the owner to wait on our table.

After our meal James accompanied me to the other albergue, the one we did not stay at because it was already full. There they had Internet! And they were getting ready to sing "Happy Birthday" to my thirty-two-year-old Japanese "twin." Of course James spoke up and said it was my birthday too, so they sang Happy Birthday in multiple languages to us both. I was able to check e-mail and receive birthday greetings from home. I sent a group e-mail to family saying "Hello" and "Happy Mother's Day in advance" to all the moms including my own. It felt good to be in touch.

Later, back at our albergue, Emma and I sat outside in the court-yard on deck chairs and yakked. That's when I started to get weepy. It's been coming for days. I don't understand all the reasons. Some tears are happy tears, some sad. I understand this much: that I would love to have a romantic partner to do this trip with. I've seen Emma and Leo together, heard about James' trips with his girlfriend. Me and ___? Somewhere, God, is there a romantic, beloved soul mate for me? I'd love to have someone here who would massage my tight calf muscle, who would help me on and off with my backpack, someone to have loads of fun with, to be kind and loving to, someone to share special glances and private jokes with, and most importantly, to share these special memories of our pilgrimage experience after we return home. I am missing someone to build good memories with. Emma can see this hole in my heart, in my life. Maybe, when I get back home, I'll try speed-dating or online dating. Who knows?

Lots of love and gratitude, God, for all my sweet friends helping me celebrate my birthday, for our safe walk, for the strength and energy to follow my big dream. As a birthday gift to myself, I will plan some walking-alone time each day, not all of the time, but some, to see what will bubble up.

P.S. It's a small world! Our Danish albergue mates here in El Burgo Ranero have friends in my hometown of St. Louis! The friends own a furniture store called The House of Denmark. I am to go there on my return and tell Egon that Neil and Bieden say "hello." Also, I have been wanting to see the stars at night: the Compostella/the Field of the Stars/the Milky Way. This walk is supposed to be directly under the Milky Way. So far, it has stayed light until very late, the evening skies have mostly been cloud- covered, and all the albergues have had curfews. I have not seen a starry night sky once since my arrival in Spain. Our albergue room here has a door that opens out onto the courtyard. I will attempt to wake early enough to step outside and have an early morning stargaze. Happy Birthday to Me!

CHAPTER SEVENTEEN:
Colorful Camino "Kin" Come to the Rescue

"Go to your bosom: Knock there,
and ask your heart what it doth know."

William Shakespeare

Do we actually call into our lives that which we think about? That is the premise of the book, "The Secret," by Rhonda Byrne. It is also a basic tenet of the Abraham-Hicks teachings. The conjecture is that we attract into our lives that on which we place our focus and our energies. This was my Camino experience in a nutshell. I anticipated meeting the perfect Camino friends and "poof!" There they were! I was sure I would love Spain, that it would feel like a "magical" place for me. And, Spain was completely magical for me, in a transformative way! I worried about my money running out, and, guess what? Poof again! The Camino was a huge opportunity for me to practice trusting in the Divine—over and over and over again I practiced. I sure wish I could have learned my lessons faster and more easily! But, no…I required remedial instruction and coaching on trusting the Divine throughout the entire journey.

Saturday, 5-7-11 Camino Journal
El Burgo Ranero to Mansilla de las Mulas

Was able to wake early this morning and sneak out into the courtyard to look at the sky. I could not see any stars though, because of the cloud cover. Darn! Will try again. Tonight we sleep at Mansilla de las Mulas. I wish I could translate the names of these cities. They all sound like they should have really interesting meanings. Anyway, we are now in the large municipal albergue with lots of friends and familiar faces: Huin from South Korea, now living and working in the U.S.; Kim, also from South Korea; Edith (pronounced E-dit) from France; Terry from Australia; the smiling German couple who are so obviously in love/lust with each other; our new Spanish friend and roomie, Bernardo. Lots of really good people.

We enjoyed cooking at the large albergue kitchen last night, taking turns using the stove, the pots, pans, knives, and the tables and chairs. We made "James' Famous Chickpea Salad." This is perfect Camino food for me: drained and rinsed pre-cooked chickpeas, good Spanish green olives with some of the juice (or vinegar, to taste), tomatoes, cucumber, onion, garlic, and a bit of olive oil, salt and pepper. All the ingredients are readily available, packed with protein and flavor!!!

Slept poorly again last night because of leg and foot pain. I am taking Ibuprofen early tonight and hope to sleep well! On to León tomorrow where I hope to see the Casa Botines, designed by architect Antonio Gaudí.

James says he doesn't think my Camino is about one giant insight, but about many smaller insights about myself. This is true so far. I am just blown away by the love and camaraderie of the pilgrims. Today I met and chatted with Myrtle from Greece. I am loving this peaceful United Nations of the Camino!

Sunday 5-8-11, Camino Journal at León and
Monday, 5-9-11 at San Martín del Camino

Spent Sunday in León. Emma, Jack, James, and I took the taxi, along with a nice Spanish man from the albergue in Mansilla de las Mulas. We arrived in León about 10:30 a.m. and took ourselves on a tour of the main floor of a very swanky hotel, the Parador San Marcos. It was a "hospital" in medieval times, a hospice for pilgrims, and has now been converted into a five-star hotel by the Spanish government. Jack explored the idea of spending a night there, but it was way beyond my financial means. Instead, we contented ourselves with taking photos of the gloriously planted, statuary-filled court-yard and getting up close and personal with some gorgeous old tapes-tries in the lobby. I am not sure where the Gaudí-designed building can be found in León. I have given up on Gaudí for now. I need to rest. I will wait to see the Gaudí architecture in the city of Astorga, in two more days.

[There are only two of Gaudí's architectural creations situated along the Camino: one in León and one in Astorga. I was fascinated with the idea of seeing a Gaudí building, but in attempting to read and to translate the pamphlet on Gaudí, written in Spanish, I was missing a lot of the details. The Casa Botines in León is currently the home of a Spanish banking concern and not open to the public. Since arriving back home I've seen photos of the exterior online... wow! I would love to go back to León and see it in person!]

We walked through León, winding our way around town in an attempt to find the albergue at the Benedictine convent. We had to ask for directions multiple times. The convent is very secluded. We twisted around corners, alleyways, and plazas. In the end, we arrived too early and had to wait outside for an hour or more until it opened. While waiting out front I met a fellow from the U.S. who is currently living in a tent here in Spain. He is technically here illegally, as he has overstayed his visa. A little too adventurous for my taste. He actually seems more stuck/homeless than adventurous at this point.

When we were finally allowed to check in at the convent albergue, we waited in a long line which wound up the staircase. Word was coming down the stairs that there were three levels of sleeping quarters. We pilgrims would be divided up by sex and marital status: single men on the top floor, married couples together on the center floor, and single women on the bottom level. No hanky panky allowed! They did allow Emma and Jack to stay together in "Married Couple Housing," as they were mom and son, related by blood.

We met Sophie today while we were standing in line on the stairs. She is a charming young woman from Cornwall who has just completed a stint working in a youth hostel in Oxford. She has saved her funds and is ready for an adventure on the Camino. She is beginning her Camino here in León. Sophie is bubbly and sweet, full of life! I hope I will get to know her better.

After getting settled in the dorms we went out to explore León. Actually, Emma and Jack went off to explore cathedrals while James and I found a neighborhood café/bar with English language newspapers! We spent a lovely, lazy afternoon at an outdoor table drinking an assortment of beverages. I have found a Spanish drink called Limona, a soft drink, which I enjoy. Sometimes, though, when I order it, I get an alcoholic beverage of the same name. I got the alcoholic version today. I'm not sure what I'm saying wrong that's confusing the server, but I have enjoyed both versions. Truly, I am a lightweight as a drinker. Good thing we had loads of time. I read a few papers cover to cover. The Camino is really "time out of time." Ordinary time, the real world, has passed us by while we've been walking in this special parallel universe. I am now, for the moment, caught back up.

James and I ran into Claire from Ireland, an earlier walking buddy of James', and Dinah, a British chiropractor who had recently been working in the world of Italian TV. We all went to a falafel restaurant for dinner. It is lovely to be in a city big enough to support ethnic restaurants with vegetarian choices! I enjoyed the food and everyone's company and will try to connect Dinah with Cheryl, my chiropractor friend in St. Louis. Cheryl will be going on vacation to Italy this summer. I bet Cheryl and Dinah will have much to discuss!

After dinner, it was back to the convent for vespers. Translations of the service were available, packets in many languages were handed out. Unfortunately, I got a Spanish/French version as they had run out of the Spanish/English ones. The nun in charge had us all corralled in the chapel vestibule and was lecturing us on "the rules." The first rule was: turn off all cell phones. Just as she said this, her cell phone rang. Not noticing the irony, she took the call and chatted a bit while we all waited. When we finally went into the chapel, this same tiny nun— wearing a head covering almost as wide across as she was tall—was in charge! She was the conductor and we, the very focused orchestra. She let us know when to rise with a sweeping hand gesture. She lowered us by reversing her move. She was the Alpha Nun! There were two other sisters who were important to the vespers service: one who sang in a delightful voice, and one who translated: she shared the service with us in English, Spanish, French, Italian, and German.

After vespers, it was off to bed. That was fine by me. I was ready. The women's showers and first-floor dorm were being "watched over" by a hospitalero: a man! This sneaky, scummy guy kept peering into the rooms as we were washing and changing, ostensibly to see if we needed anything. Ha! I don't think so! His presence felt invasive. I would have said something to him, but I feared my inadequate Spanish would not be up to making my point. The only word I could think of was "privado" (private). I just wasn't sure that "privado" was a clear enough message. Instead, I left ASAP this morning and bad-mouthed him…not my usual style. But I was ticked off and crabby from continuing pain and the usual snorers resulting in still not enough sleep. I finally gave in last night and took an Ibuprofen around midnight. Then, I was able to fall asleep. At 6 a.m. the scummy hospitalero turned on the lights to get us up and out of the convent. Not my best morning!

León to San Martín del Camino today: Twenty-seven kilometers (over 16 miles)! A new record for me! Today I walked with James, with Sophie and, for a bit, with Julie from Chicago. We walked through the city downtown. I was able to shop at a "Euro Store" (Everything's a Euro!) for real deodorant and a replacement key-ring/flashlight. Later we walked through suburbs and into the countryside, through all manner of civilization. I actually had to move on ahead of Julie after a while because her pace was too slow for me. Shocking! I am tired and my foot hurts, but I am here in San Martín del Camino. I have showered. My clothes are washed and drying in the sun. I am sitting outside, alternately enjoying the sun and the shade. I've taken aspirin, rubbed some of James's anti-something ointment on my foot. I will take Ibuprofen tonight before I go to bed. I will be fine for tomorrow.

Only Sophie, James, and I are in this room so far. It has bunk beds enough for ten. Emma and Jack seem to have gone off on their own. No text messages from them yet. Looks like about twenty-three kilometers to Astorga for tomorrow's trek. We may have to stay in Astorga an extra day to see both the church designed by Antonio Gaudí and the Chocolate Museum!

As we checked in at the San Martín del Camino albergue this afternoon, we placed our dinner orders. We were served our food hours later, all of us pilgrims seated together at a long table. I enjoyed everyone's company. There is a group of priests staying here, *all in civilian garb, all very genial, regular guys. After dinner Sophie was tired and went right to bed. James asked if I wanted to walk down to the other albergue in town, to see if there was anyone else there we knew. This is what extroverts do! I went along "for the ride," which was, fortunately, only a few blocks' walk down the street. We did indeed run into people we knew: Inga and Kenneth. They are a friendly Danish couple, both strapping and strong, handsome and beautiful, and married long enough to have kids and grandkids. We heard the story of how they first met as children: their families shared a vacation property. I just love them! They are so sweet together! That's what I want!*

Tuesday, 5-10-11, Camino Journal
San Martín del Camino to Astorga

Made it to Astorga after a long, hot walk from San Martín del Camino. James, Sophie, and I began the day walking together, taking a break for a late breakfast. Sophie shared stories of her colorful kin and her romantic attachment back in Cornwall. She described Cornwall in such loving terms, that I was ready to rush there to visit. It is the realm of King Arthur, and for me, that is magical. There's so much of England, of Great Britain generally, that I want to see. And Italy, and Cuba, and on and on. How to do this? No clues yet. James and I enjoyed Sophie's company until Santibanez de Valdeiglesia where she decided to stop for the night. We left her at a small albergue with a long, narrow, peaceful-looking courtyard.

The rest of the walk was okay. No unusual climbs, roads about average in rockiness. James, moving at a faster pace than I, was walking up ahead. I was doing well by myself, finding all the way-marker signs, some of which were simply yellow arrows painted on stones in the center of the road. By the time I caught up with James, he had made new friends: Thalles and Flavia. They are a fun and funny young couple; relative newlyweds, originally from Brazil but now living in Australia. James, Thalles, and Flavia were all laughing together when I got there. They had met because James had decided to "use the facilities" in the woods. He had first scoped out the terrain for maximum privacy and was just about to make his contribution when he heard a friendly voice call out to him. Although he could not see Thalles and Flavia where they were sitting, they could see him. They had decided a friendly "hello" in advance would be kinder than an embarrassed greeting later. When James heard their call, he made a choice to zip up and hold it. Of course, being a friendly fellow, he took this as an opportunity to make new friends, as opposed to "making water."

I walked into Astorga chatting with Flavia. James and Thalles walked together and got to know each other. Flavia told me about their incredibly clever travel plan. She and Thalles were each able to get three months off from work. They sold what they didn't want to keep of their belongings and packed up the rest to put into storage. They moved out of their apartment, bought around-the-world airline tickets, and are now traveling the world, rent-free, for three months! Brilliant! No "keep the home fires burning" expenses! They first visited friends in Europe, now are on the Camino, and after, will go to Canada, the U.S., and finally, to Brazil to visit family before returning to Australia and picking up where they left off. What an awesome idea! I didn't even know there was such a thing as an around-the-world airline ticket. Why do we push our kids to settle down? This is so great: Sophie, Flavia, Thalles, Ernest, all the twenty- and thirty-somethings here, taking in adventures now while they are free of the responsibilities of kids, homes, etc.

As we reached the outskirts of Astorga, we met a man from Italy who told us he has been averaging fifty kilometers/ thirty-one miles per day! He is a small, wiry guy with lots of lung power. Says he climbs the Italian Alps for his training regimen. Flavia and

I both think he is kidding us about the fifty kilometers per day, but he proceeds to serenade us with Italian opera (he has a beautiful voice!) as he runs up, over, and down the three-story high metal staircase that crosses the high-speed rail tracks. At this point we believe him about his training and his daily trek. We just think he's crazy. Thalles wins my lifelong admiration when he says he found the runner guy so annoying that he wanted a gun to take a shot at him while he was running up the stairs, like in a carnival booth, shooting at metal rabbits. I needed that laugh! I am tired. We all are. That was why we both hated, and were in awe of "Alp Man's" physical prowess. We are all just whipped!

The first albergue in Astorga looked pleasant, modern, and clean, but it was full. So, on we trudged to the second albergue. It has its charms and its flaws—it is as old as time. Looks like a firetrap. The wooden support beams are worn smooth, dry, and shiny. The floorboards are bare and cracking. The stair treads are thinner in the center. This place has seen centuries of pilgrims! I have asked my intuition, and it says we are safe here. The dormitory is a huge room on the second floor with rows and rows of bunk beds. I got a bottom bunk! A few beds are on the first floor, but they are reserved for pilgrims with physical disabilities. We have seen some disabled pilgrims here and there. There was the fellow who walked with his wagon and his dogs. Homeless, perhaps? He had a disabled friend who walked with him. You hear stories of people who get stuck on the Camino, who continue to walk it back and forth, who never leave, like the tent guy I met at the convent in León. There are all kinds of characters here. I suppose someone may see me as a "character" in their story, too.

Very friendly folks here in this ancient albergue, both the pilgrims—I'm seeing lots of friends—and the hospitaleros. There's a cute Scottish guy who's volunteering here. He is studying Spanish.

This is a temporary thing for him. He doesn't know what he will do next. What is next for us all?

Wednesday, 5-11-11, Camino Journal
Second day in Astorga

Last night was the first time on the Camino that I noticed just how odd it is to be a pilgrim, to engage in normally private and personal routines in front of strangers. Well, actually, it was when flossing and brushing my teeth standing at the sink next to James, so not a complete stranger. But it hit me how intimate an activity we were engaged in: facing each other in the shared mirror and smiling through our floss and toothbrushes. Perhaps this only felt oddly intimate because it was James. Because he is someone I felt instantly drawn to when we first met. It feels rather like the discomfort of greeting a new lover the morning after the first fling, "I know you intimately, but not that well."

And, then there's dressing in public. I have been learning (re-learning) the art of dressing in public while maintaining some semblance of privacy. This was a skill I had developed as a pre-teen either at summer camp or when changing to street clothes in the car after the swimming pool. Anyway, it has been a long time. While on the Camino I have managed the trick of pulling off my PJ pants and pulling on my walking pants within the confines of my sleeping bag. The upper body, the bra specifically, is a more difficult maneuver. The trick is to take both arms out of the PJ top leaving the head in the neck hole, slide the bra on underneath and then, quickly, while no one is looking, switch to the outerwear top for the day. The goal: no exposed breasts, little exposed bra. The technique works rather well in a smaller albergue dormitory room where one can face a wall, but I learned this morning that it is far more difficult to be discreet when you are surrounded by pilgrims on all four sides. I chose not to go into the bathroom to change as there were no doors except on the *toilet stalls and a huge crowd was vying to use the toilets. James was to my left, and I was particularly careful to not aim my chest his way while engaging in the tricky bra action. He has stated clearly that he has a girlfriend, and I am taking pains not to appear to be "coming on" to him (although I would have been interested if he were single… still, it's not cool to flash-flirt). I instead turned to my right, assuming that there was an empty bunk facing me there. I had not looked. I inadvertently flashed Thalles! I was embarrassed and made a point to apologize to him later. Being one hundred percent a gentleman and living in Australia, he replied. "No worries. I enjoyed it." How funny! And that's how life goes on the Camino. No need to carry around remorse or regret. Just keep walking and feel the love!*

I kept expecting my funds to run out, and they did. I realize now that I've made the error of not understanding how credit card cash advances work. I can use my credit card just fine at restaurants, etc., but not to get cash. I need a pin number to do that, and, although I have one, it is in a drawer somewhere at home in St. Louis. Maybe Erin can help me find it when she returns home from visiting her dad in Louisiana, and maybe not. So, I will have to trust that this will all work out, that I will manage somehow. Today Thalles helped me with a brilliant idea. He had come over to see if I needed help, as I was taking a long time at the ATM machine. His Spanish is perfect and mine is paltry, so he offered to translate. After helping me to understand the pin number problem, Thalles suggested that we could all go out to eat together, I could pay with my credit card, and everyone could reimburse me in cash. Fabulous idea!

After the heart-clenching ATM experience, it was still early, so Thalles, Flavia, and I went to tour the Chocolate Museum. We saw the old equipment, admired the classic Art Nouveau advertisements, and watched the movie about how chocolate was made by hand. The

movie must have been made in the 1940s or 50s. It looked "celluloidy."
Finally, we tasted samples of the various local chocolates. Exquisite!
We then went to the post office so Flavia could mail some extraneous
items ahead to herself at the end of the Camino, and I had time to
buy a few items in the supermercado: biscuits (cookies) and yogurts.
We also had to move to the other albergue here in Astorga, as you
can't stay a second night in the same place without a doctor's certif-
icate. James, Thalles, Flavia, and I are sharing a small room—only
two bunk beds in our room! But the room SMELLS! I've checked my
belongings and it's not my stuff. It is a smell beyond body odor. We
are all accustomed to that by now. This is more of a moldy, old boot,
foot-fungus-y smell. I've opened a window hoping to air it out. It is
raining and thundering outside.

We all had a huge, late lunch together. Sophie joined us with a
new friend, Giulia from Italy. Emma and Jack, who are staying at a
hotel in Astorga, joined us too. Flavia and Thalles regaled us with the
story of all that went wrong at their wedding, including Flavia almost
missing the ceremony because of a transportation snafu. I ate most of
a mushroom pizza by myself and then paid for everyone's meal with
my credit card. Everyone reimbursed me in cash! Yay! This works!
We had a thousand laughs at lunch. Jack leaves tomorrow to go back
to work. He finally seems open, having some fun, enjoying the cama-
raderie of the Camino. I'm sure Jack will take wonderful memories
back home with him.

I want to go see the church designed by Antonio Gaudí, now a
museum of the Camino. I will have time as we are taking this second
tourist day in Astorga. I am clean, have clean clothes, and have done
my e-mailing. James is on the computer now. He may leave in a
few days. I will miss him so much if he does. Thalles and Flavia are
off reading and Skyping. I will journal, rest, and keep warm in my

sleeping bag until the weather settles down, and then, I will head out for my Gaudí adventure!

Wednesday, 5-11-11, Evening in Astorga

Early this evening, after the rain stopped, I walked from the albergue across town to the Museo de los Caminos, the Gaudí church, now a museum of the Camino. It was one of my few strikes out on my own so far. I thoroughly enjoyed seeing all the details of the Gaudí architecture and the museum's collection of Camino iconography and historical artifacts. And I enjoyed seeing it all at my own pace, in slow motion, seeing the details to the degree I wanted, reading (trying to read) all the descriptions in Spanish. Gaudí was a master—ahead of his time—his designs are still being built, as some are only now possible to construct using modern techniques and materials. I loved spending time outside afterward in the courtyard, taking photos of the huge archangel statues from every angle, until the guard told me the museum was closing and I had to leave. I am so glad I went. I'm still somewhat afraid of losing my way, and I did have to push myself to go, but it was worth it.

Archangel statue in courtyard of Gaudí-designed church,
now in the Museum of the Camino

I haven't put my boots on at all today. A sandal-only day! I hardly wore my backpack either. Haven't felt like crying for a while. Good or bad? Just is. The story at lunch of Thalles and Flavia's wedding drama put me in mind of all the wonderful romantic couples I am meeting here: Emma and Leo, how they care for each other; James and his lady friend (by story) who have romantic get-togethers in Paris and London; Sophie and her young man back in Cornwall: he gave her a solar charging station so they could stay in touch while she walked her Camino; Kenneth and Inga, the Danish couple who have loved each other since they were children; the touchy-feely German couple we see everywhere, always walking arm-in-arm; and now, Thalles and Flavia, who are young, lively, and eager to enjoy the bounty of life's experiences. All are a true joy to observe. At least now I will be able to recognize that special kind of love when it comes into my life.

CHAPTER EIGHTEEN

From Recreation to Re-Creation

"What must I give more death to today, in order to generate more life? What do I know should die, but am hesitant to allow to do so? What must die in order for me to love? . . . What life am I afraid to give birth to? If not now, when?"

Clarissa Pinkola Estés

I was in pain, sleep-deprived, and feeling romantically lonely and yet, I wanted time alone. I'm an introvert and, though I wasn't aware of this at the time, introverts need to recharge their personal batteries by spending time alone, by engaging in internal self-focus. The Camino's rigors notwithstanding, I was "losing it" because I was so desperately in need of time by myself: time to allow my own thoughts to surface, time to hear myself think, time to re-create my spiritual self. I recalled my intuitive advisor's words from my January "reading" about pacing myself and honoring my own rhythm. Nikki had told me to focus on myself, on "coming home to me." I loved my Camino friends and already had special feelings for James, but I also needed to be away from everyone: on the trail, in the café/bars, in the albergues…not so easy when walking a now very popular ancient pilgrimage trail!

Thursday, 5-12-11, Camino Journal
Astorga to Rabanal del Camino

The walk today was exhausting. Hot sun! James found more new friends: Mona and Desmond, church friends from Ireland who decided to walk the Camino together. Mona is like me in her spiritual interests. Her business card says she is a "healer." I hope we get to talk more at some point. Right now I am feeling rather fragile in my beliefs, ungrounded. After days of walking with my wonderful but non-believing friends, I have allowed my spiritual self to waver. With each of my new friends, the first time I made comments of a spiritual nature, they appeared to turn away, not out of rudeness, but perhaps to avoid confrontation. Perhaps they didn't know a polite way to respond. Perhaps they thought I was a "flake" and were too kind to say that to my face, but I think I felt it. Emma says she loves to visit standing stones—like Stonehenge—but she maintains that her draw to the stones is not spiritual in any way. And that confuses me. Bottom line: no one I've met here so far wants to discuss those topics that fascinate me: past lives, synchronicities, dream interpretation, life after death, the soul and soul contracts... There is no one here to speak with on the subjects I'd discuss with my friends at home. No one here to discuss experiences with—experiences of a non-ordinary nature. Here, the conversations revolve around the physical world: the practical, political, historical, and the ethical. I am craving dialogue about the non-physical world. I am noticing my old discomforts with spiritual thoughts resurfacing, as if the scientifically-minded me wants to step in so my new friends will accept me as "normal." I feel pulled from my center. I hope a talk with Mona, my new healer friend, will help me feel right again. I would have been happy if I could have walked more by myself today... and found a ripe fig to pull off a tree and eat. It was another day of lengthy stops to chat and to be social. After those long stops I am so stiff. My muscles have to loosen up all over again.

We arrived in Rabanal del Camino very late in the afternoon. Flavia and Thalles, who had walked on ahead, had saved places for James, Emma, and me at the municipal albergue. We showered, did laundry, and sat around visiting and taking turns with the one computer in the albergue. Sophie, Giulia, and Martin, a young man who seems to have eyes for Sophie, all joined us for an evening meal, along with Mona and Desmond. Desmond had made a very strong point of the fact that he didn't drink. But for the Camino, he did. He was very "loose" by the end of the meal. We joked and laughed until my face hurt. By that time, I was so tired I was ready to fall asleep in my dirty plate. I again paid for the meal by credit card, and all my friends reimbursed me in cash. Then we hurried back to the albergue so we wouldn't get locked out at 10 p.m. curfew. We came in tipsy and giggling. Quite a few of those already in bed in the giant communal sleeping area were displeased by our less than silent arrival.

Friday, 5-13-11, Camino Journal

Rabanal del Camino to Riego de Ambrós

Walked from Rabanal del Camino to Riego de Ambrós, the little village before Molinaseca, a good part of it by myself. Early in the day we made it to the Cruz de Ferro, the Cross of Iron. I had read about this location in multiple Camino guidebooks. Traditionally, pilgrims bring a stone from home, along with their prayers, to add to the growing pile under the Cruz de Ferro. I had not brought a stone from home, picturing the ruckus it might cause in the airport security line. I suppose I could've packed one in my backpack had I planned to offer it up to the baggage handlers, but I was determined not to let my precious, pared down belongings out of my sight. So, no stone in my carry-on, just like no scissors. [Before leaving I had cut bits of moleskin down to various-sized ovals for blister prevention, just so I could avoid bringing scissors.] *I have been on the hunt for a stone to take to the Cruz since I began my walk. There are plenty to choose from here. Every day I have picked up small stones and added them to my pocket, talking to the stones, saying, "I think that you want to go to the Cruz de Ferro!" Then later, I would add the stones to a cairn, a stone tower of flattish rocks. Here in Spain we all add to each other's cairns. In cairn building I feel myself becoming part of something that will endure. I am connected with all those who have come and laid stones before me. And I become part of the experience of future pilgrims.*

Pilgrim-built stone cairns

After all the buildup, the Cruz de Ferro disappointed me. I'm not sure what I was expecting, something miraculous or with a spiritual tug for me, but what was there was a huge, yet climbable, mound of rocks and crystals, some in little gauzy bags with notes inside. The Cruz itself was a very tall simple iron bar cross. I was not even impressed by the enormous number of stones left over the years by thousands, or maybe millions of pilgrims. Instead, I felt very little. It was nothing but a photo op: me and my amigos del Camino atop the huge rock pile, arms around each other, smiling for the camera.

[Perhaps, in hindsight, this was a clue, but at the time I wasn't conscious enough to notice it. I was living solidly, most of the time delightedly, in the camp of the social pilgrims, all the while becoming more and more removed from my spiritual self.]

I am exhausted. The downhill trek today was very hard... walking on rocky plates and gouges in the Earth. It felt dangerous, like descending the Pyrenees. I am so grateful to have my walking sticks! I don't think I would have made it down safely without the

*balance they afford me. I was being hypervigilant to not turn my
ankle or step awkwardly on my left foot and make it any more sore.
I would have been happy to stop for the day at Acebo, but the group
wanted to move on. Again, everyone stopped for a long lunch, sitting
at tables on an outdoor patio. After that hour or more of sitting,
getting up and walking again is very hard for me. My muscles have
stiffened up and are unhappy not to have a long overnight to rest. I
enjoy everyone's company, except when I don't. I am going to have
to consider planning my own day, my schedule, keeping my needs in
mind. This group has consistently taken long rest/food/social breaks
each day. I have always championed these stops to have toilet access,
but my body only wants a fifteen-minute break, not an hour or more.*

Saturday, 5-14-11 Camino Journal
Riego de Ambrós to Ponferrada

*Today I said "goodbye" to Emma, James, Flavia, and Thalles.
My plan was to talk with each of my friends as we walked, to explain
why I wanted to walk some of my Camino alone. Thalles and
I walked together first. He taught me about the Brazilian economy,
and I shared about my need for alone time.*

*I also had one-on-one walk time with Flavia and later, with James.
I wrote Emma a note last night about my desire for solitary time.
I wanted them all to understand that my needs just weren't in sync
with theirs. It feels kind of unreal. I hope these Camino friends will
be friends for life. But I know they could all just as easily become only
sweet memories. We have talked about the possibility of meeting up
later in Santiago. That would be wonderful!*

*But first, before going our separate ways, we, along with Sophie,
walked together from Riego de Ambrós to Ponferrada. Part of the
walk was very rough downhill and I was, once again, happy to have
my sticks for support. I had my silk undershirt safety-pinned to the*

outside of my backpack, still drying. On a narrow path my shirt was "attacked" by a wild rose bush, and I had to rescue it.

We stopped for a long breakfast, and later, at Ponferrada, for a drink. We all walked together until the point where we were to go our separate ways—they for another sixteen kilometers, and Sophie and I to the albergue in Ponferrada. As we stood outside at an intersection saying our "goodbyes" we were having trouble parting. There were entreaties to stay, hugs, and some tears. The leave-taking dragged on until a car crashed into a concrete trash bin just in front of where we were standing, startling us. That was the signal. It seemed to bring us all back to a sense of urgency to move on. We had been trying to ignore it, but it was time to go.

After separating from the group, Sophie and I walked a short bit more. I enjoy Sophie's company a lot, as with all the others, but it is important to me to do some of this Camino alone. She and I will probably part ways tomorrow. But, for today, Sophie and I settled in at the municipal albergue in Ponferrada and then went out for lunch to a moderately fancy restaurant on the plaza. We sat outdoors and ate and talked and laughed. I tried Sophie's pulpo, fried octopus. Chewy, but tasty. Later we went back to the albergue and did pilgrim chores: washing up, doing our laundry in the big outdoor washbasins, hanging our clothes in the sun to dry, and continuing to move them as the sun moved. We had done a groceria run after lunch and made fruit salad for dinner. Sophie has gotten in the habit of "serving tea," brewing us each a cup of chamomile tea to help with p.m. relaxation. This is definitely the way to stretch money: to have a main meal out at lunch, cook a light evening meal, and buy yogurts for breakfast next morning.

I feel fragile and would love time alone. Surprisingly, time alone is nowhere to be found here. Perhaps I will find a private space in a future albergue courtyard or...? Really, I just want time by *myself; perhaps time to do some crying. Then, I'll know better. For now, what kind of a game plan do I want to set up? I will sit with my guidebook and do some figuring.*

Sunday, 5-15-11, Camino Journal
Ponferrada to Cacabelos

This morning we breakfasted on leftover fruit salad and yogurt before heading out. Sophie is wonderful to walk and talk with. She is great at finding her way around. She's still in the period of finding her way in life, but aren't we all to a certain extent? Sophie says her dad took her exploring when she was a kid, taught her how to way-find, how to keep from getting lost on the trail. She is so much more self-confident than I am in that area. I have to really concentrate to remember the landmarks, to know which way I've come, and how to return, even from a trip to the groceria or to a café/bar. I am much better now at spotting way-marker signs than I was at the start of the Camino. Just being with perky, bubbly Sophie I am picking up some of her good energy. Thank you, Sophie!

It was a short walk to Cacabelos today, only thirteen kilometers. Sophie and I walked some of the time together, and I had some walk-alone time, too. We chatted and taste-tested the ripening cherries on the trees lining the Camino. As we walked into Cacabelos we spotted an odd vending machine carrying a whole host of items I'd never seen in vending machines: combs, toothpaste, maps, all outside next to a building, there for the pilgrim in need to walk by and make a selection. After lunch Sophie and I said, "Goodbye, for now." She left me with some raisins she'd purchased at the groceria in Ponferrada. She didn't like them, and I love dried fruit. I was tickled with her gift.

It is now 3:30 p.m. I am in the municipal albergue of Cacabelos: five euros for a double room with only two twin beds! The walls of the room only go up about seven feet, so they are more room dividers.

You can hear, but not see the neighbors. I have a Spanish female roomie: Pippa. I took a shower, did my laundry, sat in the sun: too hot; in the shade: too cool. May go and lie down for a while. I should have about ninety-five euros left. Hopefully, Erin will check the bank and let me know when more funds have arrived. Meanwhile, along with my fifteen kilometers/day goal, I will shoot for spending fifteen euros/day or less, for the next six days. Then I should have more money coming in. I have an energy bar, almond butter, biscuits, and chocolate in my bag. I will snack on this and later go find a groceria for more snacks and fruit for tonight and tomorrow morning.

Had an idea about setting up tours of Cornwall with Sophie's help, then London and surroundings with Emma, plus Ireland with Mona and Desmond: "Magical Mystical Tours" of Great Britain. Two weeks in length to fit American vacation schedules. Different time lines in history: 1200s, 1300s, etc. The tours would cover spiritual happenings in each area for that period in history. Each would be a living history, and a spiritual, magical, and mystical exploration. The tour could move forward a century every year: repeat business! This is the first idea I've had in Spain. Odd. Normally I think of myself as an idea person. Have I lost my self? Have I spent too much time being social? It is good that I am taking time to be alone now.

I was feeling almost as drained as I had felt years earlier, during my one year of teaching art in a Florida middle school. I remember explaining the assignment to the entire class and then walking around the room, checking on each student's progress. As I walked the classroom, offering encouragement, students would ask questions. In art, there is no one "right" answer, and my students' minds ranged freely. After I would explain the assignment again to each one individually—this being middle school, their brains were operating on hormones more than oxygen—they were each sure to have additional individual questions, "Could I do it like this?"

"How about this idea?" And, the ever-traumatized gifted student lament "Am I doing this 'right'?" All the hows, whys, whats, wheres, and whens exhausted me. Every day I answered hundreds of questions. I became ill with the worst case of bronchitis I have ever had, and at the end of the year, I went back into what, for me, was the much less draining field of picture framing. Others of my fellow teachers managed fine, and I was in awe of their stamina and their caring. But I learned that teaching public school was not right for me. The constant barrage of questions, the ceaseless sounds, and perpetual flow of people in my personal space drained my energy reserves. That was the mid 1980s.

A decade later, back in St. Louis, in my retail frame shop, I was continuously out in front of people. And after long days at the shop fielding questions from employees and customers, in the company of others for more time than I wanted to be, what I craved most was solitude... quiet...time to hear myself, my thoughts, my own questions. I was exhausted by the questions and even the friendly conversation of others. At the time I didn't understand that I was in need of time alone to recharge my personal battery. I later learned that my battery was desperately in need of re-charging. I never felt fully energized.

After eleven years in my own business, working at the store way too many hours per week, I closed my retail shop and brought the picture framing business to my home. There I worked by appointment only, and solitary time became more available to me. Still, there were days when just working with one employee in my basement frame shop felt difficult. My battery was just so low. Somewhere deep inside me I must have known that I would need an out-of-the-ordinary experience: a silent retreat... a pilgrimage...an Anne Morrow Lindbergh *Gifts from the Sea*-type personal retreat to a cabin by the sea, or in the country, somewhere away, alone, quiet…and to remain there as long as it took for me to feel lonely. Then, I imagined, I'd feel well, complete, safe, comfortable being with people again.

PART THREE:
My Solo Camino

DESIDERATA

Go placidly amid the noise and haste, and remember what peace there may be in silence. As far as possible without surrender be on good terms with all persons.

Speak your truth quietly and clearly; and listen to others, even the dull and the ignorant; they too have their story. Avoid loud and aggressive persons, they are vexations to the spirit.

If you compare yourself with others, you may become vain and bitter; for always there will be greater and lesser persons than yourself.

Enjoy your achievements as well as your plans. Keep interested in your own career, however humble; it is a real possession in the changing fortunes of time.

Exercise caution in your business affairs; for the world is full of trickery. But let this not blind you to what virtue there is; many persons strive for high ideals; and everywhere life is full of heroism.

Be yourself. Especially, do not feign affection. Neither be cynical about love; for in the face of all aridity and disenchantment it is as perennial as the grass. Take kindly the counsel of the years, gracefully surrendering the things of youth.

Nurture strength of spirit to shield you in sudden misfortune. But do not distress yourself with dark imaginings. Many fears are born of fatigue and loneliness.

Beyond a wholesome discipline, be gentle with yourself. You are a child of the universe, no less than the trees and the stars; you have a right to be here. And whether or not it is clear to you, no doubt the universe is unfolding as it should.

Therefore be at peace with God, whatever you conceive Him to be, and whatever your labors and aspirations, in the noisy confusion of life keep peace with your soul. With all its sham, drudgery, and broken dreams, it is still a beautiful world.

Be cheerful. Strive to be happy.

Max Ehrmann

CHAPTER NINETEEN:

Lessons and Proofs

*"Your mind is everything.
What you think you become."*

Buddha

Monday, 5-16-11, Camino Journal
Cacabelos to Trabadelo

Walked from Cacabelos to Trabadelo. Lovely to walk alone! Saw some familiar faces and new ones, too. Saw Pippa, my Spanish roommate from last night, many times. She is so sweet, but we have a huge language barrier. It is hard to have any but trivial conversations: "Where will you go tonight?" "How are your feet?" That type of talk we can do, but I want to walk alone anyway.

I slept yesterday! Had an afternoon nap followed by a stroll around the town and a bocadillo sandwich. Came back, took the Ibuprofen, brushed my teeth and was back in bed at 8 p.m. My laundry was dry and collected. I didn't hear Pippa when she came in. I was zonked! This morning I got up lazily. I was almost the last one out of the albergue and it was still early, 7:40 a.m.

I walked very slowly today. Stopped once for a té con leche caliente and ate my leftover sandwich from last night. Also, needed to use the toilet. The albergue at Cacabelos was perfect except no flushing the toilet paper…a septic tank sewage system. I wonder sometimes if

I am correctly understanding what is being asked. Really? No toilet paper? For anything? Anyway, I needed a real toilet facility. I now know three words for the toilet: baño, servicios, and aseo.

I carried with me a squashed flat roll of toilet paper for toileting emergencies, either in overused bathroom facilities, or for use in the field. It remained in a pocket of my backpack, difficult to access for most of the trip. In my over-the-shoulder purse, I carried a small travel pack of facial tissues, each of which I used thoroughly! After using a tissue for nose blowing or the occasional sweat-wiping, it would go into my pants pocket where, like a cloth handkerchief, it would eventually dry out and be re-usable… not pristine, but functional. Fortunately, the Spanish pollens did not arouse my usual spring allergies, and the tissues I saved served the extra purpose of toileting wipes when needed. Had I been at home, the notion would have been unpleasant, but here on the Camino, function and frugality trumped fastidiousness. I remember laughing at Emma's description of the somewhat private and secluded outdoor spaces, the ones multiple pilgrims would use for a needed toilet break. Emma had warned us to be careful where we stepped in those areas to avoid the wads of used toilet paper, the "flowers of the field." I was always happy if I could find an indoor facility to use, but it was good to have my recycled tissues handy for emergency toilet wipes.

Walking alone today, using my common sense to find my way, there were times I still felt unsure. I asked my intuition and made only one mistake, ending up on an out-of-the-way farm path, lined with cottonwood trees, the ground covered with cottonwood "snow." It was surreal, magical, and so beautiful. Glad I went that way. Perhaps it was not a mistake after all.

Going through Villafranca del Bierzo was fun. I went the way I wanted, got a morning ice cream treat, then found a groceria and bought packets of tea and yogurts. I followed two Spanish-speaking pilgrim men, and they put me on the path I wanted, next to a little used highway, with safety barriers, and no ups and downs! I will have enough of that for the next two days. I saw a statue of Santiago with a kilometer marker: two hundred kilometers more 'til the city of Santiago de Compostela!

Statue of Santiago past Villafranca del Bierzo

I was walking on a relatively flat highway, created by blasting through the hillsides. The blast-exposed rocky sides look familiar, like those bordering many St. Louis area highways. Here in Spain though, there are heavy-duty plastic nettings strung along the exposed rock to keep falling bits from accidentally smashing pilgrims. I ate some of Sophie's raisins: they have seeds. I enjoyed the thought that as I spit out the seeds I was starting new grape plants along the Camino: "Deborah Grapeseed" they'll call me!

Tomorrow I climb O'Cebreiro, almost as high as the Pyrenees. I have been worrying about this climb ever since I finished the Pyrenees. I hope I am up to the challenge. After that, I should be very close to Santiago. If all continues to go well, I should arrive in Santiago by 5-28 or 5-29. I am loving my slow and easy schedule: good sleep, cheap eats, stop and go when I want.

I was hearing "Camino Lessons" on my walk today:

1. Trust my instincts. Ask for guidance, or, at least, go with what seems right on a logical basis (e.g., "That path must be there for the farmer to access his crops as it goes through the rows of fields, not for pilgrims who would damage the crop." Or, "That path can't be it as it leads away from the city.")

2. At the same time, always be on the lookout for life's yellow arrows, scallop shell signs, the directional markers that are laid out for me to follow. Trust that I will find these way-marker signs, these life-direction hints.

3. Be sure to follow my Camino, my path. That's what will bring me satisfaction. Following Emma, James, Flavia, and Thalles brought love, laughter, and friendship, but at some point, it was not my path: too fast, painful feet, not resting, not walking, or eating when my body was ready, but on a schedule set up for others' bodies.

Deciding to pay attention to my own needs is a huge lesson for me. I am very blessed to be able to walk quietly and slowly, to look for the places I am attracted to stop. The other blessing of following my Camino is that I again feel open to spiritual lessons. The cynicism of my friends was not only a surprise to me, but I was allowing it to cloud something in me. Isn't that odd? That I could allow others to separate me from my hard-won spiritual connection? At least I have finally recognized it and have made a decision for me! I don't know what my spiritual growth work will bring, but I know I am definitely not ready to kiss it goodbye! I do hope I get to see Mona *and Desmond from Ireland again. I feel like I could use some time with fellow "seekers."*

The development of a personal spiritual connection had not come easily to me. In the mid 1990s, after a third divorce, with a new store to make profitable and kids to raise, I was not planning, or even looking for an opening, or an invitation to come back to trusting a Higher Source, to connecting with God or Spirit. I inadvertently set the "coming back" process in motion when I enrolled my then six-year-old child in the Unitarian Universalist (U.U.) Sunday school program. There, I knew she would be taught about all the world's religions. She would gain respect for all belief systems and all believers. I loved the U.U. religious education program for its open-minded and inclusive approach! While my daughter attended Sunday school, I went to church services where I met people who were to have a healing effect on me.

One new U.U. friend shared books, conversation, and set up a small study group to discuss our spiritual journeys. I was exposed to ideas that were new to me. The first book my new friend lent me was Brian Weiss's *Many Lives, Many Masters*. It astonished me in the credence it gave to the concept of past lives. A true story: Dr. Weiss, a psychiatrist, hypnotized a patient and asked her to go back to the time when the trauma he was treating her for first occurred. Not only did she describe herself in a scene from an earlier lifetime, but after the session ended, she was healed of the trauma! Dr. Weiss described being both surprised and troubled with what he observed. Nothing in his rigorous scientific training explained it. He had to work with this same patient in many more hypnosis sessions before he was ready to concede that her past-life experiences were affecting her current life, and that her negative symptoms were being eradicated by bringing her past lives to light.

Reading the book, I was feeling the same sense of surprise as Dr. Weiss. But because a respected psychiatrist was explaining his experience to me, because he, a person of science, felt he was being shown proof, I too could now begin to see proof. I could set aside my science mindset, gained with my first college degree, and accept a nonscientific version of "proof." For the first time since studying statistics and experimental psychology, my scientific mind could be penetrated by a spiritual validity. My mind and my soul were engaged! From there I studied and took on experiences that I hoped would lead to more "proofs"… proofs that my science-oriented brain would accept. Before heading out on the Camino, I felt God had shown me such proofs: personal examples of divine resource and divine right timing in action in my own life.

CHAPTER TWENTY:
Rocks, Roses, Excrement, and "Chewing On" Anger

"Life is the fruit of your own doing. You have no one to blame but yourself."

Joseph Campbell

When one is not focused on "the moment," the moment is missed. When one places focus on each and every moment, everything is noticed: the good and the bad, the gorgeous and the gross, the serene and the snarky. Without the distractions of my very social friends, with less pain and less exhaustion, I was walking in a "be here now" state of mind. Funny, but I hadn't realized that attention to the present moment, to now, would include attention to lesser states than the epiphany and the profound I was anticipating. Some epiphanies and profound experiences did eventually come. And sometimes I was led to spiritual lessons through experiencing anger and annoyance. Who knew?

Tuesday, 5-17-11, Camino Journal
Trabadelo to O'Cebreiro

I made it all the way to O'Cebreiro today! Twenty kilometers! And I was not exhausted! It was a big hill, but done in chunks, it was do-able. Go me! I loved walking alone today. I couldn't get enough of the paths through the woods where the overhanging trees create a spiral off into the distance, off into the mystery. This is exactly the look of the photo that was my pre-Camino "dream board," the one that felt magical to me every time I looked at it. Seeing it in person, I still feel the magic and the excitement.

Sophie and Giulia are here in O'Cebreiro, and I am very happy to see them both. I had dinner with them and with Marko from Austria. Also met José, a young, handsome, out-of-work Spanish architect who is perfectly fluent in English. I suggested that the Spanish government should hire José to re-do all the bathroom facilities along the Camino. He laughed. He has lived in the U.S., and he understands why, to me, the bathrooms here seem in need of updating. Also met Davide from Italy— another one with an eye cast in Ms. Sophie's direction. I had a delightful dinner with this new crew. They are all in their 20s and 30s. I am probably the age of their parents. We did the credit card/ repay-me-in-cash plan. Now I have twenty-five euros more in pocket. This just may work! It's funny. No one sees this as odd or problematic. I guess this proves the bond we have developed as fellow pilgrims, all wanting to help each other to reach Santiago.

The city of O'Cebreiro is a flat spot on top of a high mountain. It is an ancient city with a church and other buildings from the middle ages. Tons of tourists are bussed up here for the old town and the view. Oh my God, it is stunning! We are so high up and can see so far off into the distance! After dinner, Sophie, Giulia, and I went shopping. I was hoping to find some reasonably priced mementos to bring back as gifts. So far I have found nothing but touristy "schlock" with the exception of the two poster prints from the Chocolate Museum back in Astorga. They are rolled up in a tube in my backpack. They barely fit, but at least they weigh nothing. If I'd known how nice they were compared to these other items, I'd have purchased more at the time. Too late now.

There's no Internet in this albergue, which surprises me as it is relatively new and otherwise well-outfitted. There are clean, spacious shower facilities, but as usual, with a flaw: when the women's shower windows are open to catch the breeze, anyone walking on the path just outside can see right in. Oh, and the women's showers provided me with an opportunity to learn:

Camino Lesson #4: Always speak up. Tell the hospitalero (or the person in charge) when there's a problem. Many of us took cold showers this afternoon, thinking there was a problem with the hot water. As it turns out, when someone finally did say something, it was a simple matter of turning the hot water on, an easy fix!

Only one annoyance today: the old woman selling pancakes. As I was walking through her little village, she was standing in the middle of the road, holding a plate of thin pancakes in one hand and a shaker of sugar in the other. She was stopping everyone she could, asking for a "donativo," a donation, for a pancake. I wasn't hungry and I didn't have an interest in her pancakes, but she was truly insistent. I finally took one just to get away from her. I pulled a one euro coin from my pocket and gave it to her. At this point she began to sound even more insistent that the correct donation for her pancakes was two euros. I didn't have the Spanish skills necessary to argue with her, and I was feeling scammed, so when two other pilgrims came walking up and the pancake-seller went after their business, I used the opportunity to walk away. I ate a few bites of the pancake, and then threw it on the ground for a critter to enjoy. The air smelled of cow-poo,

*not an appetizing accompaniment to pancakes, and I was steamed!
I spent at least the next half-hour imagining, brainstorming, mind-
busting…how I could help this woman do an honorable business
and make better money: offer coffee with the pancakes, have a
small sit-down café/bar with a tiny menu, advertise a few kilometers beforehand so we'd have an appetite for her wares. This, I was
telling myself, is what a truly generous and spiritual person would
do to help her do better in life. I thought of everything I could.
I spent quite a bit of my precious life force energy on it, and for what?
I wasn't planning to go back, to share my ideas, to set up shop for her!
I did everything but drop my distaste and anger. I kept chewing on it.
I am still miffed. How to set anger down? Maybe that will be a future
Camino lesson.*

Wednesday, 5-18-11 Camino Journal
O'Cebreiro to Triacastela

*So grateful to be at the municipal albergue in Triacastela. Walked
from O'Cebreiro this morning. The walk was beautiful, starting from
so far up that the cities below and the bottoms of the surrounding
mountains were all covered in fog. All I could see were the mountain-
tops poking out of what looked like water, but was actually fog. These
are the "floating islands" I had read about. I took multiple photos.
I hope the photos will accurately show what I have seen, will give
the feel of being there. I took a photo from just outside the albergue
yesterday afternoon, looking off into the far distance.*

Floating Islands

I made sure to include a Camino sign in the shot as a place marker. This morning, I took a shot from the same spot, with the same sign in the foreground and with the foggy "floating islands" now in the distance. I took lots more photos as I descended O'Cebreiro. I just couldn't get enough of the fog! The weather was fine. It spat rain the last hour of my walk today, but it still hasn't poured. I think I've been extremely lucky as far as weather goes on this trip. There's only been a tiny bit of precip while I was actually walking the trail. Mostly it has rained late in the day or at night. I did just over twenty kilometers (thirteen miles) today, much up and down. Very proud of myself. I am doing it! If I feel pain when I am walking, I lead myself in a guided meditation. This meditation came to me earlier in the year when on a pre-Camino walk. I imagine the "effervescent energies of optimal health" slowly flowing through every part of my body. This liquid healing energy gradually winds its way from head to toe, repairing, restoring, and lubricating as needed. When I am walking by myself and noticing my aches and pains, this meditation

seems to ease my discomfort and to energize me. I find myself using
it at some point almost every day.

Before I began my Camino, I had been in the habit of doing ten or more minutes of stretching in bed each morning. Suggested to me by my chiropractor and by an earlier physical therapist, the regular routine of mainly hip-related stretches and self-massages each and every morning preceded my daily walk. The goal: to keep the psoas tendons crossing my hips from becoming overly tight and affecting my stance and my gait. That old song, "the hip bone's connected to the thigh bone…" was so obviously true in my body: if my hips were "off," so eventually were my knees, ankles, and my flat feet. My arch-less feet, after years of wearing fashionable footwear with inadequate arch supports, were likely the original cause of the ankle, knee, and hip issues. The morning "bed-cer-cizes" as I dubbed them, in addition to good shoes with appro-priate arch support, had made my knees happier, and my hips, comfortable.

On the Camino I had planned to continue my regular morning stretch routine but quickly figured out that the close quarters of the albergues—bunk beds packed tightly together, right up to the walls—left little stretching space. The cramped and dirty floor space was never an option. I did my best with the few stretches I could perform in my individual sleeping space.

James and I had tried a few standing stretches, the type runners do, as we left the albergues each morning. And if we headed out and forgot to stretch, we reminded ourselves of Leo's comforting assertion that a gentle walking pace had been the ideal stretch for centuries of pilgrims. Was this true? Did it matter? Beginning with a slow and easy pace was the best option we had for staying in good alignment, for keeping our sore lower extrem-ities from revolting. Now, walking alone in the Spanish woods,

I would add in the Optimal Health Guided Meditation, thinking it through as I walked, imagining the liquid energies flowing through me. It worked. I don't know how or why, but afterwards I always felt better. [See the index for the Optimal Health Guided Meditation, page 281-286]

The albergue here in Triacastela is almost perfect. So far I have a private room! I don't know what happened to Sophie and Davide. I saw them earlier on my walk. They must have found another albergue. The water is shut off in this albergue for an hour. Glad I have already showered and done my wash. I am eating some of my bocadillo sandwich and chips from earlier. Then, I will lie down and rest, and read. I found a book in English here in the albergue. This is so exciting! I have been so bored, so hungry to read, that I have taken to "reading" my Spanish/ English dictionary. This book is a novel about World War I, four hundred and fifty pages in length. A novel about a world war is not what I would normally choose to read, but here, a book in English is like gold! I am thrilled! Maybe I'll get up and be social later, maybe not. This albergue has no Internet. Perhaps I will go find an Internet café.

People leave books at the albergue where they complete their reading for another pilgrim's reading pleasure. I had left my copy of "I'm Off Then," the Camino memoir by German comedian Hape Kerkeling, in Orisson, the first albergue of my trip, where I finished reading it. I had had nothing with me to read since, except for the pamphlet in Spanish on architect Antonio Gaudí, a tiny thought-for-the-day book, and my pocket dictionary.

Thursday, 5-19-11, Camino Journal
Triacastela to Samos
Eleven kilometers today, a short walk. I felt tired: lots of sun, lots of ups and downs, and at the beginning, lots of walking along

the side of the highway, my least favorite terrain. Lots of time alone though. All good. There were some lovely smells (oodles of roses and other flowers) and some shit smells (literally). Excrement is every-where. I am walking cow paths, sharing the road with the cows and the cow-herders.

Rock is the building material of Spain. The roads we pilgrims walk are rocky. I have taken close-up photos of the rocks sticking up in the path, so my friends and family will understand what this terrain is like. Rocks are painted with yellow arrows, as way-marker signs. Small rocks are laid together to form direc-tional arrows, and messages are written on flat rocks with magic marker from one pilgrim to a pilgrim friend walking behind. I have passed rock huts by the side of the road. Homes and court-yard walls are built of stone, and there are lots of stone cairns, which I add to as I feel so moved. Today I saw a lovely little spiral made of small stones on the side of the road. I took its picture twice, once as a close-up, and once with the background of the mountainous Spanish landscape off in the distance. I have no idea who created the small stone spiral, but I so appreciated its simple beauty.

I am in a pricey, private albergue in Samos, the first albergue I came to. I am in an upstairs room with a balcony overlooking the monastery of Samos…a perfect view. This albergue cost eleven euros. I paid six euros for the washer and dryer. I also spent one euro on tea this morning and two and a half euros at the supermercado down the road: yogurts, a Limona soda, bananas, and a package of macaroons. I am over my daily budget, but not too far off when averaged with yesterday. Whoops… forgot about the three euros charge for the monastery tour. That was worth it, though.

I toured the monastery earlier today with Sophie, Davide, and a few others. The Samos monastery is built around a central court-yard, a beautiful garden. We were taken upstairs to see the floor where priests would have slept (still do sleep?) in their individual cells. The hallway walls are painted with a mural that begins with angels in heaven and, as the mural rounds the interior corners, it morphs into scenes of sin, hell, and horribly mutated creatures. On one pillar hangs a collection box (if I translated accurately) for the purpose of getting someone out of hell? I am so glad not to have been brought up in a heaven/hell tradition. To me that feels scary and awful. Hopefully, little kids just don't "get it." Like the story Emma told me of her early Catholic school experience: seeing art depicting the Sacred Heart of Jesus, which caused her to wonder why Jesus was wearing a strawberry on his chest. Emma and I had talked about my difficulty with all the crucifixion iconog-raphy in the churches we toured, and how, from a non-Christian upbringing, the portrayal of Jesus suffering on the cross seems like viewing a torture scene: not appropriate for children from my perspec-tive. The Virgin Mary, on the other hand, appeals to me immensely: her beauty, her serenity, and her compassion. I want more of her.

Our tour guide was taking us through the main chapel at the monastery. We were admiring all the statuary and all the gilt deco-ration, when water suddenly began to pour down onto the altar.

Men were working up on the roof and some unfortunate mishap was taking place. I noticed that all the Mary (female) statues had worried looks on their faces. While our guide was making a frantic call for help (from a phone discretely hidden next to the altar) we decided to take ourselves on a tour of the third floor. This may be where modern day pilgrims are housed. We didn't see much worth noting and left for the overpriced, jewelry filled gift shop.

Mural at the Samos Monastery

I was not able to use the Internet today. There wasn't any service in the albergue. I was told to go to the local library, which houses the town's Internet connection. I ended up taking a long walk uphill looking for the library. I guess I walked right past it, but that was fine. It is such a pleasure to walk without wearing my backpack! More smells of "shit and roses" on the library hunt. When I finally did find the library, it was locked tight. I went back to the albergue, ate and read while the lights flickered on and off due to a lightning storm.

I was inside, safe, warm, dry, and with a book to read! The horrors of WW I? I am oddly fascinated.

Friday, 5-20-11, Camino Journal
Samos to Sarria

I can't believe it's actually Friday. Where have the days gone? By next Friday I should be in Santiago at a Pilgrims' Mass. Then it's on to Finisterre. I was really beginning to believe this pilgrimage would never end. And now it does...in one week.

Sarria is fine. I picked a "dive" albergue, as I'm trying to conserve euros. As a bonus, I saw an earlier-on-the-trail friend here, Abby, from England. We visited, went to the groceria, and looked for an Internet café. The connection was very s-l-o-w. I was able to answer e-mails from both my kids. I also got an e-mail from Lindy, my friend Ellen's daughter, with whom I hope to connect in Madrid after completing my Camino. I could not, however, get Lindy's e-mail to open, and, eventually, it "went away." I will try to e-mail her directly tomorrow.

I am feeling too blah to shower and do wash. The bed in the albergue is icky, although a bottom bunk became open…yay! I had yogurt (with no spoon) and an apple for dinner. Abby allowed me to treat her at the pastelería, the pastry shop. We split a yummy, chocolate-filled croissant. I am really full.

The walk today, though much longer than the guidebook says, was beautiful. Hope tomorrow is more of the same. I love being out on my path, by myself, alone with my prayers, my thoughts, my appreciation, and with the sounds of nature. I am finding it hard to walk by myself, literally, as there are so many other pilgrims walking. I have seen groups of men walking together and praying, a group engaged in self-flagellation, and a pilgrim carrying an immense cross. Then there are the bicycle pilgrims. They speed by, except for times when they have to walk their bicycles up extremely steep and rocky paths.

Their ride can be physically more difficult than my walk! There is the occasional horse-riding pilgrim too, and the day-trippers—the pilgrims who wear day-packs loaded only with sunglasses, a bottle of water, and, perhaps, a meal and a sweater. Their luggage is portered to their pensions or hotels. The day-trippers are not allowed to stay at the albergues. As we get closer to Santiago, the guide book says there will be "bus pilgrims" too, those who will walk for a day or so, just to get the feel of the Camino. I spent some time today walking with Andrea from Germany, with Helen and Lynn from the U.S., and with Abby. Mostly though, I walked alone as much as possible. When I heard people come walking up behind me, I stepped over to the side of the path, said "Buen Camino" and made a gesture to show that they were welcome to pass me. I have even heard pilgrims chatting on cell phones. This, I don't understand. If you want to walk and experience the Camino, be here on the Camino! Ah, well. Let it go. Don't chew on it, Deb.

[It appears that this is in no way a new complaint. A friend shared this quote with me: "What business have I in the woods, if I am thinking of something out of the woods?" This is from Henry David Thoreau's 1862 essay titled, "Walking." Henry is definitely a kindred spirit!]

The trails are well marked. I am finding my way easily except in town. I got turned around this afternoon after Abby and I parted ways, post-chocolate croissant. I inadvertently took myself on a small tour of Sarria in the process of finding my way back to the albergue. I had to ask for directions multiple times before I found my way back. This turns out to be to my advantage though as I have now learned how to exit Sarria tomorrow morning. All good!

CHAPTER TWENTY-ONE:
On Miracles and Bathrooms

"When we operate from a higher level of consciousness, we stop perceiving problems and instead perceive situations that are neither good nor bad; they simply are. When we do so, we start to see that an opportunity lies in every situation if we simply look at it from a different level of awareness."

Alberto Villoldo

What constitutes a miracle? It might defy the laws of nature, as we understand them. It might be perfect in scope and in timing. It might fill a deep need. For me miracles come complete with a lesson and generally stand in sharp contrast to my normal life. I wonder if perhaps all "non-normal" moments may be components of miracles. I haven't personally experienced the stopping of time or bright lights of divine intensity, but I have heard voices, had a "knowing" to pay attention—that something meaningful was taking place. And on a few occasions, I have been blessed to experience a sense of stillness and completeness. I am pleased to remember the events described here as personal experiences of miracles. No matter what their size—and the ones in this chapter were small in scale, no parting of the seas took place—they felt non-ordinary in nature, perfect in timing, and gave me the opportunity to learn needed lessons.

Saturday, 5-21-11 Camino Journal
Sarria to Mirallos

What an interesting day so far. The municipal albergue in Sarria turned out to be fine. I slept well because the person originally in the bottom bunk left, and I was able to move down to a much better bed. And in a private corner! This morning I woke and got ready quickly. I had filled my water "bladder" last night and was out the door at 8, into a foggy morning. But I had read the time wrong. It was actually 7 a.m., an unexpected and wonderfully early start to the day! I knew just where to go to exit Sarria, courtesy of having lost my way yesterday afternoon. As I walked I was conscious to let everyone pass me by, including four Spanish men, praying as they walked. I have been craving solitude, and I had plenty of time this morning. I walked today on a flat, tree-lined path in cool shade. As I walked I decided to meditate on a spiritual question to take my mind off my money worries:

What if there is a Higher Power directing my path?

Walking with my loving, yet skeptical friends for the first part of my Camino, I had allowed their skepticism to infect my hard-won spiritual reserves. I now had thoughts of doubt popping back into my head.

Was I, in any way, special enough for God to watch over me? Was I really expecting to have a spiritual experience on the Camino? Was there more to the Camino than just making new friends and having an adventure? Perhaps I was imagining something more because I wanted there to be more.

What if there is a Higher Power directing my path?

I asked this question over and over, hoping for answers. At one point, I saw a small brown bird standing on the path about twenty feet up ahead. I kept repeating my question as I walked towards the little bird. The bird did not budge until I was within about two feet of him. Then, a fast walking pilgrim came rushing up from behind me and scared off my little friend. "Thanks, God. That was a sweet sign, the bird waiting for me."

What if there is a Higher Power directing my path?

After a few more kilometers I saw an old gentleman farmer, pitchfork in hand, standing with his dog in the middle of the road. I smiled at him and said "Hola." I have been happy with my pre-Camino decision to smile at everyone, as everyone has smiled back! The farmer began to speak to me. I was able to translate some of what he said courtesy of my high school Spanish from forty-odd years ago, but some I just "understood." I didn't know the vocabulary, but I "knew" what he was saying!

"¿Está una peregrina?" Are you a pilgrim? "Sí," I replied, "Yes." He asked me if I was going to Santiago. "Yes." He asked if I would pray for him when I got to the cathedral in Santiago. "Yes!" He told me his name was Dionysius. Then he reached into his pocket and gave me an orange, which I gratefully accepted. "How perfect," I thought, "to receive fruit from Dionysius, the God of wine and fertility!" I thanked Dionysius. Then we smiled at each other, said "Adiós" and "Buen Camino," "Goodbye and have a good Camino," and I was on the path again. I immediately began to pray for Dionysius, for his long life, for his good health, and for whatever else he felt he needed.

As I continued to walk, I again began to hear myself stewing over money concerns. I was determined not to place my focus on my worries, as that seemed pointless, but instead, to look for spiritual lessons.

What if there is a Higher Power directing my path?

Along the road I saw a sign advertising the upcoming albergue in Ferrerios. The cost for a night's lodging: fifteen euros, way more than I wanted to spend! I was calculating how to best manage with *my limited cash reserves, fretting about whether to spend the night in Ferrerios or to walk on to the next city, Portomarín. "Focus on your meditation, Deb" I told myself.*

What if there is a Higher Power directing my path?

About ten kilometers further I said, "Buenos días" to an older woman standing at her courtyard gate trying to coax her little dog back into the yard. She asked in Spanish if I was a pilgrim and where was I planning to spend the night. I told her that I was a pilgrim and that I was planning to spend the night in Ferrerios. She asked me to wait and went briefly into her house. When she returned she handed me a small flyer in Spanish for a restaurant about one kilometer past Ferrerios in Mirallos. "Sounds like 'miracle,'" I remember thinking. She kept talking to me in Spanish, but I wasn't translating effectively, I didn't understand what she was telling me. Finally, out of frustration, she pointed down to the flyer, where it said "Dormir Gratis," Sleep Free. I finally got it. She was telling me about a free albergue! I was filled with joy! She could see that I was moved to tears. We hugged and exchanged kisses on the cheek.

And so, here is my Camino lesson for today. Should I choose to accept this bounty of gifts: sweet, welcoming creatures of the nature kingdom, people who remind me that my prayers do make a difference, and "angels" who magically appear to meet my needs...and I do choose to accept these gifts...then I can conclude that there is a Higher Power at work here, directing my path. This is an awesome way for a skeptically inclined soul like me to feel connected to the Divine. I love having these experiences...having a kind of proof.

Right now I'm sitting in front of the free albergue in Mirallos, next door to the town's tiny church. I have selected my free bed and have showered. The water got cold quickly, but there was natural heat coming in from the skylight, and it was tolerable. I have washed my clothes and hung them on the line in the sun to dry. I've eaten decent food: pasta with tomato sauce and cheese, plus fried eggs and potatoes, all from the land right here in Mirallos. I've talked with Natalia, the Spanish owner/operator/cook/waitress. I asked her why she chooses to offer lodging in her albergue for free. Natalia says that she appreciates her quality of life, living in a beautiful area of the world, raising her own farm-fresh foods, and cooking with them. She told me that she makes money from the restaurant and just wants "to give back…to see the pilgrims smile." Yes, all kinds of miracles! I am feeling trust in a kind and loving Higher Power once again. There's a plaque hanging on the restaurant wall that I loosely translate as: "Here live a happy old couple… along with their happy, old parents." To me, it epitomizes what Natalia says about life here in this ruggedly beautiful countryside, the benefits of fresh air and fresh produce, and being able to live a life that is generous in every way.

I asked Natalia if I could help her in some way. Could I stamp the "credentials," the pilgrims' passports, for her? She has been so busy! But for the moment, there are mainly locals inside, and I see no pilgrims coming. So I'll sit here in the shade, across from a rustling cottonwood tree and an open field. I have finished reading the four hundred and fifty-page book on World War I, "Birdsong." I would never have read it at home, but here…a book in English…my mind is starved for reading! I spotted a Spanish fashion/celebrity magazine in the sleeping area, about Príncipe Guerrmo (Prince William) and Princesa Kate's Royal Wedding. I will attempt to read it later.

5-21-11 Later in Mirallos, 6 p.m.
E-mail to my niece, Grace:

hi gracie,

i can´t use the capital letters on this computer, so this will be all little letters. hope you don´t mind. i miss you and am really excited to see you in june. i was thinking about you today while i was walking and about how much i enjoyed your e-mail letter. just as i was thinking about you i saw a really big slug. slugs are snails without their shells. i thought to myself, grace would love to see this slug....so i took a nice closeup photo of it....just for you.

see you soon...with the slug photo and a few more i thought you might like. i took photos of storks sleeping in their nests very high up on the church steeples. lots to tell you.

i love you so much...and your mom and dad...see you soon. hope all is well and that everyone is healthy and excited about the upcoming family reunion.

love,
aunt deb

Camino Journal from Mirallos (continued)

I'm bored! I'm clean, have eaten, have e-mailed Grace and Erin, also Lindy, about plans to meet her in Madrid. Have more or less finished the day-to-day planning for the balance of this walk. I have attempted to read the magazine on the royal wedding. I enjoyed all the photos and tried to make sense of the captions and the stories. I have nothing else to read. When Natalia gets back I will pay her for my lunch and my Internet time, eat a little bread and cheese, and fill my water bladder. Then what? I can write. I had not wanted to fill up all the pages in this little travel journal, but, at worst, I will purchase an additional small notebook.

So, what to write? How about the "Five-Star Rules for Camino Baños, Servicios, Aseo" (Bathrooms, Services, Cleanliness)? I've been joking about these, but here they are...

To get five stars the bathroom must have:
- *User-controlled lighting*
- *A toilet seat*
- *Soap, toilet paper, and hand towels or dryer*
- *Privacy*

• *Must be clean!*

If they don't have lights I can control and a toilet seat, they automatically lose all points.

Here's what I recall from the group meal back in Astorga when we laughed about all the possible Camino books we would write. Our planned titles:

- *"Why Fifty People Should Not Sleep In One Room" by Jack*
- *"Toilets of the Camino" by me*
- *"What Every Good Albergue Needs" by the whole crew*
- *"Never Seen Camino Scenes" Emma's photo exposé of some trashed Camino views*
- *"The Social Camino" by James*
- *"Dropping In and Dropping Out" by Leo*
- *"Tales of Peeing/Weeing on the Camino" subtitled, "How to meet new friends on the Camino" by the crew*

Other possible Camino book titles:

- *"St. John to Santiago…Where We Slept, and Where We Lay Awake in Pain, Listening to Snorers"*
- *"Darling Old Men and Women of the Camino"*
- *"Two Caminos: Shit and Roses"*

And here, out of boredom and with delight at having given myself permission to "use up" my journal pages, I began to write my Camino story in more detail. Many of those details were later added into this book in their correct time sequence.

Another day of pleasant sun and puffy clouds. This is my last week of walking. How will it feel to reach Santiago, to be done walking?

CHAPTER TWENTY-TWO:
Setting Intentions

"Imagine your departure as a metamorphosis. Through simple acts of intention and attention, you can transform even a sleepwalking trip into a soulful journey. The first step is to slow down. The next one is to treat everything that comes your way as part of the sacred time that envelopes your pilgrimage."

Phil Coustineau

The idea behind "setting intentions" is that one is asking for, praying about, and, in some sense, programming the future. It's like an athlete visualizing every move in the upcoming game, seeing it all happen in advance, seeing him/herself in complete control, with all the plays made to perfection for the team's or the individual's ultimate victory. I suppose it is also similar to rehearsing for a play, for a musical performance, or a dance revue. The more rehearsal/practice the performer puts in, the more the script, the notes, the moves become internalized and on autopilot, the more free the performer becomes to focus on adding the emotion that makes their part sparkle. For me, "intending" included an experimental component—learning to trust in a Higher Power. And the sparkle was my delight in succeeding. I had been practicing this art of intending, imagining all the attributes I hoped to find at my albergue at day's end. And some days I arrived to find exactly the albergue specifications I had requested. Intending was really about making a connection with Spirit, one in which I spoke my requests and allowed Spirit to show me how easy life could be if I'd agree to let go of fretting and worrying.

Sunday, 5-22-11 Camino Journal
Mirallos to Gonzar

I had a chance to chat with Gratzia from Italy last night at the Mirallos albergue. She's a high school math teacher who has traveled extensively. She is studying English. I remember very little of my college Italian but, with the help of the Spanish/English dictionary and both of us understanding a bit of Spanish, we were able to communicate—until the TV in the restaurant was turned on. Then, we just couldn't hear the sounds of each language well enough. We were missing some clues, and we needed all the clues. I gave up the effort and went to bed. I actually slept pretty well.

Today I have walked farther than I had planned. I stopped earlier in Portomarín, but felt bored, unhappy with the thought of overnighting there, so I walked on to Gonzar instead, a total of seventeen and a half kilometers (eleven miles). So far my day's expenses have been: breakfast at the free albergue in Mirallos (tea with lots of milk and toast, three and a half euros), and a frozen lemon-lime treat (1 euro) in Portomarín. I am checked in at the municipal albergue in Gonzar. The albergue cost is five euros. I'm now sitting at the neighboring café/bar lunching on a tortilla bocadillo, an egg and potato sandwich, and a Coke (five euros more): fourteen and a half euros for the day. Okay! 3:05p.m. Now what? I've done my hand washing of clothes. What can I do with the rest of my day? I am in a tiny town, really just a rural excuse to house and feed pilgrims. Lots of French is being spoken around me. I will write.

The walk to Gonzar today had some wonderful moments. At one point, I practiced intending what I wished for, seeing it as real in my mind with the expectation that it would be so. I was looking for a nice place to stop and rest, to eat my orange from Dionysius. I wanted a picnic table made of stone or concrete, not splintery wood, and I wanted it to be in the shade. Shortly after declaring my intentions, I came upon Thomás from Germany. I have seen Thomás just about every day for the last week. Each morning we sit, drink our morning beverages, and make polite conversation. We don't walk together because I want to walk alone, and he walks faster than I do. Thomás is reserved, quiet, and very pleasant. Thomás sat in a small neglected garden, in front of a house with a "for rent" sign. Roses were growing up into the garden's apple tree. There was a fig tree with figs close to ripening and, in this magical overgrown Eden, were two concrete picnic tables just as I'd been intending! Of course, with the house vacant, the garden had been left to nature: knee high weeds were all around. But I was able to sit, to take off my left boot, and massage my sore foot. I ate my orange and relaxed a while. Before I left I took a photo of Thomás and the "rose/apple" tree. I promised I would send it to him when I got back home.

Except for the weight of the backpack pulling on my shoulders, I am very happy walking in the cool of the morning, in the dappled shade. I am content to walk at my pace, to stop and smell all the roses. This spring Spain is covered in roses! And I stop whenever I please to take as many photos as interest me. I am happy to be completing this journey soon. I've planned everything out to the degree I can, knowing that all days are subject to change if either I or the Divine wants them to be changed. I am content to let everyone pass me by…this is not a race.

Thomás in the rose/apple garden

I enjoy feeling solitary and dislike hearing folks talking loudly in back of me, so I keep waving to them to pass me. I smile, and wish them "Buen Camino" as they sprint ahead. I walked off the path today, into a little clearing, just because I wanted to, no other reason. I came out of the clearing as two Spanish men passed by, praying out loud. This is a great chance for me to practice being aware of what I want, so I can ask for it and stand behind it. I am learning to ask: "Do I want to walk on? Am I happy with this albergue? Do I want a meal now?" Sometimes I pray as I walk. I have prayed for all to feel the peace I feel here. I've prayed for answers to life's questions and for health and happiness for us all. I have been enjoying bird symphonies, the play of shadow on the road, the way the trees overhang the path, causing it to appear to spiral off into the distance. I love this "time out of ordinary time."

My only problem today is: what to do with myself. This is not just a "what do I want?" question. It is a "what do I want that

I can do?" and that is very limited. No Internet. No shops. Nothing to read.

No one I want to talk with. Just me here, waiting for my clothes to dry and now lying on my bunk, writing.

CHAPTER TWENTY-THREE

Finding Perfection or the Gonzar "Troubles"

"We are holy creatures living among other holy creatures in a world that is holy. Some people know this, and some do not. Nobody, of course, knows it all the time."

Wendell Berry

"The single most effective way to deflect the impact others might have on our lives is to assign them to a category to which we do not ourselves belong. In this case, the category can be too high – they are holy, saints, miracle workers, spiritual giants – or low – they are fools, gullible, out of touch, extremists. Either way, we are safe from them and the challenge of their lives."

Daniel Taylor

My friend Victoria always used to tell me: "It's all perfect." I would reply sarcastically, "Yeah, right." Somewhere along the line I realized that what Vickie said was true. I just needed to add a second part to her comment. Now I completely agree with her: Everything is perfect...even if I don't know why yet. I deeply believe this to be true and yet, sometimes life just hits you hard. Some lessons are more painful than others. I'll say more about this "lesson" towards the end of this chapter, as I don't want to give it away… but it was perfect!

Monday, 5-23-11
Gonzar to Palas de Rei

Eighteen kilometers today. I don't know that I walk "well" as per Dina and Nemo from South Africa, my roomies in this albergue in Palas de Rei, but I got here! All good! Dina did tell me that I am to stand up ramrod straight when walking while wearing my backpack. Pulling my shoulders forward, leaning forward while I walk, that's what's causing my achy shoulders. Thank you, Dina!

The German women from yesterday's Gonzar "troubles" are here in this albergue room too. How awkward. Here's what happened yesterday:

I was sitting at the café/bar in Gonzar. I had previously settled in at the albergue, my washing and showering complete. I had eaten my lunch and was sitting on the sunny patio of the café/bar, writing in my journal. In an effort to follow the warm, spring sun, I had asked the women at the table next to me if I could join them. The two women were from Germany. They both spoke English well, and we ended up chatting about the usual pilgrim topics: where we were from, how the walk was going, how our feet were feeling. They asked what I thought of the municipal albergue next door. I said it was cheap, clean, but probably had too few toilets. As the number of toilets was not a deal-breaker for them, they said they would check it out after their meal.

I saw them later in the day approaching my lower level bunk at the far corner of the dormitory room of the albergue. They asked if the bottom bunks near me were taken. There were clothes on the bunks, but the beds were not "made up": the sleeping bags had not been unrolled. I said that I thought the bunks were taken. I had earlier met the French couple whose belongings lay on the bunks. One of the German women asked me if the people were older? Were they women? I answered that they were about her age (mid to late 60s). To my surprise, the two German women began to move the belongings from the two bottom bunks to the top bunks and to settle themselves in on the bottoms. I didn't know what to do. I had spoken what I knew and had been ignored. Meanwhile, two boys from a loud German family of six who had arrived earlier were leaping from their bunks to these top bunks in an effort to help the two German women rearrange. This is not the standard, accepted pilgrims' practice. You do not move someone's belongings without first asking permission.

When the French couple, the original claimants to the lower bunks, came back they were horrified. They asked me what had happened. I said the briefest version of it and that I was sorry, that I had tried. The hospitalero was called in. The two German women were told to pack up and leave. I later asked what became of them and was told that they had been given a small room on the first floor usually reserved for handicapped pilgrims. My guess is that the women felt embarrassed and chagrined, but probably slept better than the rest of us (28) in the dormitory room. The French couple chatted with me as they made up their beds. It was an awkward situation. I was unhappy to have been put in the middle, but it did not become an "international incident" and all was settled peaceably, without requiring embassy staff input.

Meanwhile, one of the boys from the loud German family, the one bunking above me, was veering into my personal space. He persisted in talking to me when I was obviously keeping to myself. He was wearing next to no clothing and hanging his laundry from the railing of the bunk bed. As he stretched his arms up to hang clothing, his partial nakedness was literally in my face. He, along with the rest of his family, seemed to lack an awareness of personal space, at least by my American standards. These were not children, but young adults. I was beginning to wonder about "the Germans."

My impression was that they were loud, aggressive, they took over others' space, and they were comfortable with their bodies (read: changing clothes publicly with no attempt at being discreet). They seemed to be unconcerned with courtesies and convention. I realized that there might be cultural differences at work here. Also there was a distinct possibility that I was tired and crabby.

At this point I chose to pick up the tiny Thought for the Day traveler's companion book given to me by my friend, Nayana. I opened the book at random and asked to be given a Higher Thought to focus on. I opened it to this:

> *"Look for perfection in others, your very search will give you abundant joy. Look for perfection in your own nature. Your very search will awaken you to love perfection evermore."*

> *—Sri Chinmoy*

"Okay, I will look for perfection," I thought. "I will look for perfection in this German man/boy on the bunk above me. And later, he closed the blinds when he saw me trying to go to sleep while it was still light out. He waved "hello" and "goodbye" and gave me the peace sign. He was very sweet. I see some perfection.

Fast forward to this morning: from my position washing at the sink in the women's bathroom I could hear one of the other German family members speaking with her dad in the adjacent hallway. She spoke with a pronounced stutter. A heavyset young woman, she had shied away from me when I'd said "Hola" to her the day before. I had the impression that she might be handicapped in some way. I could hear her father responding tenderly to her. He called her "Liebchen" (dear or sweetheart) and spoke to her in the softest, sweetest German I have ever heard. "A very loving family," I thought, "and it's amazing that they are all doing the Camino together. More perfection!"

Later this morning when I saw Thomás, my German friend, at the café/bar, we began our usual catch-up over coffee and tea. Thomás told me he had spoken to the head of the German "family." That the "family" was actually two caregivers and their four mentally challenged adult charges, all walking the Camino together. Now it all made sense: the bounciness and inappropriate loudness of the group, the sweetness of the boys, wanting to help me sleep better, and wanting to help the two German bunk-stealing ladies, the shyness of the stuttering German girl.

I am in awe. The Camino is an arduous undertaking for anyone in good physical and mental health. To be willing to take on the responsibility for four mentally challenged persons, walking over difficult terrain, with LOTS more physical demands than in everyday life, that kind of perfection inspires such admiration in me! I was amazed to see it and grateful that I had been looking for it.

After returning home, Thomás was kind enough to send me the article from a German newspaper about the group of special needs pilgrims. In the photo they looked so happy and proud! I was equally happy and proud for them. I'm still in awe of them and their caregivers.

I know what it is to live with someone with special needs. My sister is more profoundly handicapped than any of the German youths in the "family" group, and I am in awe of my sibling's caregivers at the group home where she now lives. I could not do what they do. I know myself. I'm not being modest. I could not. I had a very clear idea what was being asked of this group's caregivers. I was humbled by their patience, their goodness, and their willingness to be of service. If walking the Camino absolves pilgrims of their past sins, I think these care-givers deserve special dispensation to cover any and all future sins, too!

A funny story from today's walk:

Today I passed by an old gentleman who was out in his yard, hoeing his large vegetable garden. He had created an elaborately dressed female scarecrow (a piece of orange plastic pipe with a face painted on it, wearing a tapestry dress and a fancy hat). I said "Hola" and tried to say how pretty she was. He said that this was his "companion" and that he liked her because she didn't speak back. I understood enough to get his jest. I waved a "naughty boy" finger at him and we both laughed and said "Adiós." I kept walking — and laughing.

I spent much of my walk time today being mindful to be here now. It is increasingly difficult to stay here on the Camino, as I get closer to the end. My mind goes to the future: imagining sharing the experience when I get home. Imagining how I will describe this... how I will tell these stories.

CHAPTER TWENTY-FOUR:
From Boredom to Blink!

*"The life of every man is a diary in which he means
to write one story, and writes another; and his humblest
hour is when he compares the volume as it is with what
he vowed to make it."*

James M. Barrie

Boredom is…well…boring. I was sorely missing my favorite stimulation at home: reading. When I found books in English on the Camino I'd speed-read them. In this last week of walking I'd found two books! Four hundred and fifty pages each! I voraciously consumed each one. I still wrote daily journal entries. I walked slowly each day, finding my way with no trouble, and literally stopping to smell every rose bush I passed. I ate the same foods every day…boring, boring, boring! Even the scenery, though refreshing, lacked the feeling of mystery I'd enjoyed earlier on the path. In short, I was ready for the walk to end. The sameness of each day had surpassed my original feeling of being on an adventure. I wasn't homesick, not in the usual sense of missing familiar surroundings or longing to see loved ones, but I was craving sensory stimulation. Perhaps, if I had thought to, I could have created a daily spiritual practice: a time for meditation, for prayer, for a conscious reflection on spiritual gleanings. But I didn't. Again, another reason to go back…

Tuesday, 5-24-11, Camino Journal
Palas de Rei to Melide

Not wanting to write much. I'm in a private albergue: Twelve euros. More than I wanted to spend, but I never could find the municipal albergue, not until after I'd checked in here. Then I found it across the street, hidden from my view by shade trees. At that point, I had already walked a kilometer or so out of the way, almost out of Melide. So when I reached this albergue, I was ready to stay. I am not excited to be here. The rooms are OK, but the bathroom seems to lack privacy for showering: one male and female toilet stall with slight wall between and a shower for all twelve of us in the room. Oh, well. I will wear my same stinky clothes tomorrow and not worry about showering.

My bunkmate is an older German man with incredibly good health genes and a serious sense of wanderlust. He has trekked in the Libyan desert among other places. He told me about a web-cam in Santiago, in the Prazo Obradoiro, the plaza in front of the Cathedral. I will try to set something up with Erin so that she and other family members can see me in the plaza at a planned time. I can wave to them. Cool!

I think I'm done with this walk on some level. I will continue to physically walk, of course. I will reach Santiago in three days. I will do my best to keep my "be here now" focus. Had the usual tortilla bocadillo and Limona for lunch, I used the Internet, bought yogurt, biscuits, and an orange for dinner. And I was able to get some euros from the ATM, courtesy of Erin depositing a check. Got e-mails from Thalles and Sophie. I hope to see all my Camino friends again, somehow. Maybe they'll come visit me? I hope to see them in Santiago and, perhaps, in Finisterre. Looking forward to meeting Lindy in Madrid.

The walk today was not exciting. I kept looking for beauty, smelling roses, but I really want to be done. I will be. Soon.

Wednesday, 5-25-11 Camino Journal
Melide to Arzúa

A fine walk today, about 14 kilometers. Arrived in Arzúa around noon, tired out. I left this morning about 7:15 and took only one break for tea. Pretty good…almost 4 kilometers/hour. And I was taking every opportunity to stop and smell the roses, to take photos. The next two days are more likely to be 20 kilometers each. I hope I do well. My shoulders have been doing most of the complaining, usually later in the day. Standing stubbornly straight does help. Thank you Dina from South Africa, for your backpacking advice. I only wish we'd met a month earlier!

I have finished reading a second four hundred and fifty-page book. I found this second English "treat" at my albergue yesterday: Stephen Clarke's "Merde, Actually." Again, not a book I would've chosen to read at home… it is fluffy and funny, but it is stimulating enough to make for enjoyable reading here. It is weird to have nothing much to do in the afternoon. I ate a boring tortilla bocadillo, potato chips, and a Coke. Got to the albergue, washed my clothes and myself, and then went back to the café/bar for a Limona and to read. Thomás came walking up and we chatted a while. He's doing his second Camino, this one starting from Salamanca. He showed me some photos: flat, dull, nothing. But, he says he had times on this walk when his mind "went quiet." I have not had that experience. The meditative state has not been one I have achieved on my Camino, not so far. On the contrary, my mind has been full of sights and sounds and my own thoughts: some fearful… the money worries and pain, and some joyful… the beauty of this more pristine and ancient part of the world. I tend to consciously engage in thought. When my mind begins to quiet I rev it back up: with mantras, with guided meditations, with song! I sing the hymn, "Morning Has Broken" every morning, either quietly to myself, or, if I'm alone, out loud. Without effort, show tunes and music from my teens and twenties come to me unbidden. Perhaps there will be another Camino in my future, one with "quiet mind" time. I'd like to have that experience, too. My guess is I would have to be walking a different Camino route, a less traveled one. But, even then, Thomás and I are very different people. My mind might home in on Broadway show tunes, even on the Salamancan trail. Quién sabe? Who knows? Maybe I will "go quiet" in the next two days, or maybe not. What is, is.

This morning I enjoyed the peace and freshness of the euca-lyptus groves. The cow poop smell was completely gone the second I stepped into the trees' territory! The scent is like Vick's Vapo Rub, but milder and less astringent. It is gently stimulating. I experimented by paying attention to my nose as I walked in and out of the groves. It was a 100% reversal of cow patty odor! Mom Nature is awesome!

Eucalyptus Grove

Two more days of walking. I will make an effort to wake early and be on the road by 7ish, into the cool part of the day. I have forty-five euros on me now. I may have to get to an ATM and take more out so I can pay for an albergue in Santiago. It is so weird to have NOTHING to do! The computers here are in use and I don't want to wait in line for a turn just now. Instead, I am sitting on the albergue's back patio waiting for my socks to finish drying. This sunny day is perfect for washing clothes "a mano," by hand, and having them dry quickly in the hot sun. My bed—bottom bunk, no one on top yet—is right near the sliding glass door onto the patio. Just like sleeping on the porch at home. I love it! 5:25 p.m. I don't want to sleep or eat more just now.

I met another sweet, older Spanish man at a café/bar this morning when I stopped for tea. He told me that I seemed like a nice lady, that today would be hot, and that the farmers need the rain. He said I should sit and meditate by the little stream I would come to shortly. I found the little stream, but I wasn't alone there, so I just stood and gazed for a few moments. The gentleman also said something that made me cry... What was it? I remember him saying, "Life is over in a blink." I'm sure that's what it will feel like when I'm back home, that the Camino was over in a blink. Now though, it seems to go on forever.

For the next two days here's what I'd like, what I intend:

- *Cloud cover while walking, but no rain during the day.*
- *More time in the eucalyptus groves, hearing the birds, being by myself as much as possible.*
- *Some insights; words from a Higher Source, a going deeper or "going quiet."*
- *Cheap, comfy, sleep-promoting albergues, showers, and toilets with privacy.*
- *Good and healthy food.*
- *Some friendly faces in Santiago.*

A thought from this morning's walk: What if everyone had access to natural beauty, to Mom Nature? Would we all be happier, less prone to violence, to jealousy and ill will? This feels true to me. It is hard to conjure up anger, distrust, or any other negative emotion while taking in this invigorating air and the beautiful vistas.

OK, at 6 p.m. I will find a groceria, do a stock-up, and eat. I would love to get a quick peek at email, too. Back from checking email: Erin, Sophie's update on the Amigos del Camino, and friends from home...all read and answered. Have been to the groceria. Bought more yogurt, biscuits, and fruit. At this rate, with so much daily walking, I am still losing weight. That wasn't my plan, but is a nice side benefit. In my email I told Erin about the web-cam in Santiago. I will find out later if she thinks she can access it. Hope to see Sophie and maybe Giulia in Finisterre. There's a possibility of seeing some of the group in Santiago, but they may all have left by the time I arrive. How will it feel to be in Santiago and not know anyone? I guess that's either how it will be, or not.

Thursday, 5-26-11, Camino Journal
Arzúa to Arca O Pino

The walk today was about nineteen kilometers. Mostly level and off-road wooded paths. Bird song. Lots of eucalyptus trees!

Fresh smells! Very pleasant. My feet hurt a little. I felt weak early on and stopped to eat some peanuts and dates. At a café/bar later I ate yogurt, more dates, biscuits, and tea. For whatever reason I feel tired and still a bit weak. Had a pizza today for lunch. They try but they just don't do vegetarian food well. The crust was rock hard and tasteless. The topping was cheesy/veggie, but with no tomato sauce. I am making a pizza ASAP when I get home: one week from today!

As for tomorrow, my last day of walking the Camino, I am happy to have it be at an end, and happy that the beginning of the day, as per my guidebook, will be through more eucalyptus groves. The guidebook says it is twenty kilometers with some hills and a steep decline going into the city of Santiago. The book says I will be heading into Santiago with the "bus pilgrims," the ones who are just walking that last little bit to get the feel of it. Sounds like it will be crowded. I may want to begin the day with a real breakfast, with a serious hit of protein. The guidebook says it is seven kilometers to the first café/bar, and I want to make sure I have the sustenance I need to walk well.

I am getting myself worked up over the last week of travel. Just as I have gotten the hang of life on the Camino it is once again time to learn something new: getting around by bus, train, and whatever other transport I will need to get to Finisterre, to Madrid, and then, home. Time to be kind and gentle with myself. "Deb, you will get it all worked out. All will be well."

5:30 p.m.… What to do for a few hours? At 7ish, when everyone goes to dinner, I will refill my water bladder and pack as much as I can to be ready in the morning. I've read the V-Z entries in the Spanish/English pocket dictionary, looked back through half the photos in the camera. I've rested, massaged my feet, rubbed lotion on my skin. Not much to write about. No big stories… just, the realiza-tion—the hope—that my new Camino skills will be of help to me in other new areas of my life.

I will miss the peace and joy of being alone, walking in the Spanish woods, through the spiraling paths. I'll even miss walking near the highways (a little), but I am so ready for mental stimulation: books, newspapers, radio. I am ready for foods with flavor! And I am hungry for normalcy, whatever that looks like. I promised myself I would wait until I was on the plane heading home to write a "to do" list so I can "be here now."

CHAPTER TWENTY-FIVE:

Graduation!

"Shared joy is a double joy;
shared sorrow is half a sorrow."

Swedish proverb

My "graduation" from the Camino felt like a "finishing" in the sense of finishing a woven cloth or a knitted item: the raw edges must be worked so that they do not unravel. The two days I spent in the city of Santiago de Compostela were the finishing touches of my Camino: they offered meaningful and memorable completions. It was important to me to share the end of this journey with friends. And I did. It was important to get my Compostela, my "diploma." Got it. I hoped the end of the Camino would have a spiritual feel. That also came to pass. I even had the unexpected chance to "drop" some anger. And, as in life generally, I found good humor blessed my experiences.

Friday, 5-27-11 Camino Journal
Arrived in Santiago!!!

I have arrived in Santiago and received my Compostela, my certificate of completion! My walk was uneventful. I enjoyed the eucalyptus groves. At one point I realized that I was walking near the Santiago airport. I could see and hear the planes. Back to civilization. Saw Thomás at the top of the hill just before the descent into Santiago. There is an albergue on this hill, statuary, and some sort of monastery. I walked on ahead saying to Thomás that I hoped to see him later in Santiago. His wife is to meet him there and then they will have a vacation together. Maybe I will get to meet her as well.

I arrived in Santiago about 1 p.m. After the long downhill trek into the newer part of the city I was tired, my shoulder still sore from the backpack. I checked into the Albergue Aquario. A pamphlet for Albergue Aquario had attracted my eye at an earlier albergue, and I was drawn to the idea of stopping there. It is a hoot! It's decorated all "flower child-y" with the look of a hippie compound from the 1960s. I laugh every time I walk inside: peace posters, psychedelic art, and India print wall hangings. I took photos for my kids and for James. James had made a snide comment about my brush with "hippiedom" at the teepee albergue. I'm sure he'll be happy to know I'm staying at the Albergue Aquario with "my people." My children have always referred to me as their "hippie mom." Staying here is so in character!

I arrived at Albergue Aquario early enough in the day to score a lower bunk. I showered, left my backpack, and then walked into the Santiago city center feeling refreshed and only lightly loaded. The path into the old city, to the Cathedral, goes through a medium-sized sprawling city with Camino signage that is far from prominent. I had been given directions for the walk by the hospitalero at Albergue Aquario, but I had to ask for directions and follow other pilgrims to find my way. I entered the old city feeling somewhat sorry for myself. As per yesterday's e-mails, James, Leo, Emma, Thalles, Flavia, and Sophie will all have left Santiago. I am regretting not ending my walk with them. I have been wondering if I would see any friends or any familiar faces here in Santiago.

I heard someone yelling "Deborah! Deborah!" and turned around to find Ernest from South Korea flagging me down. What a wonderful feeling! I have an amigo del Camino here in Santiago! Ernest was on a city bus heading from the cathedral back to his albergue on the outskirts of Santiago when he noticed me. He pulled the "stop" cord, and hopped off the bus to see me! I felt so warmly welcomed! We went to a restaurant where I was able to charge food and drink for us. And we caught up on all we had seen and done since our last meeting. Finally, we exchanged e-mail addresses and hugged goodbye. Ernest will be leaving from the Santiago airport tomorrow to fly home to South Korea, to find a new job, and hopefully, a new girlfriend. I am so glad we got to see each other again!

Back to finding my way to the cathedral: the streets of the old city of Santiago seem to follow no plan, only that they all lead to the cathedral.... eventually. I finally curved in a fortuitous direction, went past the corner where the bag-pipers were playing [the Camino was formerly a Celtic pilgrimage route, remember?] *and I was in the square, the Praza Obradoiro, directly in front of the cathedral.*

There I saw protestors, just like the 1960s-70s Vietnam war protestors, but the folks here in the square are protesting for jobs. I also saw Thomás and Birgit from Germany. More friendly faces! Birgit confirmed that the rest of the "amigos" had left Santiago yesterday. Sad, but expected. Next step: find the pilgrims' office and get my Compostela.

[The Compostela is the "diploma," the official document stating that the pilgrim has walked at least the last 100 kilometers to Santiago. The folks in the pilgrims' office check the stamps on each pilgrim's passport indicating that the person stayed at the albergues along the way and is therefore a legitimate and "complete" pilgrim.]

The Pilgrims' Office, like so much here in Santiago, is not well marked and was difficult to spot, but I eventually found it, and waited in a short line for my turn. My passport was checked, my name was added to the list, my country of origin noted for inclusion *at the Pilgrims' Mass to be celebrated tomorrow morning, and my Compostela was prepared for me.*

The Compostela is written in the traditional Latin, and my name was added with a Latin spelling: DEVORAM for Deborah. The Latin reads:

CAPITULUM hujus Almae Apostolicae et Metropolitanae Ecclesiae Compostellanae sigilli Altaris Beati Jacobi Apostoli custos, ut omnibus Fidelibus et Perigrinis ex toto terrarum Orbe, devotionis affectu vel voti causa, ad limina Apostoli Nostri Hispaniarum Patroni ac Tutelaris SANCTI JACOBI convenientibus, authenticas visitationis litteras expediat, omnibus et singulis praesentes inspecturis, notum facit : Devoram Weltman hoc sacratissimum Templum pietatis causa devote visitasse. In quorum fidem praesentes litteras, sigillo ejusdem Sanctae Ecclesiae munitas, ei confero. Datum Compostellae die 27 mensis Maii anno Dei 2011

Canonicus Deputatus pro Peregrinis

My Compostela

English translation:

The CHAPTER of this holy apostolic and metropolitan Church of Compostela, guardian of the seal of the Altar of the blessed Apostle James, in order that it may provide authentic certificates of visitation to all the faithful and to pilgrims from all over the earth who come with devout affection or for the sake of a vow to the shrine of our Apostle St. James, the patron and protector of Spain, hereby makes known to each and all who shall inspect this present document that Devoram Weltman has visited this most sacred temple for the sake of pious devotion. As a faithful witness of these things I confer upon him [or her] the present document, authenticated by the seal of the same Holy Church.

Given at Compostela on the 27 of the month of May in the year of the Lord 2011.

Deputy Canon for Pilgrims

Afterward, I saw a group of young American pilgrims, three male friends, whom I had met a few days previously. They too were looking for the pilgrims' office. I was able to point them towards the right doorway just before the line got really long. I saw them later at the Albergue Aquario and they told me how grateful they were that I had helped them. What goes around really does come around here. We all help each other. We are community!

After getting my Compostela I went to the cathedral. There I performed one of the traditional acts of the pilgrim: I climbed the tall stairwell in back of the altar. The stairs lead up to the life-sized statue of Santiago. Each pilgrim may hug the statue, in essence hugging St. James, and giving thanks for his/her safe arrival. I did this and found myself overcome with emotion. I am so grateful to St. James, to all who have helped me, and to all who have guided my path. Next, I said my prayer for Dionysius, the farmer I met on my way to Mirallos. I prayed for his long, healthy, and happy life. Afterward, I walked around the church, poking my head into small chapels off to the sides. There was one chapel that called to me. I saw others sitting in there, praying quietly, and I joined them. I don't know what this chapel was about, or what I was feeling, but there was something special there, some kind of peaceful energy. I will have to go back.

Cathedral of Santiago de Compostela, a detail

Saturday 5-28-11, Camino Journal
2nd day in Santiago

I am now sitting in the square, across from the cathedral. It is 3:30 p.m. I am waiting until 4 p.m. when I will wave to family on the web-cam, assuming I've located the correct camera. Then I will head back to the albergue. I took twenty euros more out of the bank. I can get no more. How can I be most practical with these remaining funds? I have forty-plus euros left and the credit card to cover four days lodging, food, and transport. I can get the bus to Finisterre, back to Santiago, and then the train to Madrid all on credit card. Taxi to the airport? Maybe I can do the "dine out, pay with credit card and have Sophie give me cash back," assuming we meet up in Finisterre. Anyway, I have no option but to trust that all will be well, and to be better prepared when I travel the next time.

I'm sitting here on the pavement in the square with the protestors. They are protesting Spain's current high unemployment rate, especially for students and those newly graduated from college. There is a police officer watching. All is quiet. Everyone's having lunch. They have set up a food tent to hand out meals to the protestors camped out in this tent city on the square. This is so reminiscent of Vietnam-era war protests I attended. I am one hundred percent supportive of their peaceful and attention-garnering protest!

I met Melina from Denmark last night at the albergue. She is a Reiki healer, and we had a good chat about our personal spiritual paths. At one point the conversation wound around to annoyances on the trail, and I mentioned my discomfort with the pancake-selling woman who said her pancakes were a "donation" and then complained that I didn't "donate" the correct amount. To my delight Melina had also crossed her path and had felt just as annoyed with her as I had. In a funny way, having my feelings validated by Melina was all I needed. My anger dissipated. It was gone... just like that.

Melina and I agreed to go together to the Pilgrims' Mass at the cathedral this morning, then to lunch and to "joy-shop" a bit. The Mass was crowded with pilgrims and tourists, an overflow crowd, with many standing, some milling about and poking their heads into the chapels at the sides of the main sanctuary. This church is enormous. One has to climb many stairs just to get to the entrance. The main chapel must be thirty or more feet above ground level. If there is a handicapped access, it certainly isn't obvious.

The crowd this morning was excited. We were all looking forward to seeing the giant incense burner, the botafumeiro, which takes eight men pulling its ropes to make it swing from side to side across the chapel. The botafumeiro normally is only lit and swung for the Pilgrims' Mass or if generous patrons make a request and a donation. We were all thrilled to be at the cathedral on a Pilgrims' Mass/botafumeiro day! As the tiraboleiros, the incense carriers or throwers, began to pull the rope I reached for my camera to take a photo. I ended up with an image of people's hands in the air in front of me holding up their cameras and cell phones, trying to record the scene. Although I did not get a good photo of the swinging botafumeiro, I did get a photo of a very animated crowd! I love that all the countries from which we "completed" pilgrims hail were mentioned as part of the Pilgrims' Mass. I was thrilled to be present for the ceremony, I was proud of us all, and happy for our safe arrivals in Santiago.

After the Mass, Melina and I shared lunch and did some shopping before she headed back to the albergue. I remain here in the square, the Prazo Obradoiro, waiting to be seen on the web-cam. It is very pleasant here, sitting in the shade. All I really need is a toilet, more water, and to escape from the cigarette smoke.

Fifteen more minutes 'til 4 p.m. What do I want out of the rest of this trip? I don't want to look back with regret. If it is to be, I would love to run into fellow spiritual seekers, Mona and Desmond again. I want to be in Finisterre and to enjoy Sophie's company. [Sophie and I had been in touch by e-mail and were planning to reunite for a couple of glorious tourist days together in Finisterre.] I want *to go to the lighthouse in Finisterre, see sunset at the beach, see the stars, and be open to feeling energies— like in the small chapel at the cathedral yesterday. I want to eat a chocolate croissant! And, I want to drink lots of water. When I get to Madrid, I want to find a cheap, decent place to stay, preferably near the airport. I want to meet up with Lindy and spend some quality time with her exploring Madrid. I want to end up feeling that I've had an adventure, my adventure. I want to feel that all of it was perfect.*

OK, web-cam attempted. [When I returned home I found out that no one had seen me, but it was a fun attempt!]

Later, back at the albergue:

On the way back to Albergue Aquario I found the hotel where Emma had been staying. She said she might leave a message for me at the desk. There was not a message, but I was allowed to use the toilet, normally reserved for patrons only…5 stars! I was very grateful. I also stopped on the way back at a panadería, a bakery, to buy a slice of delicious-looking dark raisin bread from the loaf displayed in the window. I am now hanging out with other pilgrims here at Albergue Aquario, sharing a meal—our own individual meals—like in a grade school cafeteria. We are sitting at long tables with benches, close enough together to share conversation. We are all pilgrims. We share this much in common. Oh, and the raisin bread in Spain is made with seeded raisins. Crunchy!

CHAPTER TWENTY-SIX:
Transformation at the End of the Earth

"Well able is Allah to save."

The Koran

"The sole problem is what the machinery of the miracle is to be."

Joseph Campbell

I must be resistant to learning what I came to this life to learn, otherwise, why would certain of my life lessons be so difficult? Why must the same lesson continually confound me? Dog my path? Here I was, at the end of my Camino, still in a panic about trusting that I would always be provided for (read: provided for financially). I seemed to have accepted that I would find my way. I was reasonably at ease with trusting my intuition. I was getting good at knowing what I wanted and asking for it. And, I was spending a comfortable amount of time by myself and with my friends. But, darn it; I was still in fear of running out of funds! This had been a concern of mine for years, long before the Camino. What would it take for me to learn this lesson?

Sunday, 5-29-11 Camino Journal
Santiago to Finisterre

I'm in Finisterre: literally, the End of the Earth! All went well except that my twenty-two euro round-trip bus ticket had to be paid for in cash, as the bus company did not take credit cards. I arrived at the Santiago bus station in plenty of time thanks to Melina who, yesterday, had shown me where it was tucked away. I found my bus at platform fourteen, not twelve or thirteen like the ticket agent told me. It was good that I listened to both my intuition and my common sense and asked some folks in the line at platform fourteen, seeing twelve and thirteen both vacant.

I sat by myself for most of the three-hour bus ride. The scenery looked the same as the Spain I had seen while walking: trees, small towns, rocky landscape, until we got close to the coastline. Then, it became very Mediterranean looking, more tropical, with watery vistas peeking around curves in the road.

I got off the bus in Finisterre and asked directions to the municipal albergue where Sophie and I had agreed to meet. Even asking for help, I managed to walk right past it twice before I finally found the low-signage, locked entrance. There I waited outside with folks who told me they had just been walking with Sophie. They passed along the message that she had stopped at the beach and would be here to meet me soon. Wonderful! We all chatted while waiting for the albergue to open and for Sophie to arrive. And Sophie did arrive. And it felt like a reunion with a long-lost friend. I was thrilled to see her!

I must say that during the no-credit-card/you-must-pay-in-cash bus ticket purchase, throughout the entire bus ride, and while I was trying to find the Finisterre municipal albergue, I did a pretty good job of trusting that all would be well, meaning: I talked myself down from mini-panic regarding my finances and how easy or difficult it would be to find Sophie. I literally had spent hours on the bus repeatedly reminding myself that all had worked perfectly so far and that I was being watched over. Then, I was in Finisterre, with Sophie, and all was well!

I could not stay at the municipal albergue. I am no longer an official pilgrim. I have no more right of hospitality. Had I walked here from Santiago and had my pilgrims' passport stamped at albergues along the way, then they would have allowed me to stay in the municipal albergue. But, as I have bussed here, I have officially stepped off the pilgrim's path. That's okay. I am in a private albergue. Sophie will join me here tomorrow night. I can pay for this private albergue by credit card. We tried to go out to lunch on the credit card but, surprisingly, that restaurant didn't take credit. Lesson learned: must ask first. Sophie and I will meet for tea later, and for some fun tomorrow: The beach? Sunset at the lighthouse?

I have settled myself into my new "home" for two nights in Finisterre, have walked around town a bit, and have taken a hysterical photo of a warning sign showing that if you drive off the dock you will end up in the water, so don't do that! Not much touristy shopping. There's a dry goods shop not far from here. I will check it out later for gift possibilities.

"Don't Drive off the Dock" Sign

Tuesday morning, two days from now, I will travel back to Santiago by bus and catch the train to Madrid. I can take a midday train to Madrid or a "sleeper." The overnight train will arrive in Madrid at 6:30 a.m. on Wednesday. That would save me the cost of a night's lodging. OK, got that mapped out: I will sleep on the train and arrive in Madrid on Wednesday morning ready to meet Lindy, to enjoy some museums, a meal out, and a night in a hotel before heading home. Truly, there are some things I'd like to see, but mostly, I am ready to be home. I will feel sad to say "adiós" to Spain, to my Camino experience, and to my Camino friends, but I am so tired of traveling. I am ready for lots of cranberry juice and rest… ready to see family and friends… ready for the comforts of home. I hate the idea of wishing the days away. On the plus side, I think I currently have enough clean socks to get me all the way back home. I'm done with washing socks by hand…yay!

What else? What do I want? To feel complete with this trip, that I did everything that was important to me. At this point I have only the next few days to make that happen: beach, lighthouse, sunset, stars, good talks and quiet time with Sophie, successful negotiation of the remainder of my travels, good tourist experience with Lindy in Madrid, safe flights home. Also, to think about why I came, what I've learned, to practice more "being here now," and to continue to trust that all is perfect, that all will work out just fine…to lose fear!

Monday, 5-30-11 Camino Journal
Second day in Finisterre

I must enjoy another bathroom laugh. My private albergue here in Finisterre has the funniest toilet setup of all! The toilet area is a large room with stalls for men on the left and stalls for women on the right. There is a ceiling light fixture that is (what else?) on a timer. If you sit too long, the light goes off. The funny part is, the light connects to a motion detector: to get the light to go back on I had to open the *stall door a bit and wiggle my leg out the door. How's that for no privacy?! Zero points! They have truly saved the best for the last!*

Two snorers on my side of the room last night. Fell asleep late. Had some urinary tract pain. Drank lots of water and had to get up to pee at 10:30. Then came a rainstorm, (a restful sound to me… good for sleeping) and snoring (bad for sleeping!). I did eventually sleep, and well, but pilgrims moving about in the room had me up at about 6:30 a.m. I stayed in bed until most had left. Then I got up, dressed and was out the door about 8ish. I saw the crowd gathering for the 8:20 bus back to Santiago. That's where I will be tomorrow morning. Went back to the same café/bar where Sophie and I had tea last night. Had breakfast tea and a croissant… not chocolate, but very good… and began to walk to the lighthouse. I stopped part of the way there. I wasn't wearing the right shoes, had on sandals, not boots, and my feet were complaining. Also, the weather was threatening rain. Instead I turned around, shopped for fruit at the groceria and then went to the dry goods store. I bought a zipper top cloth bag to help me carry my excess stuff and one gift: a decorative apron for my sister. I think everyone else will be fine with photos, stories, and thanks. I have the Mary of Miracles medal from the café/bar owner in Rabé de las Calzados. I will give that to my niece Grace. I'd kind of like to find a Camino patch for my backpack, but it's not my pack. It's borrowed. Perhaps I'll get one for a future pack.

In the afternoon Sophie, a past fan of hers, Martin, and I walked to the lighthouse to see the End of the Earth. The walk was short, only a few kilometers, an easy jaunt without backpacks. It went up a gently winding road. There was mostly foot traffic, but an occasional vehicle. It was a good thing I hadn't done the whole walk to the lighthouse by myself this morning. I had originally started down at the edge of the harbor and decided to follow the water's edge around to the farthest point west. That worked for a while…I got to see more of the harbor town and an old Crusader fort, but at some point, it looked like I was walking through backyards of homes. That was another reason I had decided to head back and find someone to ask directions. This afternoon, Sophie, Martin, and I went a totally different way, starting up the road just outside my albergue.

About my companions: Sophie is cute and vivacious and has charmed all the young men here, including Martin. Martin is a handsome young military man from Eastern Europe who is very intelligent. He speaks three languages that I know of... maybe more. I suspected I was cramping Martin's style with regard to Sophie, but he was far too kind and gracious to let it show. Martin had brought a bottle of wine to share and was planning a small burning ceremony on the rocky cliffs near the lighthouse, This used to be an "end of Camino" tradition: to burn one's shoes, smelly shirt...to burn some item that had served the pilgrim well but was no longer needed. The Spanish government has posted signs saying: "No Fires," but it is still done. Sophie's wish had been to burn a pair of smelly socks. We all perched on the giant flat rocks overlooking the waters below and enjoyed the small fire and the wine. Little lizards flitted under and around us on the rocks. We could see the scorch marks left on a nearby rock from a previous fire. We took photos, enjoyed the laziness of the day and the expansive view.

As we looked out towards the Atlantic from our perch on the rocks we could completely understand why this spot had been named the End of the Earth. Except for a small bit of land jutting out to the south of us and currently sporting a bouquet of wind turbines, water was all we could see. We could look so far out into the Atlantic that the curvature of the Earth was visible. I can imagine people hundreds of years ago, certainly thousands of years ago, gazing out into this expanse of water and being afraid to venture forth, being afraid of falling off. I wish I could have seen Finisterre then, without the lighthouse, without the well-paved road and the signage, without the vendors of touristy trinkets: owls made out of seashells and the like. I can picture this more pure and ancient scene in my imagination, and, yes, with bonfires!

Later this afternoon, while waiting to meet Sophie and Martin for dinner, I saw Diothra, the young Japanese man James and I had seen in front of a small town café/bar, alone and looking forlorn only a few weeks back. This is the same interior-focused fellow who would not smile or talk with friendly James. Diothra now looks transformed. He is sitting and visiting with friends, no longer alone. He now smiles at me and says "Buen Camino." I am so happy for him, for us all. We have all transformed, each in our own way.

At dinner, Sophie, Martin, and I shared a table with Jackie, a young medical student from the U.S. I paid with my credit card and got repaid in cash. I should have enough cash on me for the balance of the trip now. I remember that they used to collect foreign currency on return flights to the U.S. as a donation to UNICEF. If I have leftover euros I will be thrilled to donate them!

The Atlantic Ocean from Finisterre

CHAPTER TWENTY-SEVEN:
Adiós to Spain

"Be patient toward all that is unsolved in your heart and try to love the questions themselves...Do not now seek answers, which cannot be given you because you would not be able to live them. And the point is, to live everything, live the questions now. Perhaps you will gradually, without noticing it, live along some distant day into the answer."

Rainer Maria Rilke

In our lives we are constantly being given opportunities to learn, but we often miss them. We don't notice the lesson until much later and then, only with the advantage of hindsight. Looking back, culling my life for lessons, I can see many: how I respond to the "new," what are my areas of giftedness, what I do poorly, what is truly important to me, what happens when I follow my passions...

I can only surmise that it was due to the Camino's "time out of ordinary time" nature that I was able to see my lessons so clearly, that I didn't need to wait for years for the lessons to finally emerge, to stand out in sharp relief from day-to-day life. I won't say that I loved every minute of my Camino, but I would not trade away even a teeny-tiny bit. It was all perfect. I had all the "right" experiences, met all the "right" people. It was, in many ways, a very specific-to-me school of life, with an intricately personalized curriculum!

As a child and as a young adult, there were times when I wondered if I were the only "real" person... if I was actually a human rat in a lab cage, being conditioned to this life...being watched to see what I would do. Would I connect the dots and finally learn the lesson being taught? God as the Department Chair in a Universal University's Experimental Psych Lab? Now, as an adult, I am very conscious that there are certain areas of my life where I still need to learn lessons, and I wonder why some lessons are so difficult for me to master. I believe I was given this gift of the Camino to accelerate my learnings: about my fearful nature and about the divine support always available to me. Perhaps I am to share these lessons with others, to facilitate their learnings as well. I believe that we are all here to teach each other. Now, I choose to see God as the Divine Teacher... a much more loving and compassionate archetype.

Tuesday, 5-31-11, Camino Journal
Finisterre to Santiago, and hours sitting in the Santiago train station

Sophie was so sweet this morning. She had saved nectarines for us to share for a "goodbye" breakfast. We had a few minutes to chat and hug before I had to catch the bus. She is smack between the ages of my two children, but I think of her as my contemporary because of the circumstances of our meeting. I hope to keep up with her by email. Sophie surprises me by saying she is not an e-mailer, but likes to send post cards. Truly, I don't care, just as long as we keep in touch. I find I already miss her and my other Camino friends: James, Emma, Leo, Jack, Thalles, Flavia, Ernest, Thomás, Birgit, Lorne and so many more...I can't wait to e-mail and exchange photos with them when I get home. I don't want to lose my Camino friends!

I caught the 8:20 a.m. bus in Finisterre and shared the ride with Sophie's friend, Ian, from Canada. We arrived back in Santiago three hours later. Ian was very kind and helped me to find the Santiago train station. It turned out to be far across town from the bus station. After taking a city bus and asking for directions multiple times, we did eventually find the train station. I could have bought my train ticket and then gone into town to hang out with Ian... I literally have over eight hours to wait before the train to Madrid, but I am so ready to be done walking with this backpack! Instead, I will sit here in the train station, write in this journal, and people-watch for eight and a half hours! I think Ian was disappointed not to have someone to keep company with for a bit longer, but I am just too tired and I don't feel up to getting sweaty or lost... I am just done.

Instead, I have a thought I want to write about: the concept of the Camino as a school for experiential learning...learning by experience rather than study. Looking back far enough I begin to see some patterns in my life. I am realizing that every ten years or so of my life I have taken on a new "class" of experiential training, or, perhaps it is as Rudolph Steiner once wrote, "My destiny finds me."

Thinking back quite a few cycles: From defending my sister—or, at least from educating my little peers on the grade school playground—I became an early advocate of sorts. "Don't call him retarded," I would say, hearing classmates taunt one another. "That just means slow." I later found my young self advocating for a favorite teacher and for various friends when someone put them down. "You don't know what's going on in their home," I'd advise. "Cut them some slack... try to imagine yourself in their position" my grade school self would instruct. I am grateful for the gifts and lessons of my childhood: the sensitivity and empathy gained from growing up with Mom and my sister and the awareness that there is always another side to each person's story.

Likely, from my parents' perspective I was a constant source of annoying surprise. I possessed a stubbornness, a desire to stay in any fight over what felt "fair' or "right" to me. I wonder what unresolved past life relationship issues we might have been playing out. In fairness to my parents, though we never seemed to be yoked to the same cart and all pulling in one direction, I did learn important lessons from Mom and Dad in the areas of taking on responsibility and sticking up for what's "right"...for what is important:

During my teen years Mom and Dad took on big challenges. In the mid 1960s our predominantly Jewish, St. Louis suburb was almost brought to its knees by some greedy realtors. As our community became racially integrated word was spread that housing values would plummet. Homeowners were advised to "Sell now, before it's too late." My parents, I am proud to say, were voices for reason in this sea of fear and prejudice! They became involved in a local organization set up to maintain a community of racial balance and harmony. As the first black students entered the school district, there was a welcoming atmosphere. Perhaps Mom and Dad, and the other Jewish families who chose not to move, knew the painful feeling of being discriminated against. They knew that any form of prejudice was wrong and hurtful.

Another of Mom and Dad's huge accomplishments was the special-needs housing community they were heavily involved in creating. My sister now lives safely and joyously in a wonderful group home along with other mentally challenged adults and a crew of loving caregivers. When my brothers and I saw our sister settled into her new group home, enjoying friendships, dances, picnics, and other activities, we were relieved, happy, and grateful. Because of Mom and Dad's hard work we will never have to bear the burden of daily care for our sister.

I learned so much from observing Mom and Dad… about the importance of pushing through difficulties to accomplish a meaningful goal. Seeing how they were able to move past barriers to bring their ideas to fruition set a useful example for me in many areas of my life, including my quest to go walk the Camino.

In the early 1980s when I taught public school art. I learned that I love to construct lesson plans. Who knew? I enjoy getting people excited about learning new skills. I love supporting and encouraging people as they develop and learn to use their individual gifts.

Ten years later, in the 90s, I opened my own retail picture framing business. I learned that I possessed the necessary skills and toughness to be an entrepreneur. I was pleased and proud that my shop also became a place to create "work family," a place to practice creative problem solving, and a lab for combining business with spiritual growth, as in: "What will I do to feel honorable in this circumstance?" or "How do I envision the highest growth of this enterprise?" I am proud of the loving connections that were forged in my shop, the beautiful work we put out, and the business ethics we practiced.

In the early 2000s I took a series of classes from a group then called Phoenix 2000. This was experiential learning at its best: watching myself to see how I took in new information, how I responded to unfamiliar and sometimes uncomfortable stimuli, and, generally, how I managed in the world. For example, one of our class lessons involved going to a homeless shelter, cooking, and serving breakfast to the residents. I had never been to a homeless shelter before, but I had some personal fears about homelessness. I had pre-mixed a big batch of whole-wheat, chocolate chip pancake batter and I spent my time at the shelter working at the frying pan, frying up pancakes. It wasn't until the breakfast was nearly complete that one of my savvy classmates realized I had not come out of the kitchen. I had (subconsciously?) avoided the full experience of

*meeting and greeting the homeless residents. My classmates pushed
me into the dining room where I found I could easily interact with the
children, but I didn't know what to say to the adults. Finally, I spoke
with one of the women about her darling child. We ended up having
a conversation and she told me about herself: how she had ended up
at the shelter through an unfortunate financial situation, that she
was a single parent, and that she had come to the dining room late
for breakfast because she had been in her room meditating. There
was my lesson: this woman was like me: a spiritual single parent.
There was no difference between us except for circumstances.*

*As for this decade, the year 2011 has certainly brought lots of
Camino lessons. I don't think I can know them all yet. I know I'm
still learning how to deal with anger, but here's what I can say so
far: I am having lots of practice in learning to trust... to trust God,
myself, other people. I have learned that everything I pursue passion-
ately, even that which is outside of my comfort zone, will work out
well, perfectly in fact. I have learned to live with very few possessions,
almost nothing, and to feel at home. The world is opening up to me
courtesy of my wonderful new friends from all over the globe. I've
learned to get conscious about what I want, what's important to me,
what's right for me.*

*I have learned to accept tons of help, and to accept it graciously.
I now trust that I will receive help when I need it. I've worked on
"being here now" and I am learning to live more calmly and gracefully with the unknown. I am learning to stay in "excitement" rather
than in "fear." I have learned that I can do anything that is important
to me: get help to go on pilgrimage, climb up and over the Pyrenees,
walk five hundred miles, say "goodbye" to friends when it is time for
me to leave, and I can find my own way. I've learned to actively look
for perfection... and to be conscious to drop anger, or at least to not
chew on it. This has been a huge health improver! I have learned*

to allow the energies of health and peace into my being. Thank you Mom Nature! Thank you Great Creator!

Wednesday, 6-1-11, Camino Journal

I sat in the Santiago train station for many hours, waiting, reading tourist brochures and newspapers in Spanish, watching people in the train station, and watching Spanish game shows on the TV in the station café/bar. One is only allowed to sit in the station's café/bar when eating and there wasn't much food I wanted, so my TV viewing was kept to a minimum. While sipping my té con leche caliente I did watch a dating show that seemed to feature two Spanish TV stars, one male and one female. They were telling the young female contestant what she did and didn't do right regarding her date. Then there was a panel that appeared to be made up of her friends who were also telling her what to do. I'm sure I missed the nuances, but as a viewer I felt sorry for this young woman. I certainly would not enjoy having my mistakes pointed out so publicly. I hope this will be an experiential learning opportunity for her. Maybe as an outcome she will learn to trust her own judgment, to follow her own heart's wisdom.

Finally, late last night I boarded the train to Madrid. I love the Spanish people: every day is a celebration, a fiesta...even a late night train ride. Instead of quiet and sleep, the people in my car picnicked, feasted! Everyone had brought great quantities of food on board. Finally, after the food and festivities, things settled down. I was almost asleep, when the train slowed and the lights went back on: bright. We had an after midnight stop to pick up passengers. I have so much to learn about how the world works, about train schedules and customs. Perhaps I dozed lightly, but I did not get any real sleep the rest of the night.

After arriving at the Madrid train station I breakfasted with two other departing pilgrims, my last experience of belonging to a special club. The station is huge! Lots of hustle and bustle. I found the tourist information counter which was staffed by a very helpful Spanish woman who spoke English well. She explained to me how to access the pay telephones, which part of Lindy's number was necessary to input, and which was not, the country code vs. the area code. She also gave me a Metro/subway map and pointed out where I currently was. I had to call Lindy three times! The phone was "eating" euros. I could speak to her for just a minute each time. I finally gave up and put the phone call on the credit card. Hope it didn't cost too much. [FYI: It cost an outrageous amount, but I didn't know how much until I received my credit card bill a month later....]

I took the Metro and met Lindy at the station near her apartment. She was waiting for me on the stairs going up to street level, a distinctive green streak in her blonde hair making her easy to spot. Lindy is a citizen of the world. She has lived in a number of countries since her student days. She currently teaches English, sings in a band, and is studying for a Spanish proficiency certificate that will give her official translator status. We went to her apartment and visited for a while, then decided to take in a museum and do lunch—my treat— on the credit card! But first, she helped me find a tiny, comfortable, and reasonably priced room in a small hotel. I was so excited: I had a five-star bathroom complete with my own tub!

We spent a very interesting couple of hours at a contemporary art museum—one Lindy had been wanting to visit. The art was wonderful, but I was starting to have a melt down. First: hunger. Lucky for me Lindy had granola bars with her. Her mom sends them so she will always be prepared, and she was. We sat out in the museum courtyard, ate, and then went back in to see the rest of the exhibit. We were checking out the gift shop goodies when the second wave hit me: exhaustion. At that point we left, found a restaurant, and had a late lunch. More pizza… tastier than the on-the-Camino attempts! After lunch, Lindy walked me back to my hotel room, gave me detailed directions for the Metro ride to the airport the next morning, and we hugged goodbye. Another wonderful young person! How I wish I'd had some of that see-the-world spirit when I was in my twenties!

At the hotel I took a bath! The first in almost two months… glorious! I have done all my packing to the degree that I can. I'm in bed before 7 p.m. My wake-up call is set for the morning. I am watching reruns of old American sit-coms, reveling in the pleasure of not having to strain to understand the actors. I do understand a lot more Spanish now than when I first arrived in Spain, but it is still mental work, not easy and natural.

Thursday, 6-2-11
On board American Airlines, flight 69 from Madrid to Miami

Got to the airport this morning on the Metro with no problem. Good job of giving directions, Lindy! For weeks my body has complained about all the walking I've been doing. My body is now complaining about all the sitting. First, the eight plus hours in the train station in Santiago, then the train ride, and a couple of hours sitting at the airport this morning. And, now, I'm currently on my flight to Miami, sitting. After my nine-hour-long flight to Miami I will have another couple hours to wait in the Miami airport, and then, finally, my flight home! Miami is six hours behind Spain and one hour ahead of St. Louis, so when I arrive tonight at 10:10 St. Louis time, it will actually be 5:10 a.m. Spanish time, the next day… a 36-hour day! I'll try to sleep a bit now: four and a half hours 'til Miami.

Thursday, 6-2-11
5:10 p.m. Miami time/ Miami airport

Waiting for my 8:30 p.m. flight to St. Louis. Went through customs fine. Gifts of wine and chocolate from the duty-free shop are safely packed in my backpack. I have just eaten icky Chinese fast food. That's good though, as it puts me on a St. Louis sleep/eat schedule. Here are my fortune cookie messages. I got two:

"The physician heals, nature makes well."

"God looks after you especially."

Could these both be Camino-related? I think so!

PART FOUR:
Lessons Learned

SEVENTEENTH CENTURY NUN'S PRAYER

"LORD, Thou knowest better than I know myself that I am growing older and will some day be old. Keep me from the fatal habit of thinking I must say something on every subject and on every occasion. Release me from craving to straighten out everybody's affairs. Make me thoughtful, but not moody; helpful but not bossy. With my vast store of wisdom, it seems a pity not to use it all, but Thou knowest Lord that I want a few friends at the end.

Keep my mind free from the recital of endless details; give me wings to get to the point. Seal my lips on my aches and pains. They are increasing, and love of rehearsing them is becoming sweeter as the years go by. I dare not ask for grace enough to enjoy the tales of others' pains, but help me to endure them with patience.

I dare not ask for improved memory, but for a growing humility and a lessing cocksureness when my memory seems to clash with the memories of others. Teach me the glorious lesson that occasionally I may be mistaken.

Keep me reasonably sweet; I do not want to be a Saint—some of them are so hard to live with—but a sour old person is one of the crowning works of the devil. Give me the ability to see good things in unexpected places, and talents in unexpected people. And give me, O Lord, the grace to tell them so."

Amen

CHAPTER TWENTY-EIGHT:
The Post-Camino Shift

"To thrive means that we have chosen a new foundation. We've stepped into an awareness that the possibilities for love in our lives are unlimited, that abundance is ours for the asking, that what we have to bring to the table is very much welcomed, and that, if we open ourselves up and start trusting both ourselves and others more, goodness and love will flow towards us always."

Katherine Woodward Thomas

It is "so Camino" to imagine oneself differently. As the result of stepping out of the familiar and into a blank canvas of sorts you can paint yourself as blonde, as outgoing, as carefree, and no one knows any better. You can try on a new persona. See how it feels to be trusting—or loving—or religious—or open-minded, and no one knows that this is not how you've always been. But, that said, I think the out and out lie of a new self doesn't happen with pilgrims so much as that the true self emerges from under layers of shoulds, mustn'ts, limits, and regrets. The Camino is a regret-free zone...a place to say, "I'm going for it. This is what I want!"

Spain, my Camino, my sixtieth birthday on the Camino...all were more than I could ever have imagined, time out of ordinary time, producing a shift in me. I learned to trust the kindness of friends and strangers, to trust myself, and to trust that a Higher

Power is guiding my path. What I continue to learn is that my level of trusting is only as high as I allow it to be. If I fill my mind with self-defeating thoughts and worries, my level of trust goes down, down, down. For me, trusting is a very conscious process of remembering all the good that has come to me, over and over and over again. Trust has not become second nature to me, but a close friend I can call on at any time by choosing to remember all the lessons, all the gifts of my Camino.

Another big change seems to be in my reduced level of life-fears. When reading in Shirley MacLaine's Camino book about her experiences with wild dogs, I remembered feeling fear. Would I encounter wild dogs on my Camino? I had been preparing myself for that situation as best as I could on my pre-Camino walks around my home neighborhood. As the fenced-in neighborhood dogs barked (to either greet me or to scare me off), I practiced sending energies of love to all the little yippy guys. Often it seemed as if the dogs noticed an energy shift and ceased barking. I had further reasoned that in Spain I would be carrying my walking sticks and could fight off wild dogs with my aluminum "swords" if necessary. Bottom line: I had invested quite a bit of precious life energy in this and other imagined fears. And what happened? There were no wild dogs. There were some town strays and some unleashed pets, but nothing scary and wild. Instead there were opportunities to be in contact with many peaceful animals on the Camino: cows, sheep, horses, chickens, dogs, cats—all much loved and well cared for.

Sharing the Camino

When I read MacLaine's book the first time, I knew I wanted to go walk the Camino and have a spiritual experience as had MacLaine. Funny that when I read her book the second time, ten years later, just before my own Camino, I responded to the book by feeling less attracted and more repelled. In the first reading I felt strongly drawn in to all of her experiences—except the wandering wild dog packs. On the second reading, I heard a different story: more about MacLaine's annoyance with the paparazzi who sneakily followed her on the trail, and about her physical body's experiences. I suppose I was a different reader at that point: looking forward to my own mystical, magical Camino—to my own spiritual learnings to come, and I was less interested in the spiritual experiences of another. Looking back, I do remember hearing from a number of other pilgrims that MacLaine's book was their initial exposure to the Camino. I wonder how many have read her book and were put off by fear? The wild dogs stood out in the minds of many readers I spoke with! Maybe the divine purpose of MacLaine's book was to reach out to a broad swath of people, those of us for whom letting go of fear is an important component of our current life's path—wild dogs, getting lost, being alone, feeling deprived of a solid faith or trust—and to help us become intrigued, inspired, and motivated to move forward past our fears.

I once owned a poster of quotes: advice given by people in their eighties and nineties, what they wish they had known when they were younger. One sage piece of wisdom I remember: a gentleman's comment that he wished he had not wasted time in worry, as most of what he worried about never came to pass. My Camino was living proof of that. No wild dogs, no getting hopelessly lost, no running out of funds. I caught all my trains and planes. Someone was always there to help me if I needed help. Heck, a "doctor" was at my albergue when I most needed one! Now I have way fewer fears; I can live "out loud." The world is open to me. No, correct that: I am open to the world, no longer shrinking back in fear.

I still have a wish to be in a relationship. I had hopes I might meet a soul mate on the Camino. For a very long time I have not allowed myself to be in that type of experiential learning situation. I hope that will be my next and my most joy-filled life lesson. On the Camino I got to see wonderful examples of people who were living the type of relationship I wish to be in. Now, I think I will recognize good relationship potential when I connect with that special person.

In an unconscious way I think I had been hoping for a protector, a man to be there for me on the Camino. A year or so before my pilgrimage a book jumped off the library shelf at me: a Camino tale written by a young woman who had done the walk with her boyfriend. I don't remember the name of the book, but I do remember the beginning of her story. When she and her young man first arrived on the trail and went to get their credentials, their pilgrims' passports, they were each asked by the woman at the desk why they were making a pilgrimage. The young woman said she was there to heal from the death of her father. The young man (a Knight Templar in a former life?) said he was there to protect his girlfriend. Immediately I knew I wanted that, a male person to love and protect me. Although I didn't get the foot rubs and backpack-toting help I imagined a romantic soul mate would have provided, looking back, I see that I was always protected by loving male energy every step of the way. From St. Louis where my male friends were helpful and encouraging, to being guided through Chicago by my brother, and on to Paris, Bordeaux, St. Jean, and throughout my Camino, there was always a wonderful man who watched out for me. A male-clad soul made sure I got where I needed to go, shared laughter and camaraderie, gave advice, and engaged in stimulating discussion. I was getting to enjoy a plethora of men after so many years of living in a "man desert," rarely dating and having way more female than male friends.

In addition to my many knight/protectors, I began to see others of my Camino friends as archetypes: Emma, the "Trickster," mischievous and clever; Ernest, the "Court Jester," funny and wise; Sophie, the "Fair Maiden," attracting suiters and waiting to see what happens (or in Sophie's case, making the choice on what would or would not happen). In later years, as my Camino friends and I correspond, I begin to learn more details of their everyday lives and they become fleshed out, multidimensional, real people. This causes me to reflect: what archetype am I? An older "fair maiden"? A simple pilgrim? Or a divinely guided seeker? The seeker feels right to me: exploring new paths, new perspectives, new callings.

The "alligator in the canal" practical joke (pp.139-146), one of my many "letting go of anger" Camino lessons, stuck in my craw on some level even after my return home. I had told Emma and James that I would write up the story when I got back to St. Louis. When I finally did write it, there was a lesson there for me. I saw the story in the context of how I, as a Camino "baby bird," was able to successfully fly the nest. I came to see how Emma, James, and the others had given me all the tools I needed for success on the Camino: teaching me how to find the way-marker signs, how to get all my basic needs met, helping me learn the ropes of being a pilgrim, while lovingly supporting and befriending me during my period of learning. With the help of these dear Camino friends, I was prepared and then pushed out of the nest: first by my alligator-practical-joke-anger, and then by noticing a need to follow what was best for my body and soul. The end result: I did walk my solo Camino. Had I not walked by myself, I would have missed out on so much that I needed, wanted, and craved. I would have come home feeling incomplete.

I had read in Carolyn Myss's book, *Sacred Contracts*, about soul friends, those who consent to incarnate with us, agreeing to do whatever it takes to push us forward in our lives. This push might anger us and even cause us to break off a relationship, but it is done out of love and with a deep desire to help us with our soul's growth. I now see Emma and James and the rest of my *amigos del Camino* as my soul friends, risking my anger to make sure I did what I was most afraid of doing: finding my own way, risking being lost, turning over my problems to a Higher Source, and trusting in divine guidance. I honor all my *amigos del Camino*, my soul friends. All were there for me at the perfect time, being their perfect divine selves.

As for my anger with the scummy *hospitalero* at the convent in Léon (pp. 157-158), with the pancake selling lady (pp. 187-188) who tried to scam me for a bigger "donation," with the two German bunk stealing women who almost put me in the middle of an "international incident" and the loud German "family," (pp. 210-213), in hindsight, I think the larger lesson was simply to practice dropping that which I have no control over, accepting what is, and moving on down the path. I now choose to look for perfection in others, as opposed to being in judgment of them. Throwing in a sprinkle of good humor seems to help too. I find that laughing at myself in a loving way is soul satisfying and even enjoyable. I choose to be compassionate with my pouty self, even saying "poor baby" and patting my own arm when necessary. I recently read in Mark Goulston's book, *Just Listen, Discover the Secret to Getting Through to Absolutely Anyone*, about our brain's mirror neurons, those cells that help us to understand what another is feeling. According to Goulston, having people recognize our emotions and acknowledge them to us is a human need. I now see that when Melina from Denmark (in the Albergue Aquario in Santiago, p. 230) told me she, too, had been angry at the pancake-selling woman's scam, she and I were able to enjoy some of the rewards of "mirroring" each other. I felt immediately understood, and that was what finally allowed me to drop my anger. I hope Melina got the same benefit.

Even after my Camino, lessons still continued to surface. While writing about my personal history for this book I had a surprising experience. I recalled the scene from my teens in which a rabbi ignored my question about why God allows bad things to happen to people, like allowing my sister to be born with an intellectual handicap. Now as I mentally replayed the scene with the rabbi (p. 25), I wonder if perhaps I might have seen him turn away to face the back of the stage…to privately wipe away a tear... or to compose himself? Could that have happened? It was possible. Perhaps, he too had a sibling who was disabled or born sickly. Perhaps one of the rabbi's own children was born with flaws. And, perhaps, he too had railed at God. Was he silent in response to my question because he was dumbstruck—because my question hit him at a fragile moment...after the death of an innocent...or after an action he perceived to be unjust on God's part? Had I touched a raw nerve? Could what I took as distaste for my question actually have been an adult male of the time, the late 1960s, struggling to control his emotions? After fifty years of anger at this man's hurtful lack of response to my genuine and heartfelt question, in an instant all my anger dropped away. Seeing him as a person with his own struggles, I easily forgave him. And I forgave myself: for holding onto my anger at his imperfect response, for holding onto my pain all these years, for seeing my initial reaction as the *ugly truth* for fifty years! In the teachings of *A Course in Miracles*, a miracle can be defined as "a shift in how we perceive a situation"... a shift that returns us to our inner peace. This is what had happened to me—and within me— a miraculous shift in my feelings had taken place.

All in all, it was a fabulous trip! I am thrilled that I was able to go. There was more joy in this seven-week period than I could ever have imagined possible. I definitely want to go again. I'd love to volunteer as a *hospitalera*, to cook tasty vegetarian food, to plant gardens at *albergues*, and to be of service to other pilgrims. I never did get to eat a ripe fig off a tree or to see the Milky Way. I missed tons of Gaudí architecture in Léon and in Barcelona. Although Barcelona is not on the Camino, it would be a fabulous side trip. The wine fountain at the Monastery of Irache outside of Estella, serving wine *gratis* (free), a gift to the pilgrims, was closed the day we were there. It would be fun to test those "waters." The sign at the wine fountain says: "Pilgrim, if you wish to arrive at Santiago full of strength and vitality, have a drink of this great wine and make a toast to happiness." And I still need to get the quote I liked off the wall at the Austrian Albergue in Los Arcos. There are Crusader forts and ruined castles to visit. I would love to find the labyrinth that Pilgrim Bill had shown me in his Camino photos. I need to go back to the special small chapel in the cathedral in Santiago, to learn more, to feel more. I am still enamored with the idea of a nighttime bonfire on the beach at Finisterre. Plus, there are many more Camino routes. One can begin the Camino from starting points all over Europe. No question, I have more trails to follow…

I arrived home seven weeks after my original departure, just in time for a full-on family reunion: oodles of relatives, no time alone, smack back into real life and ordinary time. Two checks were waiting for me. Money was provided. The home bills were paid. Since then, opportunities to practice trusting have been plentiful. I've had opportunities to decide what I want and then to act on it. I am no longer afraid of going after my own big dreams. If this Camino big dream can work out so beautifully, why not the next, and the next? Best of all, from walking the Camino my life path is becoming clearer: sharing my life lessons with others, writing, and teaching now call to me. My life is not forfeit!

CHAPTER TWENTY-NINE

Post Camino Perspective, Two and a Half Years Out

"Pray, listen, trust, and surrender."

My friend, Alex

My very devout friend, Alex, holds as his personal mantra, "Pray, listen, trust, and surrender." I know this, as he had me frame a calligraphied version of it. My Camino experience was exactly that, though perhaps with a more metaphysical bent. I prayed fervently for assistance with money and health so that I could make the pilgrimage. My money and health fears persisted throughout the walk, especially the monetary concerns, so I prayed a lot! At some point each day I would find myself praying as I walked, sometimes with mantras or using the device of repetition, always staying in communication with the Divine.

I have been a listener since the first time I received unsolicited divine input. I remember it well. I was in the bathroom, washing and getting ready for my day. I was also steaming and stewing, thinking most unkind thoughts about someone I had previously respected. This person had recently become enmeshed in some shady business dealings, and I was very angry with him. I remember hearing the words, "People aren't perfect. Love them anyway." Mind you, I had not thought those words.

They had appeared in my head of their own accord. Naturally, I was taken aback, but at the time I knew this was a case of divine guidance. What else could it be? It was a message of love. As part of my Camino preparation, I found techniques I could use to facilitate listening for divine guidance—practical techniques, like journaling and focusing on "what I want," and metaphysical techniques, like direct writing (**pp.44-45, 66-67**), the dream board (**pp. 47-48**), and the focus wheel (**p. 47**). This last one is an exercise used to put a person in the perfect frame of mind to receive. I learned it from the Abraham Hicks book, *Ask and It Is Given.*

My Year of Trusting was 2011. I had decided to actively pursue a more trusting attitude in all areas of my life. I trusted that all would work out, that my body would be strong enough to make the daily treks, that I would be provided for, that I would meet all the right people, and have all the life experiences I was meant to have. I watched with wonder as everything I needed came to me. Even experiences that felt difficult or painful had wonderful outcomes or carried needed lessons. Since my return, when I walk I will occasionally follow the yellow arrows painted on the sidewalks and streets near my home. These are meant for the road repair or utility crews, but sometimes I decide to trust that one of these arrows is a Camino way-marker put there for me. Trusting can be fun! And, I am not the only pilgrim still looking for, and trusting that I will find, signs. I recently read a blog post from a former Camino pilgrim who was trying to decide whether or not to return to Spain for a second pilgrimage. She said that, as she was walking and pondering (now at home, in Scotland), she came to a road she had never been on before, a road that was covered in scallop shells. She took the shell road as a sign that she was being directed to a second Camino.

As for surrender, what else can one do on a five-hundred-mile walk through northern Spain but to surrender? Not knowing where I would spend the night, what I would eat, whether I would get lost or hurt, whether I would be with companions, alone, lonely? At the beginning of the day I could not know how the day would end. A pilgrimage is inherently about living with unknowns and surrendering to them. I asked God for help, I asked family and friends to pray for me, and I moved expectantly into the mystery.

Perhaps the biggest Camino lesson I received was about always being provided and cared for. This has carried on into my post-Camino life, now two and a half years out. It's funny. I couldn't see it at the time, but in looking back over these past few years, everything I've needed has been provided for me, often in unforeseen ways. My money issues, for years a huge problem, have turned around, in large part, I think, because I no longer go automatically to worry. Now, I'm much more likely to think, "I've always been provided for" and to trust that I will continue to receive what I need, what is in my highest good. Work shows up all the time. Opportunities to meet all the perfect people present themselves with some regularity. Examples: an author I admire spoke at a conference where I was to present a story I'd written. Because I now know how important it is to stand behind myself, I sent the author an e-mail and asked if she had enjoyed my story and would she give me an introduction to her publisher. And, she agreed! Also, I recently met a person who works with college students, helping them to move forward on their life paths, and she wants to hear more about the big dreams course I developed as a result of my Camino experiences. All the right books and all the perfect teachers continue to show up in my life. New friends help me learn about the art of writing, about the publishing business. I often feel grabbed by a surprising interest in a new topic. It feels as if I am being inspired to study what the Great Creator wants me to learn next.

I learned at a summer get-away with friends (six girlfriends) that I am an official introvert. By the time we were to return home from our five-day gathering, I was in meltdown-mode, crying and not understanding why. Fortunately, on the car ride home, friend Kristine explained it to me: how introverts need time alone to recharge, while extroverts recharge by being with people. This reasoning explained my discomfort with years of being on call for customers in my shop. It also clarified my serious need for time alone on the Camino: how I was losing myself, how my deep spiritual side was being overwhelmed by too much social time. I now know I need time to walk alone, to journal, to think myself back into being me. I now know to balance time with friends, family, and customers with quiet time by myself at home or out in nature. I know to watch myself so I don't leak out, don't dissipate into other people's energies.

Another big change for me since the Camino is the size of my sense of adventure: it has grown! I am open to more of life. I can be anything, do anything I want: I can be an observer at an Israeli/Palestinian checkpoint if I want; I can rent out or sell my home and get an around-the-world airline ticket like Thalles and Flavia. I have only to decide what I want. I now relish a bus or train trip as an opportunity to smile and make new friends. I recognize that those I meet might be soul friends. I am actively looking to spot them. I look forward to seeing more of my native land, and yet, I feel a deep desire to walk more European pilgrimage trails. There are more stories from the trail in my future. I trust that is true.

I was pleased to have brought in close to $1,000 in my Habitat for Humanity fundraising. It was not enough to cover the cost of a house, but perhaps we raised the funds for a kitchen? After my return from the Camino, I met volunteers collecting for Habitat at the entrance to an art show. I shared with them the story of my own Habitat fund-raiser and was delighted to have them connect me with a young man who has set up a fund-raising-for-charitable-causes-through-walking program: Jonathon Stalls from kivawalk.org. Jonathon and I were able to Skype with each other and share about our journeys. He has walked across the entire U.S.! I really can't imagine walking through big U.S. cities, but maybe some day I will. Jonathon teaches a class at the Colorado Free University. The title of his class intrigued me: "Make Your Own Mission: Radical Ideas for a Better World." It makes my heart happy to know that this generation of young Americans is capable of creating great works. I loved how the Divine set up our "chance" meeting!

Perhaps the two best long-term benefits of my Camino are my *amigos del Camino*, my wonderful Camino friends, and my enhanced self-esteem. I've been blessed and thrilled to maintain my Camino friendships—now multiple years out. Thank God for e-mail and Skype! The first month or two after we returned to our homes, we e-mailed and shared photos. It has been a joy every single time I've received a photo, an e-mail, or an actual piece of postal mail. We have shared our delight at family weddings, books published, and new jobs. We've shared our sorrows at job losses, relationship completions, and deaths. We may be spread across the world, having actually spent only a few short moments together, but we care about each other fiercely. James and I communicate regularly. We e-mail humorous YouTube videos, photos, newspaper articles, favorite music, and we catch up by Skype. We keep up on each other's travels and share about other Camino friends we've seen or from whom we've heard. We discuss work, play, families, and friends. I love to hear from him, and I'm always excited when I come across an item to email, imagining his delight at a darling child violin virtuoso or a scathing political column. For someone I've only know in person for a few weeks of my life, he is amazingly dear to me. In fact, I was so surprised by the depth of my feelings for James that I recently asked my intuitive friend, Nikki, for some "behind the scenes" insight. Her take was that James and I had lived multiple past lives together, in various forms of relationships, the most recent life as brother and sister.

That felt right to me, as the initial closeness I felt with James and the continuing desire to remain in contact was so unexpectedly strong. I shared Nikki's words with James, saying that when we first met I had felt an immediate sense of comfort with him. He said he had felt the same initial comfort with me.

I now see myself as a world citizen because I maintain these loving friendships with folks from England, Germany, Australia, New Zealand, South Korea, and Canada. Some of my sense of adventure, my wanderlust, has rubbed off on Erin, now in her twenties. She feels a huge pull towards traveling. She has already made car trips to California, to Louisiana, and to Canada. The lure to explore life beyond this continent calls to her as well. I am excited for her to be seeking out adventure, to become a world citizen. Perhaps she will visit my Camino friends on her travels. That will be another way for us to stay connected, through sharing our lodgings—they all know they are always welcome to come stay with me—and through sharing our families.

As for enhanced self-esteem, in addition to the enormous sense of satisfaction from completing my Camino and realizing my personally meaningful big dream, many friends and family members told me that I had inspired them. I had never, ever, in my whole life thought I might be a source of inspiration. What I recognized was that if I could reach for and grab hold of my own deep desire—me, an ordinary person with no special skills, no world-famous gifts or talents—perhaps others might see that they too could reach for and grab hold of their own shining stars, that they could go after what called most loudly to them, that they could become the heroes in their own life stories.

After my return from the Camino, having realized my own big dream, I read a number of books detailing various authors' experiences of realizing their own big dreams. In examining these experiences, a pattern of successfully realized big dreams began to emerge. There appeared to be stages/steps/patterns that occurred for all of us...the same stages/steps/patterns! And we were all pursuing very different big dreams. However they labeled theirs: deep desires, life goals, callings, we were all having parallel experiences.

These steps were found in all the realized big dreams I read about:

1. I know (or learn) what I want.

2. I become open to the possibility that I can have what I want.

3. I make a commitment to myself. I stand behind what I want. I do everything I can imagine to make my big dream happen, including asking for help.

4. I prepare to deal with negativity and fear, from others and from myself.

5. I place focus on the sacred quality of my big dream. I feel its power! I receive help from beyond myself.

6. I realize my big dream! I get comfortable with my own importance to the world.

7. I take time to assess what I've learned, how I've grown, how I've changed, how this new me might be better prepared for my next big dream. I take time for gratitude, celebration, centering, coming back to self.

8. Then, it's back to step 1, "What do I want?" I may feel pulled in the direction of my next big dream, or, I may take time to "lie fallow."

I had been gifted with love from so many people as a result of my decision to "stand behind myself." I received love in the form of prayers, time spent, items lent, monies and frequent flyer miles given, good wishes, intuitive support. To me the most moving part of receiving all that was shared with me was that I was asking for help to do something I *wanted* to do, not *needed* to do. I wasn't asking for help with something I needed to stay alive: for food, shelter, medical care, or even transportation help. I was asking for help with something to lift me out of the ordinary and into more. I was helped to have a life experience I wanted just because I asked. What an obvious show of unconditional love! For any one of us who lives life feeling average, ordinary, or non-special, asking for and receiving help to do what feels personally important can be a grandly affirming experience. Before the Camino I would have felt scared and ashamed to ask for help. Afterwards, I realize that asking for help is what we all must do to achieve big dreams. If I want to teach a class, to meet a person, to have an opportunity, I must be willing to share my thoughts, my goals, my desires… The mind-reading community is not as large as we'd like to believe. "If you don't ask, you don't get" is my current mantra. Rather than think, "I can't do that" or "What will so and so think?" or "What if he/she says 'no'?" I tell myself that I am just as worthy, just as loved, that the world needs my input just as much as the next person's.

Then I say a prayer for the highest good, and I hit "send," dial the number, or put the envelope in the mailbox.

———

On my return to St. Louis I gave a number of talks about my Camino journey. In the first of these talks I was given an opportunity to be provided for, even though I had not asked for any help. I had scheduled a Camino talk and photo viewing, opening the event to everyone I knew: folks who had helped fund my trip, newsletter readers, friends, and family. The problem was that the talk was to take place in my backyard during a very hot part of the St. Louis summer. I had cautioned all those planning to attend to come prepared with bug repellant, and to dress for the weather. I was worried though. Summer heat in St. Louis can be brutal. Two days before the event, out of the blue, a friend offered me a space at a local mall. I was able to contact everyone by e-mail and phone and we enjoyed that air conditioning! It was at one of these Camino talks that I first realized how much I love being a teller of tales. I was sharing the story of "the alligator in the canal" and when I got to the part where the truth came out, that the whole thing had been a practical joke, everyone in the room collectively drew in breath…a group "haaah!" The storyteller in me imagines it feels much the same as when the rookie comedian gets that first audience laugh. It was very satisfying!

Upon my return, a story was written about me in my local newspaper. I was interviewed on two radio talk shows about my pilgrimage and about the steps I took that led to realizing my big dream. I knew I wanted to write a book on my Camino experiences. My dilemma: how to find time, energy, and a publisher. God answered with a very busy work month during which I made good money, followed by a slow period. In the past the "worrier me" would have fretted the entire slow period. This new me figured God's plan was to give me some time free of the distraction of earning a living to get serious with this book. The best part was God's follow-up: an e-mail notice of a publishing contest, complete with a reachable deadline. Good one, God!

I have put back on my pre-Camino weight. It was wonderful to be the slimmer-bodied version of me upon my return, but over a few holiday seasons the weight has come back. Bottom line: I miss the daily Camino walking. I haven't walked as regularly as I had planned since my return. I love to walk…once I get out on the path. But there are often so many items that get put before walking in my priority sequence. Although I know my body is merely here to truck my soul around, I am wildly grateful for my good physical health. I want to continue to climb hills and mountains, to backpack into the unknown, to make friends wherever I go, and to receive meaningful stories from the Divine. I want to continue to be a strong woman, with sixty-something years of this-life experience. I want to live my life watching for all the good that is coming my way. I love my life. It is most definitely not forfeit!

Why are some of us called to the Camino, some to Mecca, some to the Grand Canyon or to the Great Wall of China? The easy answer to me is: a "past life" pull. But, who can say this is true? I recently had the thought to ask my Camino friends about their original motivations for walking the Camino. I was wondering if anyone else, like me, had felt "pulled" to walk the Camino from the first moment they heard of it. One friend said that he had accidentally come to the city of Santiago on his way home from Portugal. There in the Praza Obradoiro, in front of the cathedral, he first saw pilgrims and first learned about the pilgrimage trail. He said he was "immediately intrigued." It captured his imagination as a "parallel world" he knew nothing about. Others of the friends spoke of their reasons for going in more traditional terms: going to have an adventure in the outdoors, going to spend time with a parent or a friend, going to deal with anger or dissatisfaction, or to feel peaceful during a between-jobs period. Some of these friends' pilgrimages ended in interesting and surprising outcomes. One felt the "...presence of past pilgrims in the churches" and found peace there, even though she is not a religious person. Another met the romantic partner of his dreams at the very end of his Camino. They now have a darling son together and are a happy family. And my dear friend Ernest has become philosophical about his Camino. He said it healed him, that other pilgrims listened to him, gave their best advice, and through conversations with "precious Camino friends" he found out who he is. We were able to reflect back to Ernest how creative, funny, adventurous, persistent, and very kind he is. He wrote that "Life is like the Camino: muddy hill, dry and boring Meseta, smelly road, fresh morning, and people who raise me up." My friend Melina from Denmark, whom I didn't meet until the Albergue Aquario in Santiago, shared that she originally went "...to have an exciting holiday experience and to think through my life." She further shared that she said goodbye to her younger brother who had followed her since 2003 when he died. Melina said that her brother, in spirit form, had been a huge help to her and guided her life, "... until he told me on the way to the Iron Cross [the Cruz de Ferro] that now he had to proceed." Her brother asked Melina to leave a stone at the cross for him, and after, she said, "He was gone." She said it was a fantastic experience!

My friend Ian said that the Camino was plan B for him. Plan A had been a sailing trip around the Mediterranean on a one-hundred-year-old restored sailing vessel, but that trip got cancelled due to the boat owner's poor health. Ian said he still had time off and was looking for an adventure. The Camino, the Christian pilgrimage route, did not call to him, but when he read about the pre-Christian pilgrimage to Finisterre, to the place once thought to be world's end, where the ocean continued west until it spilled off the plate of the earth, then he felt pulled in with a "compelling force." Ian made a point to ask other pilgrims what had drawn them to the trail and was fascinated to hear how many felt "irresistibly compelled." There were varieties of compulsions: religious callings, petitions of prayers to be made, spiritual summons, personal growth reasons, or a trust that the unknown reason for their call would present itself. And perhaps, like Ian, some became inspired by a bit of history that seemed somehow present tense and familiar.

It is equally likely that we are pulled to our callings to meet up with a soul-friend—one whom we agreed to connect with at a certain point in this life…Or perhaps there is a heritage connection to a place—to the very molecules of soil and air—that is passed on to us through our genes. Perhaps we had a teacher whose glowing description of a place or a period of history was enthralling, enticing, and memorable. Perhaps our love of music, art, stories, or foods of a particular culture draws us to visit or to live in that part of the world. And perhaps, a life of steadfast country-of-birth-culture is the correct life path for some of us.

It is worth noticing our pulls, our excitement, our sensual delight in certain smells, tastes, or sounds. It is worth reaching back into our childhood memories: what stories we loved, our favorite activities, our favorite subjects in school. Were we captivated by stories of our grandparents in their youth…imagining the world they grew up in…the old country, the customs, the cuisine?

And we might look at our family of origin's physical attributes: my Jewish ancestors likely hailed from both Eastern Europe (the history I know) and, going by skin tone and hair texture, from the Middle East, or possibly from Spain. Perhaps some of my distant relations were Sephardic Jews, expelled from Spain during the Inquisition. Some of them might have become *conversos*, converts to Christianity, either sincerely changing their belief systems, or becoming "secret Jews." I can't fathom a genetic link in my heritage reaching back to Ireland, but perhaps I had Spanish/Jewish ancestors who intermarried with persons of Celtic bloodlines? When I get to this point in my wonderings I happily remind myself, that I can't know this now, but I will look forward to finding out all my juicy past-life histories when I am next between lives, and in the meantime, I have trails to walk and stories to tell. My life is not forfeit.

Appendix

Guided Meditations by Deborah Terra Weltman

To get the most from doing a guided meditation, either:

Record the meditation for yourself, speaking slooooowly!
Sit comfortably with your eyes closed. Relax and listen.

Or, have someone read it to you.

Or, you can listen to Deborah's guided meditations by visiting her web-site: TerraArtPublishing.com and clicking on the free Guided Meditation links.

Have a notebook and pen ready to write about your experience at the end of the meditation. There will be a number of "prompt" questions to help your remembering process. It is not important that you recall every tiny detail. Trust that you will retain what is most important for your personal growth.

Pilgrimage to Essence of Self Guided Meditation

A pilgrimage is a journey, perhaps a long one, made to a sacred place, a place of devotion, a place that is honored, and that honors you.

As you head out on your personal journey, it is important to be relaxed and open to whatever learning is to come.

Please close your eyes and take a deep breath, hold for a count of 3 (1-2-3) and breathe out fully, expelling any concerns in your life outside of this room.

Again, inhale deeply. Hold for 3 (1-2-3) and exhale any anger, jealousy or guilt.

Once again, take in as full a breath as you can. Hold for 3 (1-2-3). Release your breath and any nagging fears.

You are now prepared for the joys and blessings of what is to come.

With your eyes still closed, picture yourself now in your warm home. It is winter and outside it is cold, snowy and icy. You have decided to go out for a walk and you dress warmly putting on many layers, plus a hat, scarf, mittens, boots and a heavy coat. Ready now for an adventure, you head out the front door and immediately begin to slide… down the front walk… down the driveway. You are feeling safe and in control of the sliding, in fact, it is more of a controlled gliding that you are doing. You feel very balanced and very comfortable. "This is fun!" you think. With arms out to the side, you imagine yourself on a ski board, coasting down sidewalks and streets.

You glide to a beautiful snow covered park. Entering the park you alternate between walking on the crunchy, snow-covered grass and gliding down the icy glazed-over pathways. You are very engaged in the joy of this "walk & glide" and don't notice until it's too late that the pathway you have been gliding on dips. You find yourself gliding down into the dip, picking up speed, and, too late to stop, you realize you have fallen into a large hole. You are not alarmed as you find yourself floating… as if attached to a parachute. You have a brief thought of Alice and her rabbit hole and you wonder what YOUR rabbit hole might hold for you.

As you float gently down, you become aware of the layers of rock and dirt, the changes in their color, sheen, and texture. Compacted limestone, carbonous organic matter, "layers of life" you think. You float down for quite a while… alert and calm… thinking about these many "layers of life" that you are passing through. [pause]

You land gently. All your body parts are in good shape. No bumps or bruises (perhaps because you were so well padded by your heavy winter clothing). You look up… a LONG way up… You can see sky at the top of your rabbit hole. You look around you at the area where you have landed and you can see another light source: from an open door. You walk to the doorway and step out onto a beautiful countryside: gentle rolling terrain all swathed in green. You notice a path a little ways ahead. It leads to a mountain.

"What is it about this mountain?" you think. "Why do I feel so drawn to it? This is more than just a gentle curiosity. It's almost a magnetic pull". You have never wanted anything so much in your life as you want to go to this mountain. You set off at once. The magnetic pull only increases, as you get nearer. As you approach more closely, you can now see multiple paths leading up the mountainside and you begin to understand: you are going on a pilgrimage to find your Highest, truest self…the essence of you! You don't entirely understand how you got here or what you might learn, only that you are very excited to find out what is so important for you to learn on this pilgrimage walk to your Highest Self.

When you reach the mountain's base, you are near the start of many trails: some that are well trodden and some that look passable, but have rarely been walked. "Which path to take?" As you think this question a voice in your ear says to you, "Follow the light". You turn quickly to see who has spoken, but you see no one. "Follow the light?" you think. "Yes", the voice answers, "We each have a path that is special to us. Watch for yours. See it light up". Without turning to look this time, you say, "Thank you" and look more intently at the paths.

There are cleared paths: some paved, some dirt. There are rocky paths: some that are easy for a good climber with a good pair of hiking boots to navigate, and some that will require great effort to go each step. And there are paths of every degree of variation in between. Some of the paths crisscross and take on new characteristics for a time. Many paths are still too far away to be seen clearly. As you scan back and forth among the many paths, you do see one that has begun to glow. [small pause]

You rush towards it, YOUR glowing path. What does your path look like? Is it smooth and at a gradual incline? Is it full of rocks and roots to step over? What plant life do you see? Will you be walking in a pleasant shade, in darkness? Under a blistering sun? Or in a gentle light? What other sounds, smells and sights are you aware of? [pause] Notice what you see on and off the path as you walk. What do you hear, touch, smell? [pause]

After walking for some time, you become aware that your winter weather clothing is making you uncomfortably hot. You stop and shed your coat, mittens and cap. "There, much better", you think. You set off on your path once more, noticing a dark area up ahead. Your steps become slower. You realize that there is a small wood ahead that you will have to pass through. The closer you get, the darker it gets. But you are very much feeling the "move–on" message of the mountain, so into the dark wood you step.

Your eyes have become accustomed to the low light and you keep walking on your path. Your path is still glowing, but at a barely perceptible level. You keep walking, more slowly now, because you have become more aware of your other senses: hearing, touch, and smell. All are feeding you new information. They are telling you that there is something alive up ahead and it is moving towards you. What to do? You start to pick up old fears… to walk with those fears… to run with them… until, ahead in the darkness you see a pair of eyes staring at you. Now you can smell fear: your own. Before you reach panic-mode, the same voice from earlier says to you, "Wait. What's up ahead is your Shadow Self, a hidden part of you that you don't know, but that you fear. This is your opportunity to get to know it, to befriend it. Go to it with an out-stretched hand and an open heart. Your Shadow Self has much to share with you about your fears: the ones which are controlling you without your knowledge".

You are steadied by the voice and by the mountain's pull and you continue forward through the dark toward the eyes of your Shadow Self. As you get closer you begin to see an outline of your Shadow Self. You stretch your hand out to it and greet it with all the love you can call up. "This is not so scary", you think, now ready to learn whatever there is to learn from this experience. Your Shadow Self leads you to two flat rocks where you sit down and get to know each other.

You say, "What may I call you?" Now listen for that name. [pause]

You say, "I'm told that you have something to share with me". Now listen for that message. [pause]

And, now, your Shadow Self surprises you with a gift. You hold it, feel its weight, you note its details. Does it have a smell, a sound, a texture? [pause] After enjoying the gift you tuck it safely into your pocket.

You thank this previously hidden part of yourself, your Shadow Self, for sharing the message and the gift. You are no longer afraid, but very grateful. You rise to take your leave. You bow to each other and see a light of heart-connection energy that binds you together. Your Shadow Self now smiles at you and waves you on through the remainder of the woods.

The trail is a long one. You travel it over many levels of the mountain, sometimes switching to a new path as you are led by the light. At times you become aware of carrying too much weight, making your climb more difficult. You shed more layers of clothing and whatever else you no longer need: whatever is no longer necessary for your protection, what is too heavy, too restrictive, or that which no longer feel like it is right for you. See yourself laying down that which no longer serves you... now. [pause]

You shed layers of fears. Mostly this occurs as you switch to a new path. There, you are conscious to lay down false fears that caused you trouble on the previous path segment, and to replace those fears with the excitement you feel about venturing onto the new path. See your self laying down fears and picking up excitement... now. [pause]

As you walk, you also shed old dreams that are no longer your true dreams. In their place you pick up a dream that completely resonates with your heart. See yourself picking up your heart-felt dream now. [pause]

You shed old hurts as you walk. They come off you like old rattle-y skins, leaving you with a youthful excitement. You plant these old hurts along the trail, watering them with forgiveness and watching the miraculous flowers that grow. See yourself shedding and planting old hurts now. See yourself adding the hydrating properties of forgiveness now.

You realize that there are few things in this physical world that are important to you. Really, only love is worth carrying all the way to the top of the mountain. So you make a conscious choice to carry only love and to lose all that is unlike love. By the time you reach the mountaintop you are a sleek, lean, loving machine! As you gaze down at the land on the opposite side of the mountain, you are swept with the desire to be with love, to be with your family, your friends, your heart's work. And you realize, crestfallen, that you don't know how to get to, how to re-enter, that love.

"Never fear", says the voice. You look up to see an angelic presence who smiles at you and reaches out for your hand.

"Your heart is so full of love and so relieved of all that had dragged it down before, that you can now fly with me. Come, we'll fly to wherever your heart says", the angel tells you, As you touch hands you are once again aware of the sensation of floating, only this time, you are floating down the mountain, close enough to see other pilgrims on their paths to the mountain top. You wave to them and yell words of encouragement.

You can see all you have left behind: old hurts, old dreams that no longer connect to your heart, old fears, including the fear of your Shadow Self. You recall the talk with your Shadow Self and the gift you received. You recall all the clothing (the costumes of life) that you chose to leave behind. You are so grateful to have successfully shed that which no longer serves you.

The angel shows you back to your "rabbit hole". You are so full of love, and so light of worry, that you float up to the top… to the park, where the snow and ice has melted. You walk back to your home, enjoying the sunshine and the smiles you exchange with others. You see someone who reminds you of your Shadow Self and you smile warmly at each other.

You are aware of your heart connection, aware that your heart is always communicating its deepest desires to you. You are excited to be focusing on that heart connection and on the useful information it brings to you.

When you have arrived at your front door, you enter and are back in this current time and place, remembering all that you learned, all that you shed, and all that you gained on your pilgrimage to the sacred mountain that is You.

When you are ready, please open your eyes and write down all your experiences on the "pilgrimage": How did your path look? Was it easy or difficult to traverse? What message and gift did you receive from your "Shadow Self"? What fears did you leave behind? What past dreams (no longer your true dreams) did you shed? What hurts did you slough off, plant, and water with forgiveness? Did you pick up new heart-felt dreams or desires?

You may want to look for symbolism in the nature of your path and in the "gift" you received. You may want to ask others who have "walked" this guided meditation to brainstorm with you to discover any hidden symbolic messages.

Optimal Health Guided Meditation

[Do some gentle stretches before you begin this guided meditation. Either lying, seated, or standing, do a few minutes of whatever stretches feel best to you: Then, sitting or lying comfortably, close your eyes, take easy, natural breaths, and listen to the meditation.]

Doctors have always known the power of our minds to control our health: people who receive placebos do heal…folks who hear a negative diagnosis may go down-hill quickly, or, conversely, may summon their will and choose to fight their illness.

What if…it is possible to consciously direct our optimal health…through creative visualization…creative imagining? Let's try that now. Feel free to adapt whatever feels most powerful and productive to you into your future health meditations.

Notice how your body feels after doing the gentle stretches. You may feel relaxed, refreshed. You may feel energized. Perhaps, you "tingle". Mentally, carry this feeling of "tingling" to the top of your head. Imagine an opening there at the crown of your head… an opening for God, angels, Divine Beings who are here to assist you…to pour the "energies of health" into your body. You might also see the special health energies as emanating from the well wishes or the prayers of loving friends. Or, these special health energies may come from your Highest Self…your soul…the part of you that is in constant and direct communication with the Divine.

From wherever these energies originate, from whatever source, notice now that tingling sensation at the crown of your head. It is the energy of optimal health. It is ready to enter your physical body…your "Earth suit"…to heal, to cleanse, to lubricate, and to revitalize your organs, bones, muscles, glands…all of your body's systems…to renew each and every cell.

Imagine now, you opening your crown chakra, the energy center at the top of your head. You become aware of the tingling energies of Optimal Health entering at the top of your head… bubbling, effervescing, flowing…around and through your skull, your brain, your sinus cavities…opening blocked channels, lightening your load. What feels like a bubbly, energized liquid now begins to flow through you, a carbonated beverage of health! As it reaches the backs of your eyes, your vision becomes sharper. It makes its way through the sinuses and the rear of your nasal cavity, clearing all your passageways for the breath of life to flow easily. As it enters the canals of your ears, the bubbly liquid energy removes old blocks, those that have kept you from really hearing the words, thoughts, and feelings of others.

This effervescent energy now slides down the back of your throat, loosening stuck words, especially those which, when shared, will serve to increase love, happiness, and cooperation. Your throat feels refreshed, as if you have just had a delicious drink of cool, sparkling spring water. The energy also acts as a lubricant, increasing the range of movement in your neck. You can now turn your head in all directions, swiveling so as to be able to see all sides of a situation. In your imagination, you see your head rotating to both sides and up and down with ease.

Your neck feels so fluid… It feels as if your head is attached to your body with a sturdy and flexible ball joint. Perhaps you can see all the way behind you… to where you've been. You can see past patterns that have contributed to ill health: whether what you ate, breathed in, or took in on an emotional level. You see behind you now how the past has affected you, or might continue to affect you physically. And you are now joyously aware that the effervescent energies of Optimal Health continuously flowing through you can heal your negative patterns and ill health.

This healthy energy now bathes your thyroid gland. The cells of your thyroid, many of which have been overworked by lifestyle stresses, are being renewed. Feel the tingle? You might also feel or see a very gentle ray of sunlight now being directed at your thyroid gland, at the base of your neck. Imagine a slim ray of sunlight shining through a tiny hole in the clouds.... streaming directly towards your body... towards your neck. This light energy is working in conjunction with the liquid energies of Optimal Health. Each of your cells has its own healthy light signature. If your cell's optimal light signature has been altered, this directed ray of sunlight, in conjunction with the bubbling energies, will now restore all your altered cells to their corrected settings. Feel this gentle restructuring process taking place... now.

From the thyroid, the bubbling, liquid energy of complete wellness now moves into your heart where it permeates all the chambers and fizzes into the blood vessels, gently cleansing them of debris and floating away any non-functioning cells. See damaged cells restored to their intended functions as the gentle ray of healing light shines on them. Feel all the walls of your heart's chambers and of your blood vessels as they are restored to their original state of elasticity.

From your blood vessels, the effervescence now moves to your lungs, where all the lobes are opened wide. All damaged cells and structures can now be repaired and restored. Visualize the gentle, directed ray of sunlight adjusting your cells to be at their peak performance. It is a pleasure to breathe in and out.

Now see, feel, and perhaps hear the bubbling health energies traveling through your esophagus, and descending into your stomach. Feel the combination of the bubbly cleansing and the restorative light. From your stomach, the energies and the light move to your liver to offer a gentle cleanse, and then, rumble gently through your intestines. You may feel gassy. Know that whatever gasses are released from your digestive tract are carrying away impurities. They may be unpleasant when they emerge, but they are oh so much better outside of you. Again, shine a gentle ray of perfect sunlight on your digestive tract and see any damage becoming repaired.

Your kidneys, bladder, and urinary tract are thrilled to feel the effervescent healing energies and the light healing energies as they enter, cleanse and restore. You may notice feelings of thirst more so than normal. You will honor your body by quenching that thirst with cool water, which will serve to wash away any lingering impurities. Focus now on the bubbles, the light, and your freshly restored urinary tract.

Your reproductive organs and glands are now excited to be in the healing spotlight. As you feel the rush of fizzing healing energies and as you visualize the gentle healing light being directed their way remember that, especially in the reproductive system, Optimum Health differs depending on your stage of life. The reproductive system helps us to create offspring …until the stage of life when its function changes and it works with us hormonally to FEEL youthful. Your hormonal and reproductive systems function at the best level for your stage of life. Feel the bubbling energies and the gentle ray of light as they restore your cells to optimum function. Feel your hormone levels in perfect balance to keep you fertile…OR energetic…OR youthful. Feel your reproductive organs now working with efficiency and loving commitment to you.

Notice the effervescent healing energies spreading throughout your body…through your bones…feel their strength. Shine gentle light on your bones and feel any breaks, tiny cracks, or weaknesses becoming repaired. Feel in perfect alignment.

Your muscles, joints, and tendons are asking for healing, for increased strength, and flexibility. The healing energies feel like millions of tiny bubbles at each joint…clearing away restrictive debris, and lubricating as they work. The joints have complete ease of motion… the tendons and muscles are completely in sync with the joints. Shine gentle light on your muscles, joints, and tendons now, removing any impurities and realigning any irregularities, increasing strength.

If you have pain or difficulty with joints or any body part, now focus extra attention there. Allow the tingles, the fizzes, the bubbles, AND the gentle light to bathe that area, to caress it, and to tease out any discomfort, removing non-functioning cells as well as any old thought patterns that impede your health or your sense of well-being. Take a few moments now to relax into these areas of extra need. Feel the tingles. Bring in the light. [pause]

Now, expand the tingles throughout your body…. feel them from the crown of your head, down through the palms of your hands, into the tips of your fingers. Gently shake your hands, causing the healing energies to lodge there. At the end of this meditation, you may use the energy now in your hands and fingers, to bless and heal your food. Holding your hands above your food, focus the effervescent energies of Optimal Health onto your food. You may add a blessing such as: "Please bless this food that it keep me healthy, vibrant, energetic, and able to follow my path with grace and ease". Now, when you eat, you will be absorbing the most health-promoting aspects of that food.

And finally, expand the tingling energies all the way down your torso into your thighs…your legs, your feet, your toes. Focus on allowing the tingly feeling all the way to the very tips of your toes, so that it almost leaks out. Gently shake your feet to lock in this healing energy. Now, when you put your feet down, focus the healing energies from the soles of your feet and the tips of your toes into the Earth. You may add a blessing or a prayer, such as:

"May my healing energies be connected with the energies of this planet and all who live here. May we always live and work together in harmony".

Relax now...allowing your focus to rest on the healing effervescent energies circulating in your body... and on the gentle light which is restoring altered cells to their corrected settings. [pause]

When you are ready, open your eyes. Note the new, sparkling cells and increased elasticity you can feel in all areas of your body. Feel the sense of comfort and well-being in your newly energized Earth-suit. Feel the effervescent energies still residing in the palms of your hands, in your fingertips, in the soles of your feet and in your toes. Know that you can fill your body with these energies any time you desire. And, when you next step out into the sun, see that gentle ray of sunlight caressing and fine-tuning your cells, keeping them operating at the level of Optimal Health.

Reflection Questions for Book Clubs or for Individuals

*"The purpose behind questions
is to initiate the quest."*

Phil Cousineau

Please use the following questions for any purpose that best serves you: journaling, seated or walking meditation, deep discussion with friends, with your book club, or in any group where members wish to become more open and vulnerable with each other.

1. Do you see yourself as a rationalist or an ir-rationalist? Could you go after a personal Big Dream even if it looked like an irrational choice to your friends and family?

2. Have you ever received Divine Input... through dreams, messages, "knowings", song lyrics or other synchronous experiences? Example: seeing a bumper sticker on the car in front of you that answers the question you were just thinking about?

3. Fear: What are you afraid of? Have you been scared to death to do something and done it anyway? Share your story of "Courageous You".

4. Who or what do you absolutely trust? Not just lip service, but stake-your-life-on-it trust? Yourself? Your spouse? A Divine Being? How does this trust play out in your life? Are you constant in your trust-level or does your trust-level fluctuate with circumstances?

5. What is your Big Dream? How might "standing behind your Big Dream" look?

6. Funks and stuckness? How do you lift these fear-focussed feelings and move forward? Do you make lists, exercise, journal, relax, meditate, work harder, flip to excitement? What works for you? You may want to share tips among your friends.

7. Do you have a personal mantra? What is it and why does it feel right for you? What is the story of how you came to adopt this mantra? Is there a mantra you would like to adopt?

8. Have you ever asked for Big Help? For a need? For a want? What was your experience of asking for Big Help? Who helped you? Have you helped others with their needs and wants? How did you feel when receiving help? When giving help?

9. What areas of life seem the hardest and most challenging for you? What life-lessons might you be in a position to learn because of your challenges? What life-lessons can you share with others?

10. Do you know what you want? Your "Top Ten"? You might share with your friends something you want but think is impractical, illogical, or just not possible. Ask them to help you see it as possible. Ask for a new perspective.

11. Worry: How do you feel when you know someone is worrying about you? Has what you've worried about come to pass or has worrying been a waste of energy? Do you have any un-worrying tips that work for you? Share your tips with friends and hear theirs.

12. What is your experience of being immersed in another culture? Is there a particular culture that calls to you? Could you imagine yourself having led a past life in that culture?]

13. What is the size of your sense of adventure? Is it a perfect fit for you or might it need to expand? What, to you, is the purpose of adventure?

14. Is there a "Scamming Pancake-Selling Lady", a "Scummy Hospitalero", or an "Alp Man" who has made you angry? Are you still "chewing on" that anger? How might you drop your anger by asking others to "mirror" you... to share their feelings from similar circumstances?

15. Describe your adult version of "A Terrible, Horrible, No Good, Very Bad Day". How did you cope? Humor? Friends? Escape? What works best for you?

16. Are there "Protectors" in your life? "Soul Friends"? Angels? Teachers? Who performs these functions/roles for you? For whom do you fill these roles?

17. How do you know when you've had either too much time with others or not enough? Do you need quiet time away to recharge your batteries (an introvert) or do you recharge by being with others (an extrovert)?

18. With whom do you "look for perfection" rather than going to judgment?

19. Who inspires you? Why? Who do you inspire?

20. Do the Guided Meditation, "Pilgrimage to Essence of Self" with a group of friends and discuss your meditation experiences. Allow the others to help you decipher the symbolism in the information you received.

Bibliography

Adair, John, *The Pilgrim's Way, Shrines and Saints in Britain and Ireland*, London: Thames and Hudson, copyright © 1978.

Brierly, John, *Camino de Santiago, Maps – Mapas – Cartas*, Findhorn Press, Forres, Scotland, copyright © 2011.

Byrne, Rhonda, *The Secret*, Atria Books, a trademark of Simon & Schuster, New York, NY, copyright © 2006.

Cameron, Julia, *The Artist's Way: A Spiritual Path to Higher Creativity*, G.P. Putnam's Sons, New York, NY, copyright © 1992.

Campbell, Joseph, *The Hero with a Thousand Faces*, Princeton University Press, Princeton, NJ, copyright © 1972.

Chinmoy, Sri, *The Life-Illumining Traveller's Companion*, Agni Press, Boston, MA, copyright ©1993.

Clarke, Stephen, *Merde Actually*, Black Swan, an imprint of Penguin Random House UK, London, Copyright © 2006.

Coelho, Paulo, *The Pilgrimage*, Originally published as the Diary of a Magus, English version copyright © 1992 by Paul Coelho and Alan R. Clarke. HarperCollins Publishers, New York, NY.

Cron, Ian Morgan, *Chasing Francis: A Pilgrim's Tale*, Nav Press, Carol Stream, IL, copyright © 2006.

Cousineau, Phil, *The Art of Pilgrimage: The Seeker's Guide to Making Travel Sacred*, Conari Press, San Francisco, CA, copyright © 1998.

Davies, Bethan and Cole, Ben, *Walking the Camino de Santiago*, Pili Pala Press, Vancouver, BC, copyright © 2003.

Estés, Clarissa Pinkola, *Women Who Run with the Wolves: Myths and Stories of the Wild Woman Archetype*, Ballantine Books, New York, NY, copyright © 1992.

Faulks, Sebastian, *Birdsong*, Hutchinson, an imprint of Cornerstone, Penguin Random House UK, London, copyright © 1993.

Farrell, Joseph Pierce, *Manifesting Michelangelo; The True Story of a Modern-Day Miracle That May Make All Change Possible*, Atria, a division of Simon & Schuster, Inc., New York, NY, copyright © 2011.

Gould, Joan, *Spinning Straw into Gold: What Fairy Tales Reveal About the Transformations in a Woman's Life*, Random House, New York, NY, copyright © 2005.

Goulston, Mark, *Just Listen: Discover the Secret to Getting Through to Absolutely Anyone*, AMACOM, a division of the American Management Association, New York, NY, copyright © 2010.

Harper, Hill, *The Wealth Cure: Putting Money in Its Place*, Gotham Books, Penguin Group (USA) Inc., New York, NY, copyright © 2012.

Hicks, Esther and Hicks, Jerry, *Ask and It Is Given*, Hay House, Inc., Carlsbad, CA, copyright © 2004.

Hodge, Susie, *The Knights Templar: Discovering the Myth and Reality of a Legendary Brotherhood*, Hermes House, London, copyright © 2006.

Kerkeling, Hape (author) and Frisch, Shelley (translator), *I'm Off Then: Losing and Finding Myself on the Camino de Santiago*, Free Press, a division of Simon & Schuster, Inc., New York, NY, copyright © 2009.

Lindbergh, Anne Morrow, *Gift from the Sea*, Pantheon Books, an imprint of Knopf Publishing Group, New York, NY, copyright © 1977.

MacCoun, Catherine, *On Becoming an Alchemist: A Guide for the Modern Magician*, Trumpeter Books, an imprint of Shambhala Publishers, Boston, MA, copyright © 2008.

MacLaine, Shirley, *The Camino, A Journey of the Spirit*, Pocket Books, a division of Simon & Schuster, Inc., New York, NY, copyright © 2000.

Michener, James, *Iberia*, Fawcett Crest Books by Ballantine, New York, NY, copyright © 1968.

Myss, Caroline, *Sacred Contracts: Awakening Your Divine Potential,* Harmony Books, a division of Random House, New York, NY, copyright © 2002.

Peirce, Penney, *The Intuitive Way: A Guide to Living from Inner Wisdom*, Beyond Words Publishing, Inc., Hillsboro, OR, copyright © 1997.

Raju, Alison, *Pilgrim Guides to Spain (Finisterre)*, Confraternity of St. James, London, UK, copyright © 2004.

Roman, Sanaya and Packer, Duane, *Creating Money, Keys to Abundance*, H. J. Kramer, Inc., Belvedere Tiburon, CA, copyright © 1987.

Rupp, Joyce, *Walk in a Relaxed Manner: Life Lessons from the Camino*, Orbis Books, Maryknoll, NY, copyright © 2005.

Schucman, Helen and Thetford, Bill, *A Course in Miracles*, Foundation for Inner Peace, Novato, CA, copyright © 1975.

Steinbach, Alice, *Without Reservations: the Travels of an Independent Woman*, Random House, New York, NY, copyright © 2000.

Taylor, Daniel, *In Search of Sacred Spaces: Looking for Wisdom on Celtic Holy Islands*, Bog Walk Press, Arden Hills, MN, copyright © 2005.

Thomas, Katherine Woodward, *Calling in "The One": 7 Weeks to Attract the Love of Your Life*, an imprint of the Crown Publishing Group, Penguin Random House, copyright © 2004.

Villoldo, Alberto, *Courageous Dreaming*, Hay House, Carlsbad, CA, copyright © 2008.

Weiss, Brian L., *Many Lives, Many Masters*, A Fireside Book, published by Simon & Schuster, copyright © 1988.

Author Bio

Deborah Terra Weltman is a seeker of the best in humanity. She loves to look for the personal gifts and genius in each person she meets. She deeply appreciates the humanizing qualities of the arts and the nature world. And, she loves to brainstorm, to explore life issues from a creative, inspired, or shifted perspective.

In her past lives Deborah feels sure she was previously a pilgrim on the Camino de Santiago, a perpetual seeker. She's also certain she lived a life on the tiny island of Iona, where she was, in some way, involved in creating The Book of Kells.

In this life, Deborah walked away from her spiritual nature, her true Self, for thirty years. In her late 40s she was finally able to reawaken to her spiritual (not religious) path. After reading Shirley MacLaine's book about the Camino de Santiago, Deborah felt lit up with desire to walk the Camino, to have a spiritual experience on the pilgrimage trail... but it took her ten years and a "Divine Threat" before she fully stepped into her deep Camino desire.